Summary Guides

Maths 8

Natalie Caruso

First published in 2024, reprinted in 2025.

Insight Publications Pty Ltd
3/350 Charman Road
Cheltenham Victoria 3192
Australia

Tel: +61 3 8571 4950
Email: books@insightpublications.com.au

www.insightpublications.com.au

Summary Guides – Maths 8 / Natalie Caruso

ISBN: 9781923154551

Edited by Dr Geoffrey Marnell
Proofread by Owen Kavanagh and Robert Beardwood
Artwork by Artin Education
Typesetting by Aptara®, Inc.
Cover design by Melisa Paredes
Printed by Markono Print Media Pte Ltd

Insight Publications acknowledges the Traditional Custodians of the Country on which we meet and work, the Boonwurrung People of the Kulin Nation. We pay our respects to their Elders past and present, and extend that respect to all Aboriginal and Torres Strait Islander peoples.

Table of contents

Introduction

The *Summary Guides – Maths* series has been written by practising teachers who are passionate about creating user-friendly, accessible guides on mathematics.

The explanations and exercises in these guides develop core numeracy skills for personal, work and civic life, and provide the base knowledge for professional applications of maths as well as for mathematical specialisation. Maths is part of your daily life, no matter what you choose to do as an adult – it is important for thinking critically and for making sense of the world.

This book summarises key concepts in a clear and comprehensive way. It includes examples with worked solutions and step-by-step explanations, as well as exercises for you to complete. The best way to use this book is to make a habit of it, regularly working through the exercises and examples, and comparing your answers with those provided. Whether you commit to a daily, weekly or fortnightly routine, consistent practice is the key to your success.

Natalie Caruso and Insight Publications

Natalie Caruso has over 30 years of experience teaching mathematics and has had numerous leadership roles, including Head of Mathematics. She has also coordinated extension mathematics programs for students in Years 5 to 12. Natalie has authored numerous texts and study guides for students in Years 7 to 12 and has taught all mathematics subjects offered in Victoria for students in those years. She has been a VCE exam vetter and assessor, and has presented papers at annual conferences of the Mathematical Association of Victoria.

Chapter 1 – Integers

1.1 Introduction

An integer is any positive or negative whole number, or zero. Any whole number larger than zero is a **positive integer**. Any whole number less than zero is a **negative integer**. Zero is the only integer that is neither positive nor negative.

We can use a single number line to represent positive and negative integers.

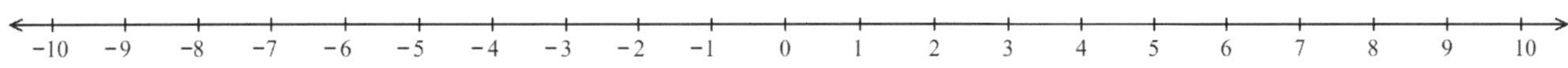

A number line is a useful tool when ordering or comparing integers.

Example

Place $>$ (greater than) or $<$ (less than) in the boxes below to make these statement true.

a. $-3 \square 5$ **b.** $0 \square -4$ **c.** $-8 \square -2$

✓ *Solution*

Working	Explanation
−5 −4 −3 −2 −1 0 1 2 3 4 5 $-3 < 5$	Mark both numbers on a number line. −3 is to the left of 5 so it is less than 5.
−5 −4 −3 −2 −1 0 1 2 3 4 5 $0 > -4$	Mark both numbers on a number line. 0 is to the right of −4 so it is greater than −4.
−10 −9 −8 −7 −6 −5 −4 −3 −2 −1 0 1 2 $-8 < -2$	Mark both numbers on a number line. −8 is to the left of −2 so it is less than −2.

Example

a. Write the integers −5, −9, 2, 0, −1, 6 in ascending order.

b. Write the integers 3, −7, 4, −9, −3, 2 in descending order.

✓ Solution

Working	Explanation
a. $-9, -5, -1, 0, 2, 6$	Ascending order means from smallest to largest. Mark each number on a number line and then list the numbers from smallest (furthest left) to largest (furthest right).
b. $4, 3, 2, -3, -7, -9$	Descending order means from largest to smallest. Mark each number on a number line and then list the numbers from largest (furthest right) to smallest (furthest left).

Exercise 1.1.1

Place > (greater than) or < (less than) in the boxes below to make these statement true.

a. $-2 \square 3$ **b.** $-3 \square -1$ **c.** $-2 \square -7$ **d.** $4 \square -5$

Exercise 1.1.2

a. Write the integers $3, -2, 5, 0, 1, -10$ in ascending order.

b. Write the integers $-4, -8, 2, -1, 1, 3$ in descending order.

1.2 Addition and subtraction of integers

The following rules apply for addition and subtraction of negative integers.

- Adding a negative integer is the same as subtracting a positive integer.
- Subtracting a negative integer is the same as adding a positive integer.

Example

Evaluate the following.

a. $5 + (-2)$ **b.** $3 - (-6)$ **c.** $-4 - 3$ **d.** $-6 + 8$ **e.** $2 - 7$

✓ ***Solution***

Working	Explanation
a. $5 + (-2) = 5 - 2$ $= 3$	Adding a negative integer is the same as subtracting a positive integer.
b. $3 - (-6) = 3 + 6$ $= 9$	Subtracting a negative integer is the same as adding a positive integer.
c. $-4 - 3 = -7$	On a number line, start at -4 and then subtract 3 by moving 3 numbers to the left. −10 −9 −8 −7 −6 −5 −4 −3 −2 −1 0
d. $-6 + 8 = 2$	On a number line, start at -6 and then add 8 by moving 8 numbers to the right. −10 −9 −8 −7 −6 −5 −4 −3 −2 −1 0 1 2 3 4 5
e. $2 - 7 = -5$	On a number line, start at 2 and then subtract 7 by moving 7 numbers to the left. −10 −9 −8 −7 −6 −5 −4 −3 −2 −1 0 1 2 3 4 5

Exercise 1.2

Evaluate the following.

a. $10 + (-3)$ **b.** $15 + (-7)$ **c.** $10 + (-5)$ **d.** $7 + (-9)$

e. $6 - (-9)$ **f.** $5 - (-8)$ **g.** $5 - 13$ **h.** $-3 + 8$

i. $9 - 11$ **j.** $-6 - 5$ **k.** $-10 - (-8)$ **l.** $-5 + (-12)$

1.3 Multiplication and division of integers

We say that a positive integer has a positive sign and a negative integer has a negative sign.

When two integers with the same sign are multiplied or divided, the result is a positive integer.

When two integers with different signs are multiplied or divided, the result is a negative integer.

These rules are summarised in the following table.

$+ \times + = +$	$+ \div + = +$
$- \times - = +$	$- \div - = +$
$+ \times - = -$	$+ \div - = -$
$- \times + = -$	$- \div + = -$

Example

Evaluate the following.

a. -4×6 b. -12×-5 c. $48 \div -6$ d. $-32 \div -4$

✓ Solution

Working	Explanation
a. $-4 \times 6 = -24$	A negative integer multiplied by a positive integer gives a negative result.
b. $-12 \times -5 = 60$	A negative integer multiplied by a negative integer gives a positive result.
c. $48 \div -6 = -8$	A positive integer divided by a negative integer gives a negative result.
d. $-32 \div -4 = 8$	A negative integer divided by a negative integer gives a positive result.

Exercise 1.3

Evaluate each of the following.

a. 3×-5 b. -4×-7 c. 8×-6 d. -9×9

e. $18 \div -3$ f. $-24 \div 12$ g. $-36 \div -4$ h. $40 \div -10$

i. $5 \times 4 \times -3$ j. $-3 \times -4 \times -2$ k. $30 \div -5 \div -3$ l. $-42 \div -2 \div -3$

1.4 Order of operations with integers

BIDMAS is an acronym for the correct order of operations in arithmetic. It applies to all numbers including integers.

B	Brackets	( )
I	Indices (i.e. powers)	$\square^{\text{power}}$
D	Division	÷
M	Multiplication	×
A	Addition	+
S	Subtraction	−

First do any arithmetic that is inside brackets.

Next do any arithmetic involving indices.

Then, moving left to right, do any multiplication or division.

Finally, moving left to right, do any addition or subtraction.

Example

Evaluate the following.

a. $-5 \times (-6 + 2)$

b. $7 - 3 \times -4$

c. $(3 \times -10 - 6) \div (-3)^2$

✓ ***Solution***

Working	Explanation
a. $-5 \times (-6 + 2) = -5 \times -4$ $= 20$	Brackets first: $-6 + 2 = -4$. Multiplication next: $- \times - = +$ and $5 \times 4 = 20$.
b. $7 - 3 \times -4 = 7 + 12$ $= 19$	Multiplication first: -3×-4. $- \times - = +$ and $-3 \times -4 = 12$. Addition next: $7 + 12 = 19$.
c. $(3 \times -10 - 6) \div (-3)^2$ $= (-30 - 6) \div (-3)^2$ $= -36 \div (-3)^2$ $= -36 \div 9$ $= -4$	Brackets first: Within the brackets perform the multiplication first: 3×-10. $+ \times - = -$ and $3 \times -10 = -30$. Addition inside the brackets next: $-30 - 6$. Start at -30 on a number line and move 6 numbers to the left. You come to -36. Index next: $(-3)^2 = -3 \times -3 = 9$. Finally, division: $-36 \div 9$. $- \div + = -$ and $-36 \div 9 = -4$.

Exercise 1.4

Evaluate each of the following.

a. $-2 \times 3 + 8 \times -5$

b. $(-4)^2 \div 8$

c. $-36 \div (-13 + 4)$

d. $18 - 4 \times -2$

e. $12 \times (-5 + 3)$

f. $5^2 - (-10)^2$

g. $(-12 \div -3 + 5) - (-2)^2$

h. $(-3 - 8 \div -2)^2$

i. $-54 \div (-3 - 3)$

j. $5 \times -2 \times -3 + 7 \times -2$

k. $(4 - 5)^2 - 3 \times -4$

l. $(5 + 3) \times (-5 + 2)^2$

Answers

Exercise 1.1.1

a. $<$ b. $<$ c. $>$ d. $>$

Exercise 1.1.2

a. $-10, -2, 0, 1, 3, 5$ b. $3, 2, 1, -1, -4, -8$

Exercise 1.2

a. 7 b. 8 c. 5 d. -2

e. 15 f. 13 g. -8 h. 5

i. -2 j. -11 k. -2 l. -17

Exercise 1.3

a. -15 b. 28 c. -48 d. -81

e. -6 f. -2 g. 9 h. -4

i. -60 j. -24 k. 2 l. -7

Exercise 1.4

a. -46 b. 2 c. 4 d. 26

e. -24 f. -75 g. 5 h. 1

i. 9 j. 16 k. 13 l. 72

Chapter 2 – Angles, lines and shapes

2.1 Complementary and supplementary angles

Complementary angles are two angles that add to $90°$. A right angle is $90°$.

Supplementary angles are angles that add to $180°$. A straight angle is $180°$.

Angles in a rotation add to $360°$.

Vertically opposite angles are equal.

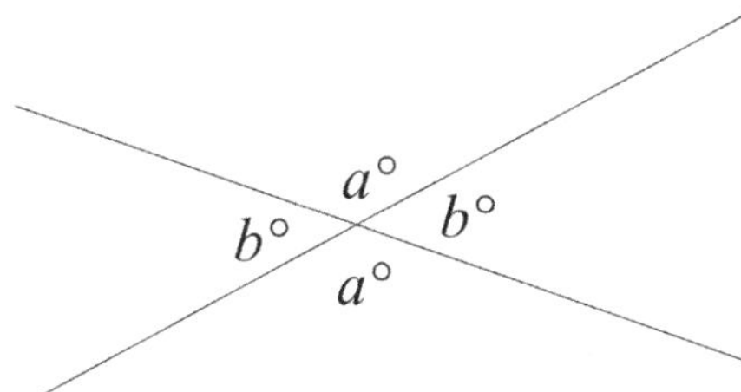

Example

Find the value of the pronumeral in each of the following diagrams.

a.

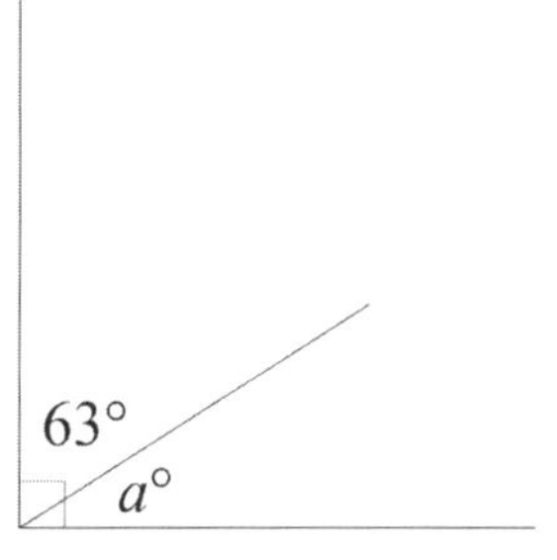

b.

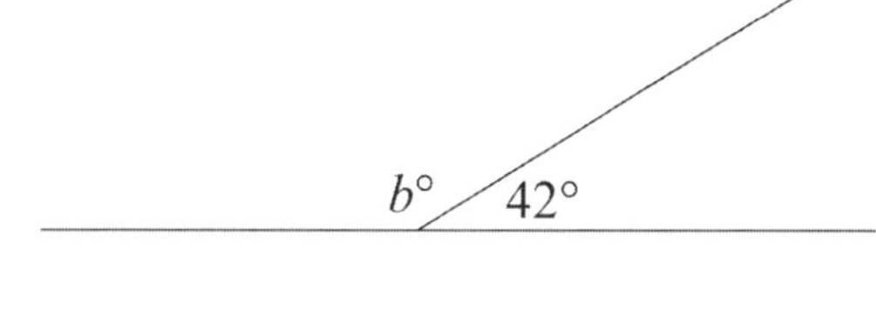

c.

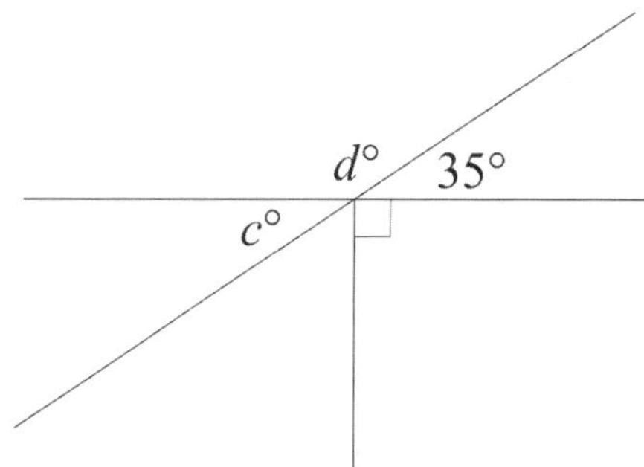

✓ Solution

Working	Explanation
a. $a = 90 - 63$ $= 27$	The angles $a°$ and $63°$ are complementary.
b. $b = 180 - 42$ $= 138$	The angles $b°$ and $42°$ are supplementary.
c. $c = 35$	The angles $c°$ and $35°$ are vertically opposite.
d. $d = 180 - 35$ $= 145$	The angles $d°$ and $35°$ are supplementary.

Exercise 2.1

Find the value of the pronumeral in each of the following diagrams.

a.

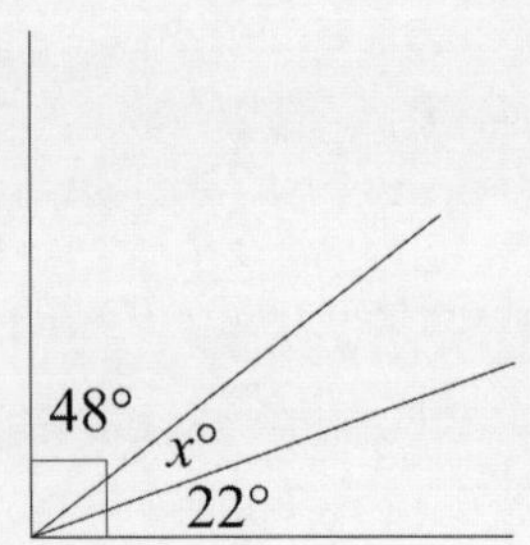

b.

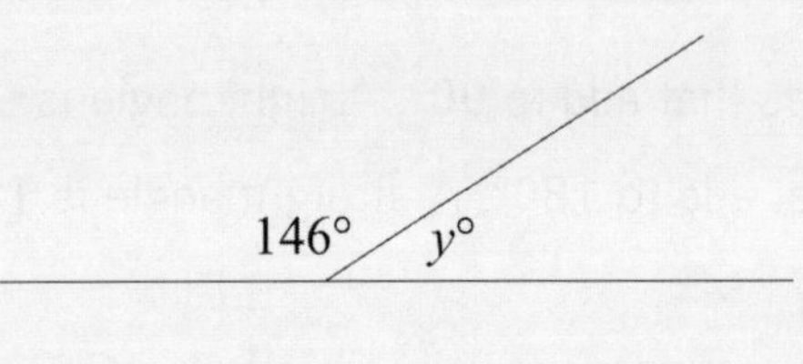

c.

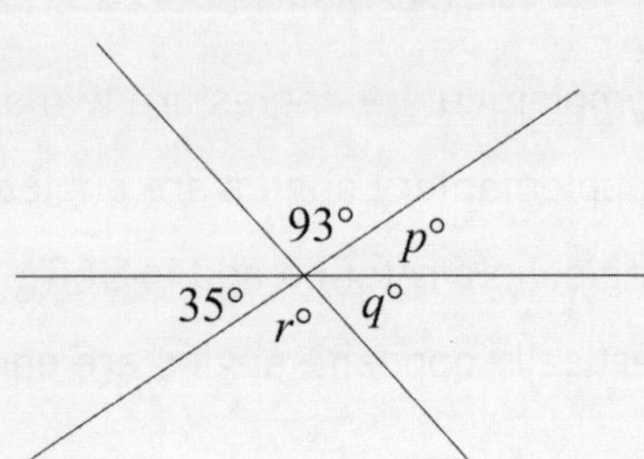

2.2 Angles and triangles

The angle sum of a triangle is 180°.

An exterior angle of a triangle is equal to the sum of the opposite two interior angles.

$$d = a + b$$

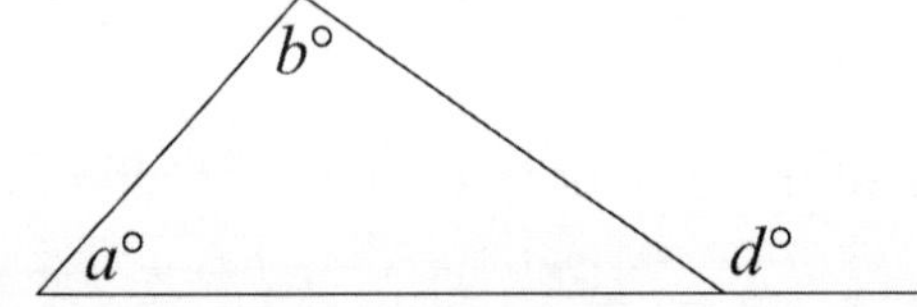

In an **equilateral** triangle (below) all sides are of equal length and all angles are 60°.

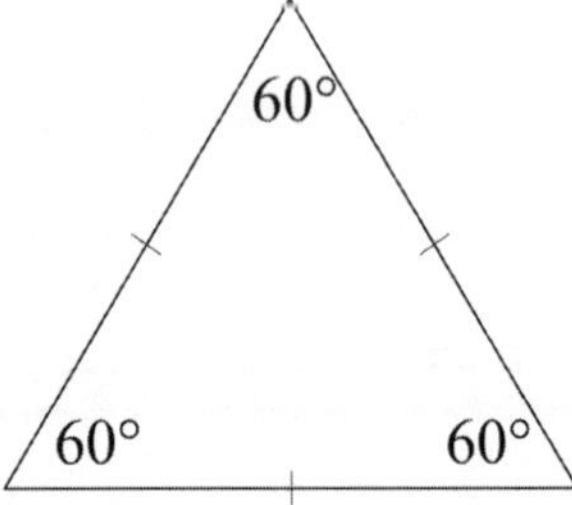

In an **isosceles** triangle (below) two sides are of equal length and the two angles opposite the equal sides are equal.

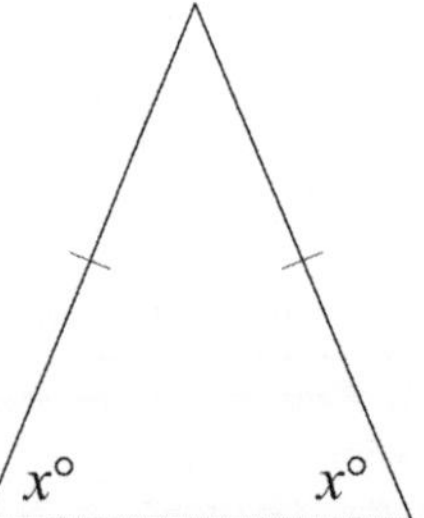

Example

Find the value of the pronumeral in each of the following triangles.

a.

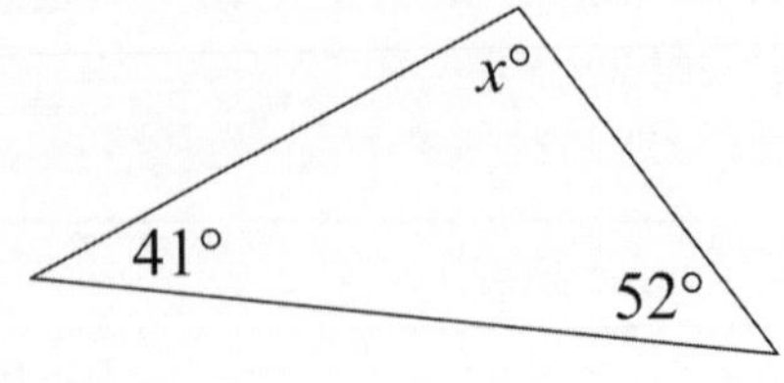

b.

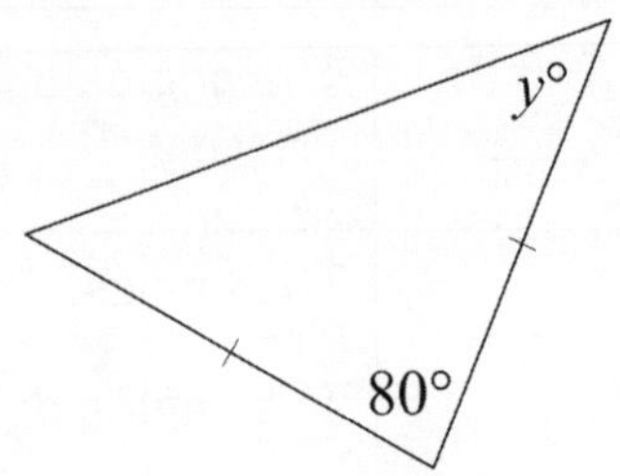

✓ ***Solution***

Working	Explanation
a. $x = 180 - (41 + 52)$ $= 180 - 93$ $= 87$	The angle sum in a triangle is 180°.
b. $y°$, $y°$, $80°$ $y = \frac{180 - 80}{2}$ $= \frac{100}{2}$ $= 50$	The angle labelled y° and the unlabelled angle are equal, since the triangle is isosceles and these angles are opposite the equal sides. The angle sum in a triangle is 180°. Since the two unknown angles are equal, subtract 80 from 180 and then divide by 2 to find y.

Example

Find the value of Z.

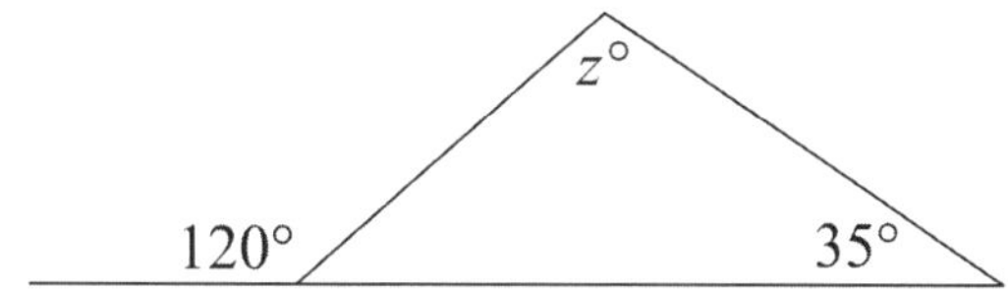

✓ ***Solution***

Working	Explanation
$35 + z = 120$ $z = 120 - 35$ $= 85$	The exterior angle of a triangle is equal to the sum of the two opposite interior angles. Solve for z by subtracting 35 from the exterior angle.

Exercise 2.2

Find the value of the pronumeral in each of the following diagrams.

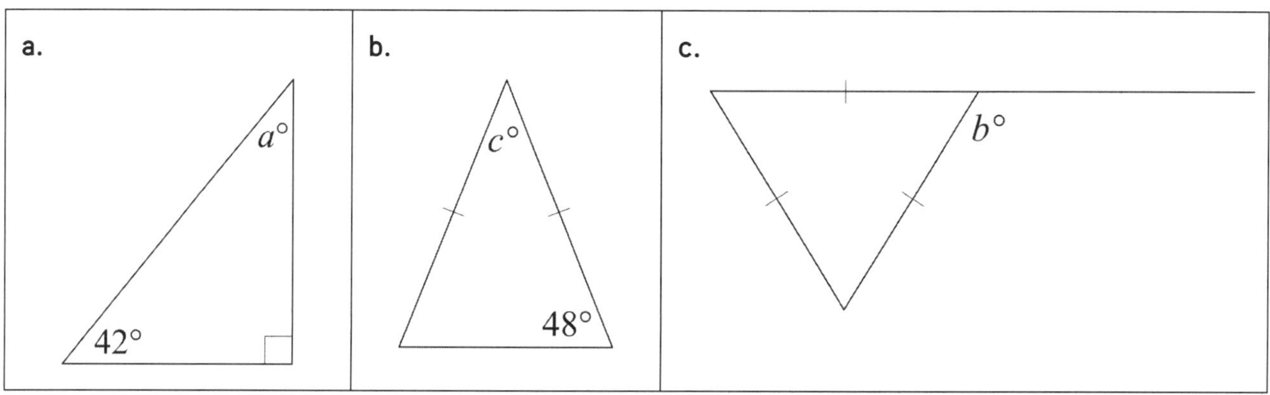

Naming triangles

Triangles can be named according to their side properties or angle properties. We have seen two types of triangles that are named according to their side properties: equilateral triangles and isosceles triangles.

A **scalene** triangle is one with all sides of different lengths. In a scalene triangle, all angles are different in size.

A triangle in which all angles measure less than 90° is called an **acute-angled** triangle.

A triangle that contains a right angle is called a **right-angled** triangle.

A triangle that contains one angle measuring more than 90° is called an **obtuse-angled** triangle.

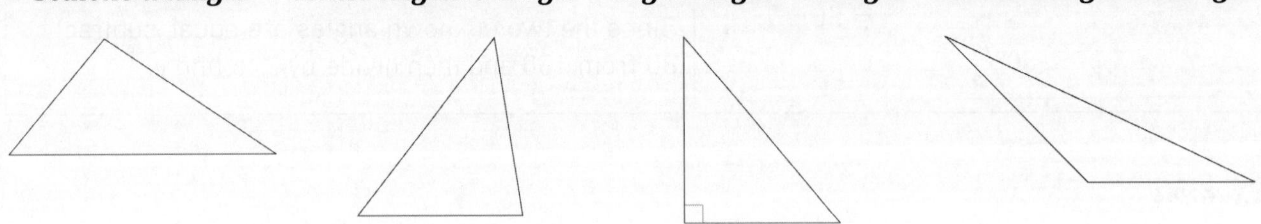

2.3 Angles and parallel lines

Parallel lines in the same plane are always the same distance from each other, so they never intersect.

When another line crosses parallel lines, we refer to this line as a **transversal**.

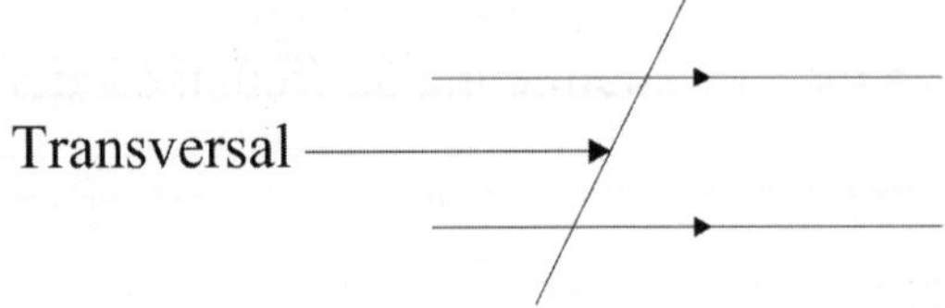

When parallel lines are crossed by a transversal, **corresponding angles** are equal.

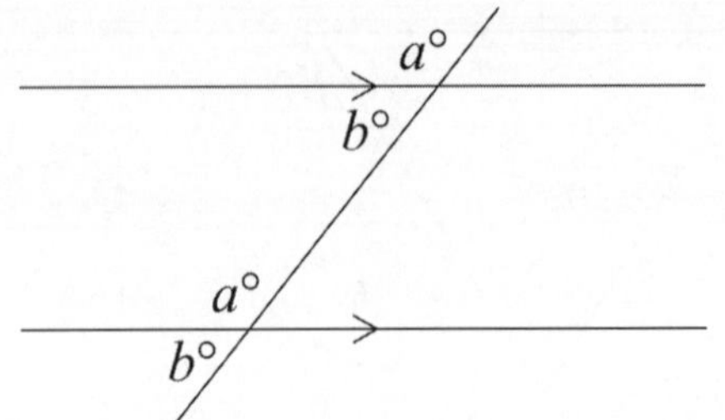

When parallel lines are crossed by a transversal, **alternate angles** are equal.

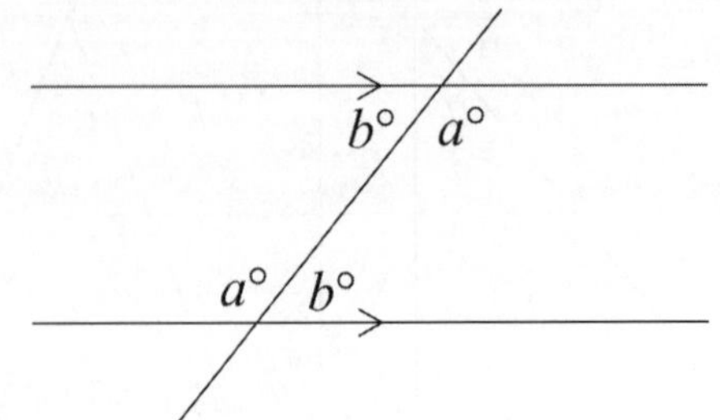

When parallel lines are crossed by a transversal, **co-interior angles** are supplementary.

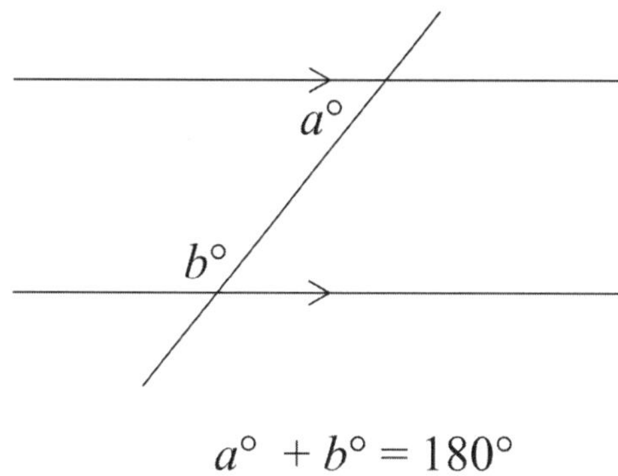

$$a° + b° = 180°$$

Example

Find the values of x and y in the following diagram.

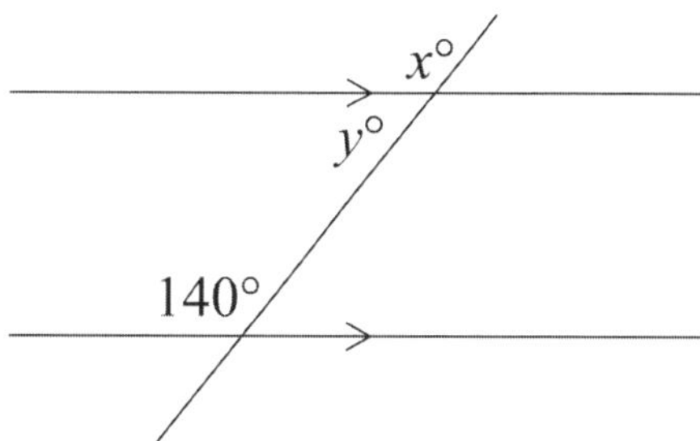

✓ Solution

Working	Explanation
a. $x = 140$	The angles $x°$ and $140°$ are corresponding angles. Corresponding angles are equal.
b. $y = 180 - 140$ $= 40$	The angles $y°$ and $140°$ are co-interior angles. Co-interior angles are supplementary.

Example

Find the values of p and q in the diagram below.

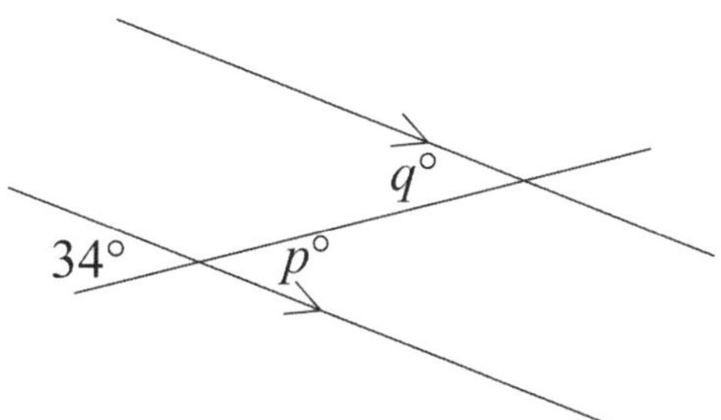

✓ ***Solution***

Working	Explanation
a. $p = 34$	The angles $p°$ and 34° are vertically opposite. Vertically opposite angles are equal.
b. $q = 34$	The angles $p°$ and $q°$ are alternate angles. Alternate angles are equal.

Exercise 2.3

Find the value of the pronumeral in each of the following diagrams.

a.

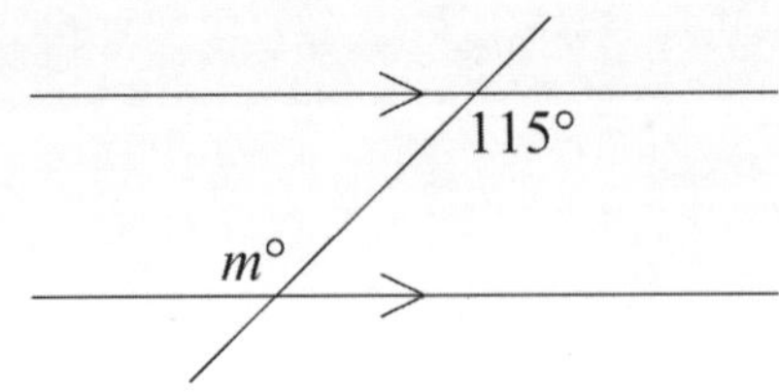

b.

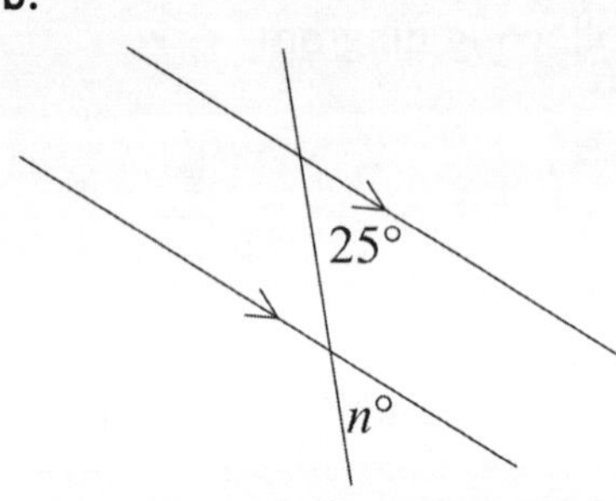

c.

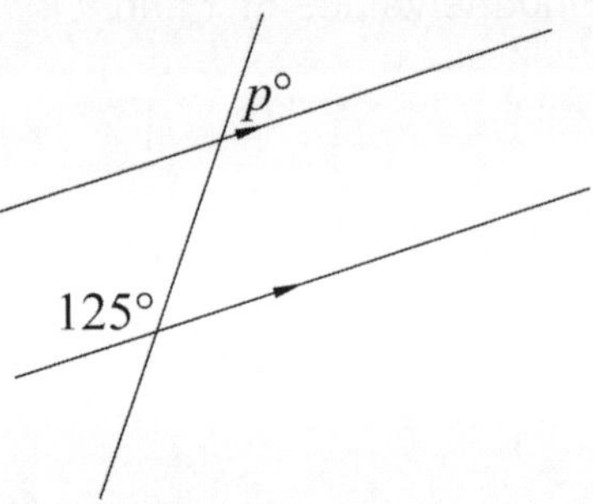

2.4 Quadrilaterals

A quadrilateral is a shape with four sides. The sum of the four angles in a quadrilateral is 360°.

Types of quadrilaterals and their properties

Square

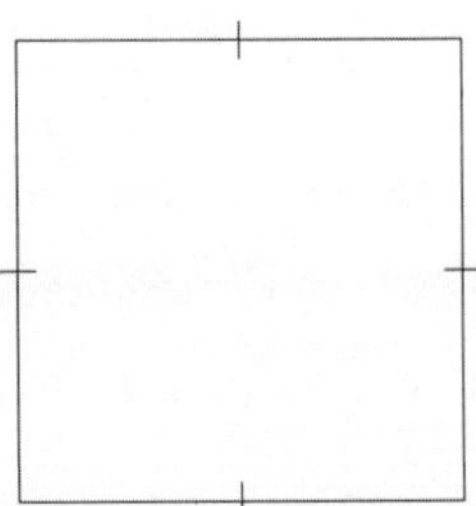

- Opposite sides are parallel.
- All sides are equal in length.
- All angles are right angles.
- Diagonals are equal in length.
- Diagonals bisect each other.
- Diagonals intersect at right angles.

Rectangle

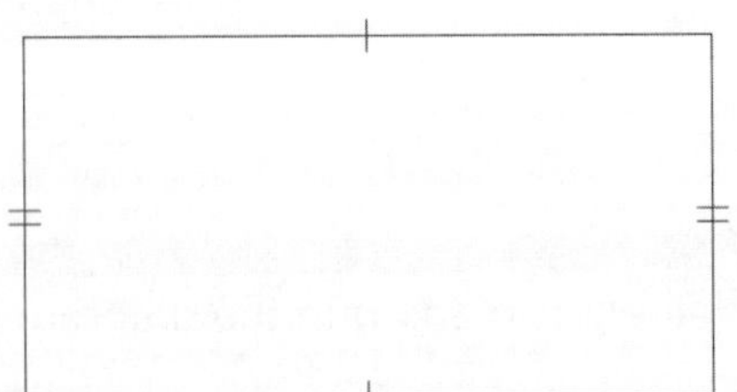

- Opposite sides are parallel.
- Opposite sides are equal in length.
- All angles are right angles.
- Diagonals are equal in length.
- Diagonals bisect each other.
- Diagonals do not intersect at right angles.

Parallelogram

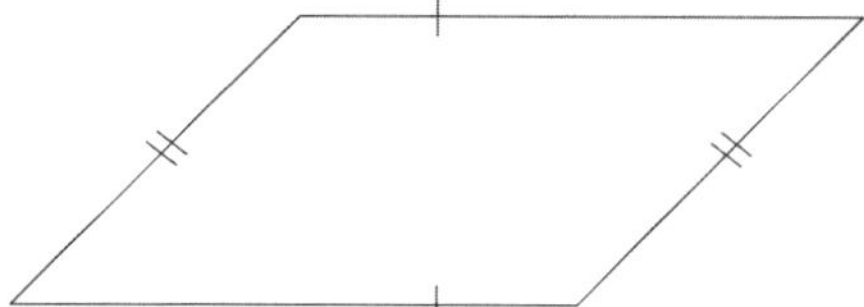

- Opposite sides are parallel.
- Opposite sides are equal in length.
- Diagonally opposite angles are equal.
- Adjacent angles are supplementary.
- Diagonals are not equal in length.
- Diagonals bisect each other.
- Diagonals do not intersect at right angles.

Rhombus

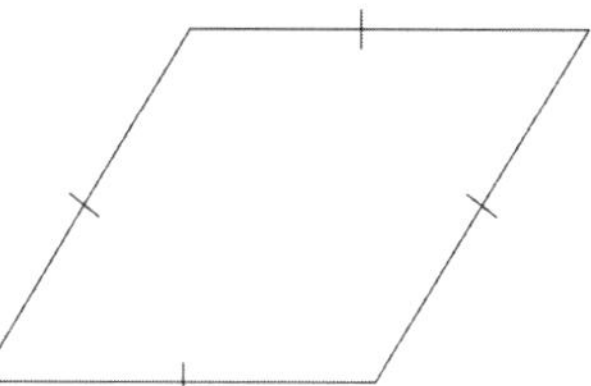

- Opposite sides are parallel.
- All sides are equal in length.
- Diagonally opposite angles are equal.
- Diagonals are not equal in length.
- Diagonals bisect each other.
- Diagonals intersect at right angles.

Trapezium

- One pair of opposite sides are parallel.
- Diagonals are not equal in length.
- Diagonals do not bisect each other.
- Diagonals do not intersect at right angles.

Kite

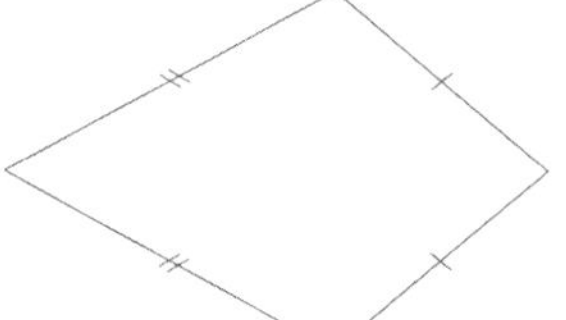

- Two pairs of adjacent sides are each equal in length.
- Opposite sides are not equal in length.
- The angles opposite the longer diagonal are equal.
- One diagonal bisects the other.
- Diagonals intersect at right angles.

Bisect means 'to cut in half'. **Adjacent** means 'next to'.

Example

Find the value of the pronumerals in each of the following quadrilaterals.

a.

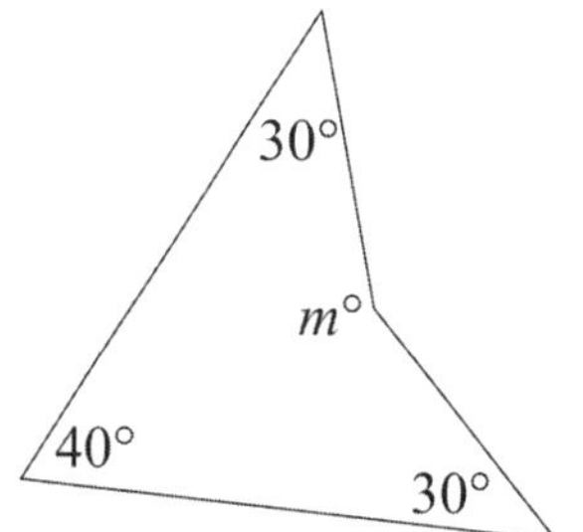

b.

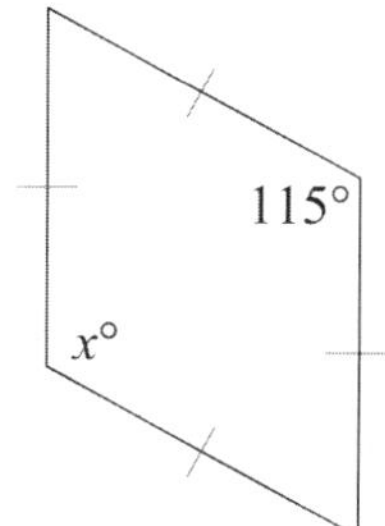

c.

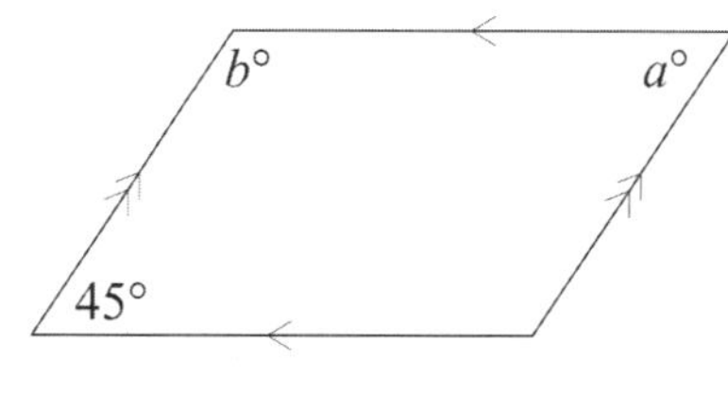

✓ Solution

Working	Explanation
a. $m = 360 - (30 + 30 + 40)$ $= 360 - 100$ $= 260$	The angles in a quadrilateral add to 360°.
b. $x = 115$	The quadrilateral is a rhombus. Opposite angles are equal.
c. $a = 45$ $b = 180 - 45$ $= 135$	The quadrilateral is a parallelogram. Opposite angles are equal. Adjacent angles are supplementary.

Exercise 2.4

Find the value of the pronumeral in each of the following quadrilaterals.

a.

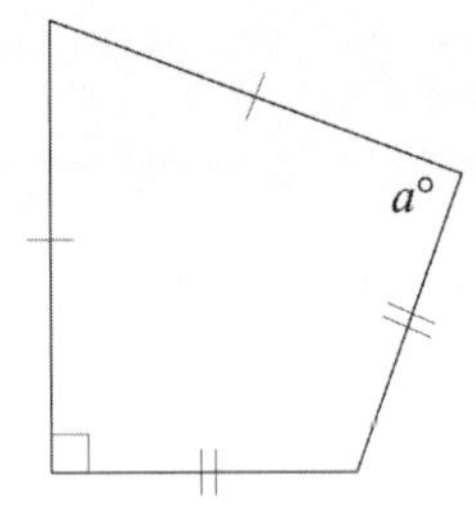

b.

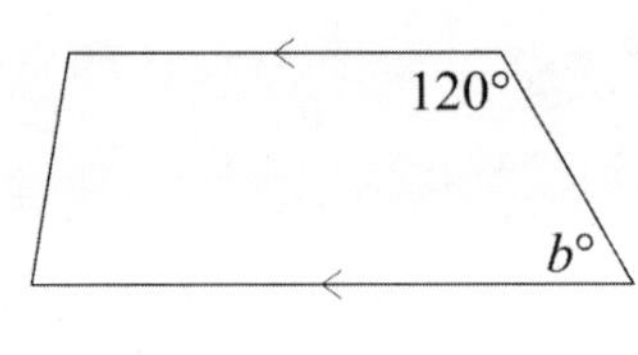

c.

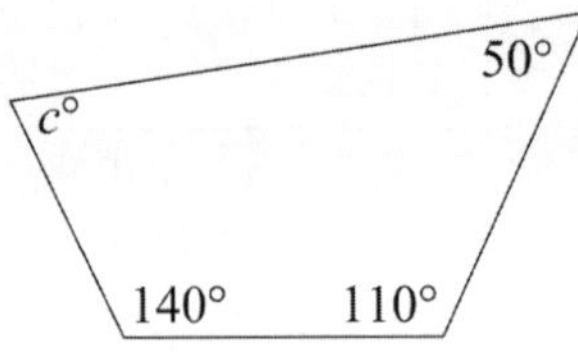

d.

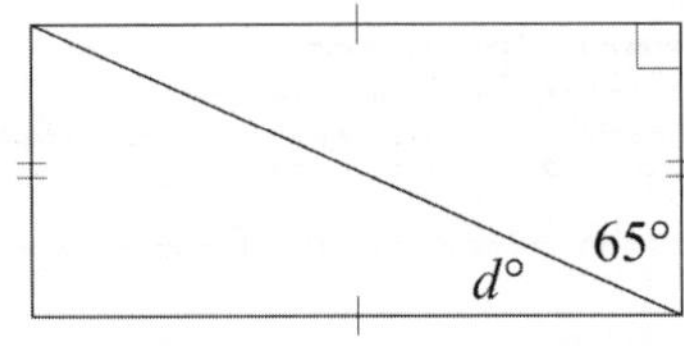

e.

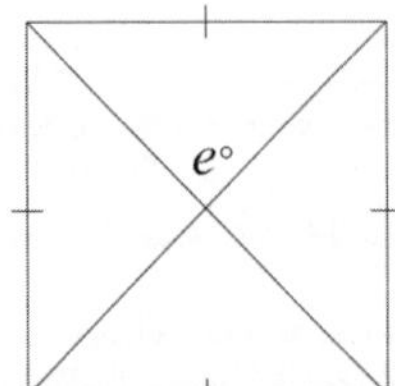

f.

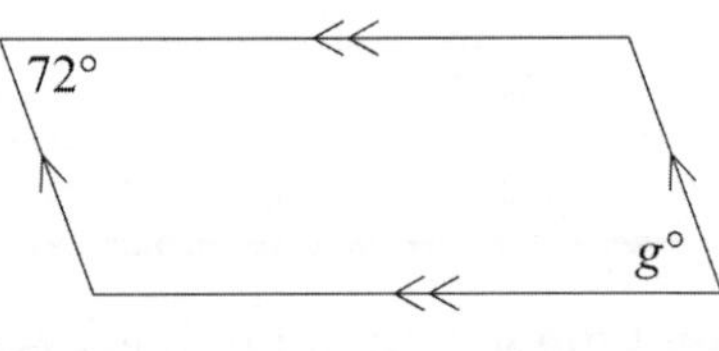

2.5 Symmetry

A line of symmetry divides a shape into two identical halves. A line about which a shape is symmetrical is referred to as an **axis of symmetry**.

Example

Determine the number of axes of symmetry for each of the following shapes.

a. a square

b. an isosceles triangle

✓ *Solution*

Working	Explanation
a. A square has 4 axes of symmetry.	Draw a square. Draw the axes of symmetry. Count the number of axes of symmetry.
b. An isosceles triangle has one axis of symmetry.	Draw an isosceles triangle. Draw the axes of symmetry. Count the number of axes of symmetry.

Exercise 2.5

Determine the number of axes of symmetry for each of the following shapes.

a.

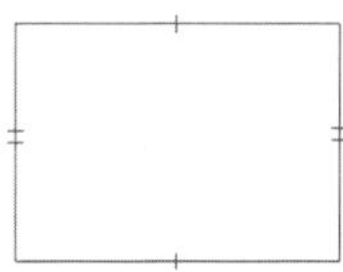

b.

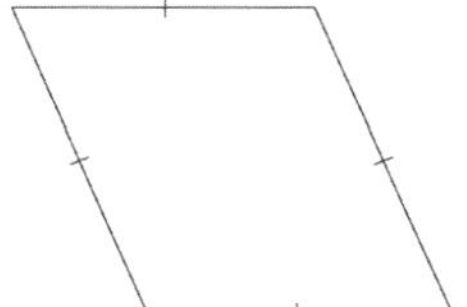

c.

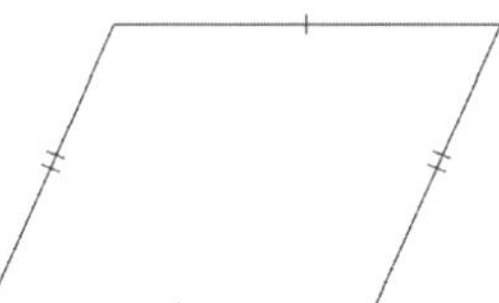

Answers

Exercise 2.1

a. $x = 20$ b. $y = 34$ c. $p = 35, q = 52, r = 93$

Exercise 2.2

a. $a = 48$ b. $c = 84$ c. $b = 120$

Exercise 2.3

a. $m = 115$ b. $n = 25$ c. $p = 55$

Exercise 2.4

a. $a = 90$ b. $b = 60$ c. $c = 60$

d. $d = 25$ e. $e = 90$ f. $g = 72$

Exercise 2.5

a. 2 b. 2 c. 0

Chapter 3 – Fractions, decimals and percentages

3.1 Equivalent fractions

Equivalent fractions are equal. Given a fraction, another equivalent fraction can be found by multiplying or dividing both the numerator and denominator by the same number. This is illustrated below.

$$\frac{2}{3} = \frac{10}{15} \quad (\times 5 \text{ top and bottom})$$

$$\frac{33}{88} = \frac{3}{8} \quad (\div 11 \text{ top and bottom})$$

Example

Rewrite $\frac{2}{5}$ as an equivalent fraction with a denominator of 15.

✓ Solution

Working	Explanation
$\frac{2}{5} = \frac{2 \times 3}{5 \times 3}$ $= \frac{6}{15}$	The denominator of the given fraction is 5. Multiply the denominator by 3 to obtain the required denominator: 15. Now multiply the numerator by the same value: 3. This produces a new fraction that is equivalent to the given fraction.

Example

Rewrite $-\frac{5}{6}$ as an equivalent fraction with a denominator of 24.

✓ Solution

Working	Explanation
$-\frac{5}{6} = -\frac{5 \times 4}{6 \times 4}$ $= -\frac{20}{24}$	The denominator of the given fraction is 6. Multiply the denominator by 4 to obtain the required denominator: 24. Now multiply the numerator by the same value: 4. This produces a new fraction that is equivalent to the given fraction. **Note**: since the original fraction was negative, the equivalent fraction must also be negative.

To simplify a fraction, divide both the numerator and the denominator by their highest common factor.

Example

Simplify the fraction $\frac{18}{30}$.

✓ ***Solution***

Working	Explanation
$\frac{18}{30}=\frac{18\div 6}{30\div 6}$ $=\frac{3}{5}$	The highest common factor of 18 and 30 is 6, so simplify the fraction by dividing the numerator and denominator by 6.

Example

Simplify the fraction $\frac{32}{72}$.

✓ ***Solution***

Working	Explanation
$\frac{32}{72}=\frac{32\div 8}{72\div 8}$ $=\frac{4}{9}$	The highest common factor of 32 and 72 is 8, so simplify the fraction by dividing the numerator and denominator by 8.

Exercise 3.1.1

a. Rewrite $\frac{3}{8}$ with a denominator of 24.

b. Rewrite $-\frac{7}{15}$ with a denominator of 60.

Exercise 3.1.2

Simplify each of the following fractions.

a. $\frac{4}{28}$ b. $\frac{6}{18}$ c. $\frac{35}{50}$ d. $\frac{32}{56}$ e. $\frac{18}{48}$

3.2 Arithmetic with fractions

Fractions can only be added or subtracted if they have the same denominator. We make the denominators the same by first finding their lowest common multiple. We then multiply the fractions by the same number so that each fraction has the lowest common multiple as its denominator. We can then add or subtract the numerators.

Example

Evaluate $\frac{3}{8}+\frac{3}{4}$.

✓ Solution

Working	Explanation
$\frac{3}{8}+\frac{3}{4}=\frac{3}{8}+\frac{6}{8}$ $=\frac{9}{8}$	The lowest common multiple of both denominators (8 and 4) is 8. To make both fractions have the lowest common multiple as their denominator, multiply the numerator and denominator of $\frac{3}{4}$ by 2. Add both numerators: $3+6=9$.

Example

Evaluate $\frac{1}{6}-\frac{4}{9}$.

✓ Solution

Working	Explanation
$\frac{1}{6}-\frac{4}{9}=\frac{3}{18}-\frac{8}{18}$ $=-\frac{5}{18}$	The lowest common multiple of both denominators (6 and 9) is 18. To make both fractions have the lowest common multiple as their denominator: • multiply the numerator and denominator of $\frac{1}{6}$ by 3 and • multiply the numerator and denominator of $\frac{4}{9}$ by 2. Now that both denominators are the same, subtract the numerators: $3-8=-5$

Example

Evaluate $-\frac{5}{12}-\frac{1}{3}$.

✓ Solution

Working	Explanation
$-\frac{5}{12}-\frac{1}{3}=-\frac{5}{12}-\frac{4}{12}$ $=-\frac{9}{12}$ $=-\frac{3}{4}$	The lowest common multiple of both denominators (12 and 3) is 12. To make both fractions have the lowest common multiple as their denominator, multiply the numerator and denominator of $\frac{1}{3}$ by 4. Now that both denominators are the same, subtract numerators: $-5-4=-9$. Simplify by dividing the numerator and denominator by 3.

To multiply fractions we first look to see if we can cancel any factors that are common to both the numerator and the denominator. (Cancelling common factors means dividing both the numerator and denominator by a factor that is common to both.) After cancelling common factors (if any), multiply the numbers remaining in the numerator and the denominator.

Example

Evaluate $\frac{3}{5} \times \frac{3}{4}$.

✓ ***Solution***

Working	Explanation
$\frac{3}{5} \times \frac{3}{4} = \frac{3 \times 3}{5 \times 4}$ $= \frac{9}{20}$	There are no factors common to both the numerator and the denominator, so all we need to do is: • multiply the numbers in the numerators and • multiply numbers in the denominators.

Example

Evaluate $\frac{5}{12} \times \frac{21}{25}$.

✓ ***Solution***

Working	Explanation
$\frac{5}{12} \times \frac{21}{25} = \frac{\overset{1}{\cancel{5}}}{\underset{4}{\cancel{12}}} \times \frac{\overset{7}{\cancel{21}}}{\underset{5}{\cancel{25}}}$ $= \frac{1 \times 7}{4 \times 5}$ $= \frac{7}{20}$	First cancel common factors: • 5 and 25 share a common factor of 5, so divide both numbers by 5. • 21 and 12 share a common factor of 3, so divide both numbers by 3. After cancelling, multiply the numbers in the numerators and the numbers in the denominators.

Example

Evaluate $-\frac{3}{5} \times \frac{20}{33}$.

✓ ***Solution***

Working	Explanation
$-\frac{3}{5} \times \frac{20}{33} = -\frac{\overset{1}{\cancel{3}}}{\underset{1}{\cancel{5}}} \times \frac{\overset{4}{\cancel{20}}}{\underset{11}{\cancel{33}}}$ $= -\frac{1 \times 4}{1 \times 11}$ $= -\frac{4}{11}$	First cancel common factors: • 3 and 33 share a common factor of 3, so divide both numbers by 3. • 20 and 5 share a common factor of 5, so divide both numbers by 5. After cancelling, multiply the numbers in the numerators and the numbers in the denominators.

Dividing by a fraction is the same as multiplying by its reciprocal. To find the reciprocal of a fraction, swap the numerator and denominator. Therefore

$$\frac{a}{b} \div \frac{c}{d} = \frac{a}{b} \times \frac{d}{c}$$

Example

Evaluate $\frac{3}{8} \div \frac{1}{2}$.

✓ ***Solution***

Working	Explanation
$\frac{3}{8} \div \frac{1}{2} = \frac{3}{8} \times \frac{2}{1}$ $= \frac{3}{\cancel{8}_4} \times \frac{\cancel{2}^1}{1}$ $= \frac{3 \times 1}{4 \times 1}$ $= \frac{3}{4}$	Dividing by $\frac{1}{2}$ is the same as multiplying by its reciprocal, which is $\frac{2}{1}$. Cancel common factors: 2 and 8 share a common factor of 2, so divide both numbers by 2. Multiply the remaining numbers in the numerators and denominators.

Example

Evaluate $2\frac{1}{3} \div 6$.

✓ ***Solution***

Working	Explanation
$2\frac{1}{3} = \frac{2 \times 3 + 1}{3}$ $= \frac{7}{3}$	Convert $2\frac{1}{3}$ to an improper fraction.
$2\frac{1}{3} \div 6 = \frac{7}{3} \div \frac{6}{1}$ $= \frac{7}{3} \times \frac{1}{6}$ $= \frac{7 \times 1}{3 \times 6}$ $= \frac{7}{18}$	Since 6 is equivalent to $\frac{6}{1}$, dividing by 6 is the same as multiplying by $\frac{1}{6}$. There are no common factors to cancel, so multiply the numbers in the numerators and denominators.

Example

Evaluate $-\frac{5}{6} \div -\frac{2}{3}$.

✓ Solution

Working	Explanation
$-\frac{5}{6} \div -\frac{2}{3} = -\frac{5}{6} \times -\frac{3}{2}$	Dividing by $-\frac{2}{3}$ is the same as multiplying by $-\frac{3}{2}$.
$= \frac{5}{6} \times \frac{3}{2}$	When you multiply two negative numbers, the result is positive, so the – signs can be removed.
$= \frac{5}{\cancel{6}_2} \times \frac{\cancel{3}^1}{2}$	Cancel common factors. 3 and 6 share a common factor of 3, so divide both numbers by 3.
$= \frac{5 \times 1}{2 \times 2}$	Multiply the remaining numbers in the numerators and denominators.
$= \frac{5}{4}$	

Exercise 3.2

Evaluate the following.

a. $\frac{2}{5} + \frac{3}{10}$

b. $\frac{3}{8} + \frac{5}{12}$

c. $\frac{11}{12} - \frac{1}{4}$

d. $-\frac{2}{3} + \frac{1}{2}$

e. $\frac{5}{6} \times \frac{3}{7}$

f. $\frac{7}{12} \times -\frac{9}{14}$

g. $\frac{1}{6} \div \frac{3}{4}$

h. $-\frac{3}{10} \div -\frac{5}{12}$

3.3 Decimals and fractions

To convert a fraction to a decimal, divide the numerator by the denominator. The result is either a terminating decimal (that is, one with an end) or a recurring decimal (that is, one that goes on forever).

An example of a fraction that is equivalent to a terminating decimal is $\frac{1}{2}$, since it is equivalent to 0.5.

An example of a fraction that is equivalent to a recurring decimal is $\frac{5}{12}$, since it is equivalent to $0.4166666\ldots$ We usually put a dot above the digit that repeats in a recurring decimal, so $0.4166666\ldots$ would be written as $0.41\dot{6}$.

Some fractions are equivalent to decimals where a group of digits repeats. For example, $\frac{2}{7} = 0.28571428571428\ldots$ Note that the digits 285714 repeat. In this case we can indicate a repeating group either by placing a dot above each digit in the group, or placing a line above all the digits that repeat. So we write $0.28571428571428...$ as either $0.\dot{2}\dot{8}\dot{5}\dot{7}\dot{1}\dot{4}$ or $0.\overline{285714}$.

Example

Convert each of the following fractions to a decimal.

a. $\frac{3}{5}$ b. $\frac{2}{3}$ c. $\frac{5}{8}$

✓ Solution

Working	Explanation
$\frac{3}{5} = 0.6$	Divide 3 by 5.
$3\overline{)2.{}^{2}0{}^{2}0{}^{2}0}$ with quotient $0.\ 6\ 6\ 6\ldots$ $\frac{2}{3} = 0.666\ldots$ $= 0.\dot{6}$	Divide 2 by 3.
$8\overline{)5.{}^{5}0{}^{2}0{}^{4}0}$ with quotient $0.\ 6\ 2\ 5$ $\frac{5}{8} = 0.625$	Divide 5 by 8.

Exercise 3.3

Convert each of the following fractions to a decimal.

a. $\frac{3}{4}$ b. $\frac{7}{20}$ c. $\frac{5}{6}$

3.4 Decimal arithmetic

To add or subtract decimals we first write the numbers under each other with their decimal points aligned. Then we add or subtract.

Example

Evaluate $19.53 + 8.36$.

✓ Solution

Working	Explanation
${}^{1}19.53$ $+\ \ 8.36$ 27.89	Write the numbers to be added in a vertical stack, aligned on the decimal point. Now add the numbers in the same way that we add whole numbers, working from right to left.

Example

Evaluate $9.6 - 5.12$.

✓ *Solution*

Working	Explanation
$\begin{array}{r} 9\,.\,{}^{5}\!\not{6}\;{}^{1}0 \\ -\underline{5\,.\;1\;\;2} \\ 4\,.\;4\;\;8 \end{array}$	Write the numbers to be subtracted in a vertical stack, aligned on the decimal point. Add a 0 in the hundredths column of 9.6 so that the two numbers have the same number of decimal places. Now subtract the numbers in the same way that we subtract whole numbers, working from right to left.

When multiplying decimals, the number of decimal places in the product is equal to the total number of decimal places in the numbers being multiplied.

Example

Evaluate 0.04×0.32.

✓ *Solution*

Working	Explanation
$4 \times 32 = 128$ $0.04 \times 0.32 = 0.0128$	Ignore the decimal points and multiply the two whole numbers: 4 and 32. 0.04 has two decimal places and 0.32 has two decimal places, so their product will have four decimal places.

Example

Evaluate 0.3^2.

Working	Explanation
$3 \times 3 = 9$ $0.3 \times 0.3 = 0.09$	0.3^2 means 0.3×0.3. Ignore the decimal points and multiply 3 by itself. 0.3 has one decimal place, so the product of 0.3 with 0.3 will have two decimal places.

When dividing a decimal by a whole number we simply divide as normal.

When dividing a number by a decimal, we multiply both parts of the division so that we can divide by a whole number.

Example

Evaluate $7.6 \div 5$.

✓ *Solution*

Working	Explanation
$\begin{array}{r} 1.52 \\ 5\overline{)7.^{2}6^{1}0} \end{array}$ $7.6 \div 5 = 1.52$	Divide 7.6 by 5 using the same method as when dividing a whole number.

Example

Evaluate $14.53 \div 0.2$.

✓ *Solution*

Working	Explanation
$\begin{array}{r} 72.65 \\ 2\overline{)1^{1}45.^{1}3^{1}0} \end{array}$ $14.53 \div 0.2 = 145.3 \div 2$ $= 72.65$	Multiply 0.2 by 10 to obtain a whole number (which is 2). If we multiply one number by 10 we need to multiply the other number by 10: 14.53 multiplied by 10 is 145.3. Divide 145.3 by 2. This is the same as dividing 14.53 by 0.2.

Exercise 3.4

Evaluate the following expressions.

a. $11.76 + 5.23$ **b.** $37.49 + 42.8$ **c.** $10.76 - 4.29$ **d.** $18.4 - 11.59$

e. 12.2×15.3 **f.** 1.2^2 **g.** $27.69 \div 4$ **h.** $12.42 \div 0.3$

3.5 Rounding decimals

To round a decimal number to a particular number of decimal places:

1. Locate the digit after the decimal point in the place you need to round to. For example, if rounding to 3 decimal places, locate the digit in the third place after the decimal point. Call this digit d.
2. Look at the digit to the right of d. If this digit is 5 or more, round up by adding 1 to d. It the digit is 4 or less, round down by leaving d unchanged.
3. Discard the digits to the right of d.

Example

Round 15.94437 to 3 decimal places.

✓ *Solution*

Working	Explanation
15.94437	Locate the digit in the third decimal place. This digit is 4.
15.944[3]7	Look at the digit to the right of the third decimal place. This digit is 3.
15.944	Since 3 is less than 5, we round down; that is, we leave the digit in the third decimal place unchanged and discard the digits to the right of it.

Example

Round 4.178942 to 2 decimal places.

✓ *Solution*

Working	Explanation
4.178942	Locate the digit in the second decimal place (7).
4.17[8]942	Look at the digit to the right of the second decimal place. This digit is 8.
4.18	Since 8 is greater than 5, we round up. Change the 7 to 8 and discard the digits to the right of it.

Example

Round 281.963 to 1 decimal place.

✓ *Solution*

Working	Explanation
281.963	Locate the digit in the first decimal place (9).
281.9[6]3	Look at the digit to the right of the first decimal place digit. This digit is 6.
282.0	Since 6 is greater than 5 we round up; that is, we add 1 to 9 and get 10.
	In this case we need to carry the 1 into the units column (that is, the column immediately to the left of the decimal point). The 1 becomes 2 and the first decimal place becomes 0.

An understanding of place value is required, as sometimes you will be required to round to the nearest tenth, hundredth or thousandth. Consider the place value diagram below.

			.			
Hundreds	Tens	Units		Tenths	Hundredths	Thousandths

You can see that rounding to the nearest tenth is the same as rounding to one decimal place, rounding to the nearest hundredth is the same as rounding to two decimal places and so on.

Example

Round 16.2435 to the nearest hundredth.

✓ ***Solution***

Working	Explanation
16.2435 16.24[3]5 16.24	Rounding to the nearest hundredth is the same as rounding to two decimal places. Locate the digit in the second decimal place (4). Look at the digit to the right of the second decimal place. This digit is 3. Since 3 is less than 5 round down by discarding the digits to the right of 4.

Example

Round 252.4655943 to the nearest tenth.

✓ ***Solution***

Working	Explanation
252.4655943 252.4[6]55943 252.5	Rounding to the nearest tenth is the same as rounding to one decimal place. Locate the digit in the first decimal place. Look at the digit to the right of the first decimal place. This digit is 6 so round up. Change the 4 to 5 and discard the digits to the right.

Exercise 3.5.1

Round each of the following decimals correct to 2 decimal places.

a. 12.4328 **b.** 197.63582 **c.** −29.896 4713

Exercise 3.5.2

Round each of the following decimals correct to 3 decimal places.

a. 445.213894 **b.** 3.1415 **c.** 27.006421

3.6 Fractions, decimals and percentages

The term 'per cent' means 'out of 100'. We can think of percentages as being fractions with a denominator of 100.

To convert a fraction or decimal to a percentage, we multiply by 100.

Example

Convert 0.92 to a percentage.

✓ Solution

Working	Explanation
$0.92 = 0.92 \times 100\%$ $= 92\%$	To convert a decimal to a percentage, multiply by 100. (This is the same as moving the decimal point two places to the right.)

Example

Convert $\frac{3}{5}$ to a percentage.

✓ Solution

Working	Explanation
$\frac{3}{5} = \frac{3}{5} \times 100\%$	To convert a fraction to a percentage, multiply by 100,
$= 3 \times 20\%$	Divide 100 by 5 first.
$= 60\%$	Multiply the remaining numbers.

To convert a percentage to a fraction or a decimal, we divide by 100.

Example

Change 64% to a fraction.

✓ Solution

Working	Explanation
$64\% = \frac{64}{100} = \frac{16}{25}$	To convert a percentage to a fraction, divide by 100. Divide numerator and denominator by 4 to simplify the fraction.

Example

Change 12.5% to a decimal.

✓ ***Solution***

Working	Explanation
$12.5\% = \frac{12.5}{100}$ $= 0.125$	To convert a percentage to a decimal, divide by 100. This is the same as moving the decimal point two places to the left.

Exercise 3.6.1

Convert each of the following decimals to a percentage.

a. 0.3 b. 0.57 c. 1.2

Exercise 3.6.2

Convert each of the following fractions to a percentage.

a. $\frac{7}{10}$ b. $\frac{3}{4}$ c. $\frac{4}{5}$

Exercise 3.6.3

Convert each of the following percentages to a decimal.

a. 14% b. 0.3% c. $5\frac{1}{2}\%$

Exercise 3.6.4

Convert each of the following percentages to a fraction.

a. 36% b. 42% c. $3\frac{1}{4}\%$

3.7 Finding a percentage of a quantity

Finding percentages without a calculator can be done by dividing and multiplying.

Take 100% to be the whole quantity. Then:

- to find 1%, divide the quantity by 100
- to find 10%, divide the quantity by 10
- and so on.

Example

Calculate 12% of 500.

✓ *Solution*

Working	Explanation
1% of $500 = 500 \div 100 = 5$	Calculate 1% of 500 by dividing by 100.
12% of $500 = 12 \times 5 = 60$	Multiply the result by 12 to calculate 12% of 500.

Example

Calculate 30% of 72.

✓ *Solution*

Working	Explanation
10% of $72 = 72 \div 10 = 7.2$	Calculate 10% of 72 by dividing by 10.
30% of $72 = 3 \times 7.2 = 21.6$	Multiply the result by 3 to calculate 30%.

Example

Calculate 45% of 240.

✓ *Solution*

Working	Explanation
10% of $240 = 240 \div 10 = 24$	Calculate 10% of 240 by dividing by 10.
5% of $240 = 24 \div 2 = 12$	Calculate 5% of 240 by dividing 10% of 240 by 2.
45% of $240 = 4 \times 24 + 12 = 96 + 12 = 108$	45% is $4 \times 10\% + 5\%$

We can also find the percentage of a quantity using the rule

$$\textbf{\textit{percentage of a quantity}} = \frac{\textbf{\textit{percentage}}}{\textbf{\textit{100}}} \times \textbf{\textit{quantity}}$$

Example

Calculate 15% of \$480.

✓ ***Solution***

Working	Explanation
$15\% \text{ of } 480 = \frac{15}{100} \times \frac{480}{1}$	15% of a quantity = $\frac{15}{100}$ × the quantity. Express the quantity as a fraction (since a whole number can be written as a fraction with a denominator of 1).
$= \frac{15}{\cancel{100}_{5}} \times \frac{\cancel{480}^{24}}{1}$ $= 3 \times 24$ $= 72$	Simplify by dividing 480 and 100 by 20. Divide 15 by 5. Multiply the remaining numbers.
$15\% \text{ of } \$480 = \$72$	Include units with your final answer.

Example

Use a calculator to find 22% of \$540.

✓ ***Solution***

Working	Explanation
$22\% \text{ of } 540 = \frac{22}{100} \times 540$ $= 118.8$ $22\% \text{ of } \$540 = \$118.80$	22% of a quantity = $\frac{22}{100}$ × the quantity. Key 22 ÷ 100 × 540 = into the calculator. Include a \$ sign with the final answer. For money, decimal answers should be given to two decimal places.

Exercise 3.7.1

Calculate each of the following.

a. 10% of 60 **b.** 30% of 40 **c.** 45% of 20

Exercise 3.7.2

Calculate each of the following.

a. 55% of 88 **b.** 80% of 64 **c.** 36% of 50

3.8 Expressing one quantity as a percentage of another

To express quantity A as a percentage of quantity B, write the fraction $\frac{\text{quantity } A}{\text{quantity } B}$ and then multiply it by 100 to convert the fraction to a percentage.

Example

Express a test result of 32 out of 40 as a percentage.

✓ ***Solution***

Working	Explanation
$\frac{32}{40} \times 100 = \frac{4}{5} \times 100$	Write the test result as a fraction and then multiply it by 100.
$= \frac{4}{\cancel{5}_1} \times \frac{\cancel{100}^{20}}{1}$	Express 100 as a fraction. Simplify by dividing 5 and 100 by 5.
$= 4 \times 20 = 80$	Multiply the remaining numbers.
$\frac{32}{40} = 80\%$	

To calculate a percentage increase, use the rule

$$\textbf{percentage increase} = \frac{\textbf{increase}}{\textbf{original}} \times 100\%$$

To calculate a percentage decrease, use the rule

$$\textbf{percentage decrease} = \frac{\textbf{decrease}}{\textbf{original}} \times 100\%$$

Example

The number of students in a year level at a school increased from 120 to 150. Find the percentage increase.

✓ ***Solution***

Working	Explanation
Increase $= 150 - 120$ $= 30$	Calculate the increase in numbers.
Percentage increase $= \frac{30}{120} \times 100\%$ $= \frac{1}{4} \times 100\%$	Percentage increase $= \frac{\text{increase}}{\text{original}} \times 100\%$. Simplify the fraction by dividing the numerator and denominator by 30.
$= \frac{1}{\cancel{4}_1} \times \frac{\cancel{100}^{25}}{1}\%$ $= 25\%$	Express 100 as a fraction. Simplify by dividing 4 and 100 by 4. Multiply the remaining numbers.

Example

The price of a dress is reduced from \$250 to \$175. Find the percentage discount.

✓ ***Solution***

Working	Explanation
$\text{Decrease} = 250 - 175$ $= 75$	A percentage discount is a percentage decrease. Decrease = original price − new price.
$\text{Percentage decrease} = \frac{75}{250} \times 100\%$ $= \frac{3}{10} \times 100\%$	Percentage decrease $= \frac{\text{decrease}}{\text{original}} \times 100\%$. Simplify the fraction by dividing the numerator and denominator by 25.
$= \frac{3}{\cancel{10}_1} \times \frac{\cancel{100}^{10}}{1}\%$ $= 30\%$	Express 100 as a fraction. Simplify by dividing 10 and 100 by 10. Multiply the remaining numbers.

Exercise 3.8.1

Express each of the following test results as a percentage.

a. 21 out of 25 **b.** 14 out of 20 **c.** 22 out of 40.

Exercise 3.8.2

Ian's wage increases from \$1500 per week to \$1650 per week. Find the percentage increase.

Exercise 3.8.3

A car was purchased for \$8500 and sold three years later for \$6800. Find the percentage loss in price.

3.9 Increasing and decreasing a quantity by a percentage

To increase a quantity by a percentage, calculate the amount by which the quantity is increased and then add this to the original quantity.

Example

A bag of potato crisps contains 60 grams of crisps. If the mass of crisps in the bag is increased by 15%, determine the new mass of crisps in the bag.

✓ *Solution*

Working	Explanation
$15\% = 10\% + 5\%$ $10\% \text{ of } 60 = 60 \div 10 = 6$ $5\% \text{ of } 60 = 6 \div 2 = 3$ Therefore $15\% \text{ of } 60 = 6 + 3 = 9$	Calculate the increase by calculating 15% of 60. To do that: • Calculate 10% of 60 by dividing 60 by 10. • Calculate 5% of 60 by dividing 10% of 60 by 2. • Add the two results (since 15% of 60 = 10% of 60 + 5% of 60).
New mass $= 60 + 9 = 69$ grams	Calculate the new mass of chips by adding the increase to the original mass.

To decrease a quantity by a percentage, calculate the amount by which the quantity is decreased and then subtract this from the original quantity.

Example

A pair of runners has a retail price of \$180. At a sale, the price is discounted by 30%. What is the sale price of the runners?

✓ *Solution*

Working	Explanation
$10\% \text{ of } 180 = 180 \div 10 = 18$ $30\% \text{ of } 180 = 18 \times 3 = 54$ Sale price $= 180 - 54 = \$126$	Calculate the discount by calculating 30% of 180. To do that: • Calculate 10% of 180 by dividing it by 10. • Calculate 30% of 180 by multiplying 10% of 180 by 3. This gives the discount. • Calculate the sale price of the runners by subtracting the discount from the original price. Include a \$ sign with your final answer.

Exercise 3.9.1

The price of a bag is increased by 10%. If the original price was \$160, calculate the new price.

Exercise 3.9.2

A \$1200 television is discounted by 30%. Determine the sale price.

Exercise 3.9.3

The area of a chicken pen is 4 m^2. A boundary fence is moved so that the area is increased by 35%. What is the new area of the pen?

3.10 Finding the whole from a given percentage

If we know a percentage of a quantity, we can find the whole quantity by using a method known as the **unitary method**. This involves finding another percentage of the quantity that can easily be multiplied by 100 to find the value of 100%.

Suppose we are told that 30% of a quantity is 18. We can use the unitary method to find the whole quantity, that is, 100%. We first look for a percentage that is easy to multiply to get to 100 (for example, 10). We then calculate what 10% of the quantity would be, based on the given percentage (10% is one third of 30%, so 10% of the whole quantity is a third of 18, that is, 6). Finally we multiply the 10% quantity by 10 to get the 100% quantity ($10 \times 6 = 60$).

$\div 3$	30%	is	18	$\div 3$
	10%	is	6	
$\times 10$	100%	is	60	$\times 10$

Example

35% of Rob's savings is $2100. How much has Rob saved in total?

✓ Solution

Working	Explanation
35% is 2100	35% of Rob's savings is $2100.
5% is $\frac{2100}{7} = 300$	Divide by 7 to find what 5% of the savings is.
100% is $300 \times 20 = 6000$	Multiply by 20 to find 100%.
Rob has saved $6000 in total.	

Example

The price of a shirt is discounted by 25%. The sale price of the shirt is $150. What was the original price of the shirt?

✓ Solution

Working	Explanation
75% is 150	The sale price of the shirt is the original price (100%) minus the discount (25%), so $150 is 75% of the original price.
25% is $\frac{150}{3} = 50$	Divide by 3 to find 25%.
100% is $50 \times 4 = 200$	Multiply by 4 to find 100%.
The original price of the shirt is $200.	

✎ Exercise 3.10.1

If 40% of a quantity is 100, find the whole quantity.

✎ Exercise 3.10.2

If 8% of a quantity is 32, find the whole quantity.

✎ Exercise 3.10.3

Jesse has saved 35% of the amount required to buy a car. If the amount saved is $2800, determine the price of the car.

✎ Exercise 3.10.4

At a sale, the price of a dress is $72 after a 20% discount is applied. What was the original price of the dress?

3.11 GST

In Australia prices are subject to a 10% Goods and Services Tax, known as the GST. This means that 10% of the base price of an item is added to the price as GST. (The prices quoted in stores generally include GST.)

Example

An air fryer costs $132 before GST is added. What is the selling price of the air fryer with GST included?

✓ Solution

Working	Explanation
10% of $132 = 132 \div 10 = 13.20$ Price including GST $= 132 + 13.20 = \$145.20$	The GST is 10% of $132. To find 10% of any quantity, divide the quantity by 10. Add the GST to the base price, i.e. the price before GST is added. Include a $ sign with your final answer.

The price of an item when GST is included is $100\% + 10\% = 110\%$ per cent of the price without GST.

We can use the unitary method to find the price before GST is added.

Example

The price of a skirt including GST is $79.20. What is the price without GST included?

✓ Solution

Working	Explanation
110% is 79.20 10% is $\frac{79.20}{11} = 7.20$ 10% is $7.20 \times 10 = 72$ The price without GST included is $72.	The price including GST is 110% of the price without GST. Divide by 11 to find 10%. Multiply by 10 to find 100%.

Exercise 3.11.1

A microwave oven costs $380 before GST is added. What is the selling price of the microwave with GST included?

Exercise 3.11.2

The price of a camera including GST is $198. What is the price without GST included?

Exercise 3.11.3

The price of a bottle of perfume with GST included is $231. How much of this price is GST?

Answers

Exercise 3.1.1

a. $\frac{9}{24}$ b. $-\frac{28}{60}$

Exercise 3.1.2

a. $\frac{1}{7}$ b. $\frac{1}{3}$ c. $\frac{7}{10}$ d. $\frac{4}{7}$ e. $\frac{3}{8}$

Exercise 3.2

a. $\frac{7}{10}$ b. $\frac{19}{24}$ c. $\frac{2}{3}$ d. $-\frac{1}{6}$

e. $\frac{5}{14}$ f. $-\frac{3}{8}$ g. $\frac{2}{9}$ h. $\frac{18}{25}$

Exercise 3.3

a. 0.75 b. 0.35 c. $0.8\dot{3}$

Exercise 3.4

a. 16.99 b. 80.29 c. 6.47 d. 6.81

e. 186.66 f. 1.44 g. 6.9225 h. 41.4

Exercise 3.5.1

a. 12.43 b. 197.64 c. −29.90

Exercise 3.5.2

a. 445.214 b. 3.142 c. 27.006

Exercise 3.6.1

a. 30% b. 57% c. 120%

Exercise 3.6.2

a. 70% b. 75% c. 80%

Exercise 3.6.3

a. 0.14 b. 0.003 c. 0.055

Exercise 3.6.4

a. $\frac{9}{25}$ b. $\frac{21}{50}$ c. $\frac{13}{400}$

Exercise 3.7.1

a. 6 b. 12 c. 9

Exercise 3.7.2

a. 48.4 b. 51.2 c. 18

Exercise 3.8.1

a. 84% b. 70% c. 55%

Exercise 3.8.2

10%

Exercise 3.8.3

20%

Exercise 3.9.1

$176

Exercise 3.9.2

$840

Exercise 3.9.3

5.4 m^2

Exercise 3.10.1

250

Exercise 3.10.2

400

Exercise 3.10.3

$8000

Exercise 3.10.4

$90

Exercise 3.11.1

$418

Exercise 3.11.2

$180

Exercise 3.11.3

$21

Chapter 4 – Measurement

4.1 Units of measurement

When we convert from smaller units of measurement to larger units of measurement we divide.

When we convert from larger units of measurement to smaller units of measurement we multiply.

Each quantity that we measure has a standard unit of measurement. We use prefixes to indicate multiples of the standard units of measurement.

Prefix	Symbol	Meaning
milli	m	one-thousandth
centi	c	one-hundredth
kilo	k	one thousand

When we attach a prefix to a standard unit it tells us what the multiple of that unit is. For example, kilogram means 1000 grams and centimetre means $\frac{1}{100}$ of a metre.

The following diagrams show how to convert units.

Units of length

The standard unit of length is the metre (m).

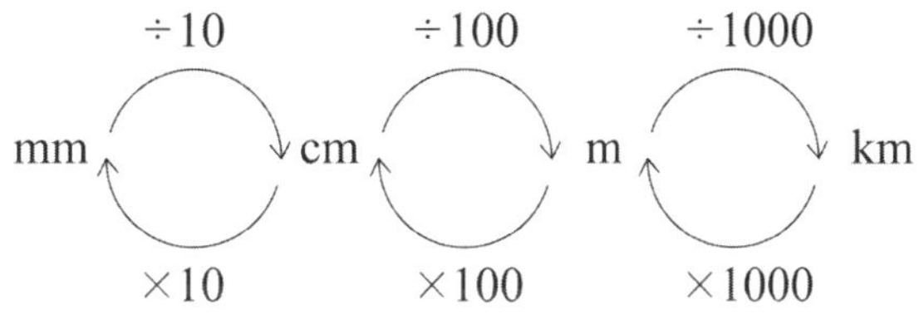

$\div 10$ $\div 100$ $\div 1000$

mm cm m km

$\times 10$ $\times 100$ $\times 1000$

Units of area

The standard unit of area is the square metre (m^2).

Large areas can be measured in hectares, where one hectare is equal to ten thousand square metres.

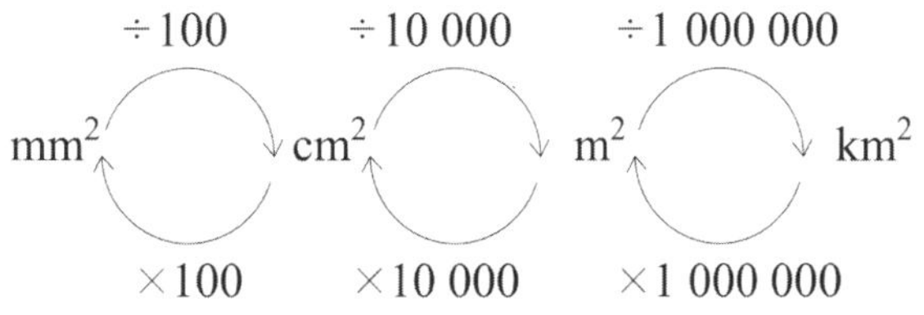

$\div 100$ $\div 10\,000$ $\div 1\,000\,000$

mm^2 cm^2 m^2 km^2

$\times 100$ $\times 10\,000$ $\times 1\,000\,000$

$$1 \text{ ha} = 10\,000 \text{ m}^2$$

Units of volume

The standard unit of volume is the cubic metre (m^3).

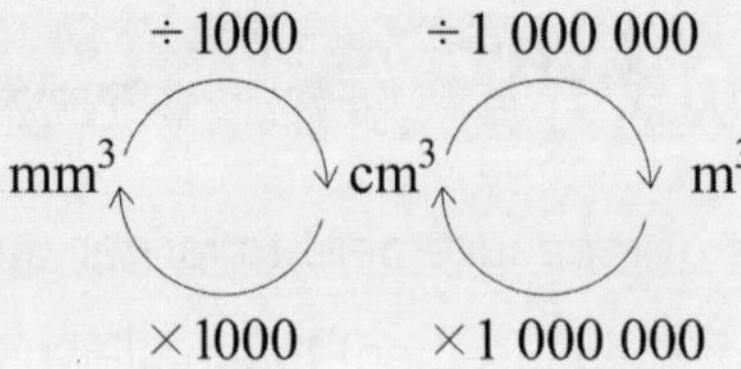

Units of capacity

The standard unit of capacity is the litre (L).

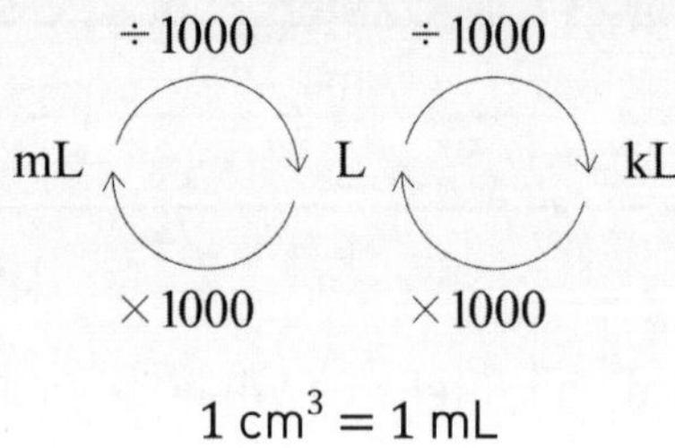

$1 \text{ cm}^3 = 1 \text{ mL}$

Units of mass

The standard unit of mass is the gram (g).

÷ 1000 ÷ 1000

mg g kg

× 1000 × 1000

Example

Fill in the following blanks.

a. 1540 mm = ________ m

b. 2 cm^2 = ____________ mm^2

c. 3 L = ______________ mL

d. $15\,000 \text{ m}^2$ = ________ ha

e. 4 m^3 = ____________ cm^3

f. 55 cm^3 = __________ mL

g. 0.05 kg = __________ mg

✓ Solution

Working	Explanation
a. $1540 \div 1000 = 1.54$ $1540 \text{ mm} = 1.54 \text{ m}$	To convert mm to m divide by 1000.
b. $2 \times 100 = 200$ $2 \text{ cm}^2 = 200 \text{ mm}^2$	To convert cm^2 to mm^2 multiply by 100.
c. $3 \times 1000 = 3000$ $3 \text{ L} = 3000 \text{ mL}$	To convert L to mL multiply by 1000.
d. $15\,000 \div 10\,000 = 1.5$ $15\,000 \text{ m}^2 = 1.5 \text{ ha}$	To convert m^2 to ha divide by 10 000.
e. $4 \times 1\,000\,000 = 4\,000\,000$ $4 \text{ m}^3 = 4\,000\,000 \text{ cm}^3$	To convert from m^3 to cm^3 multiply by 1 000 000.
f. $55 \text{ cm}^3 = 55 \text{ mL}$	$1 \text{ cm}^3 = 1 \text{ mL}$
g. $0.05 \times 1000 = 50$ $50 \times 1000 = 50\,000$ $0.05 \text{ kg} = 50\,000 \text{ mg}$	Multiply by 1000 to convert kg to g then multiply by 1000 to convert g to mg.

Exercise 4.1

Fill in the following blanks.

a. 216 cm = ________ m

b. 2.4 m^2 = ________ cm^2

c. 3 kg = ________ g

d. 1.2 ha = ________ m^2

e. 2.7 mm^2 = ________ cm^2

f. 22 mL = ________ cm^3

g. 3500 cm^3 = ________ m^3

h. 22435 cm = ________ km

4.2 Perimeter

The perimeter is the distance around a two-dimensional shape. When calculating the perimeter of a shape, we add the lengths of all sides. However, all measurements must be in the same units.

Example

Calculate the perimeter of the following shape.

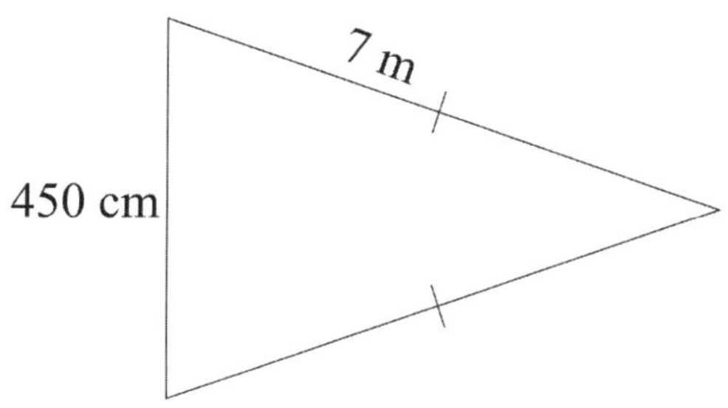

✓ Solution

Working	Explanation
$450 \div 100 = 4.5$ $450\text{ cm} = 4.5\text{ m}$ $P = 4.5 + 7 + 7$ $= 18.5\text{ m}$	All measurements need to be in the same units, so convert cm to m by dividing by 100. Add the length of each side of the triangle. Include units with the final answer.

Example

Calculate the perimeter of the following shape.

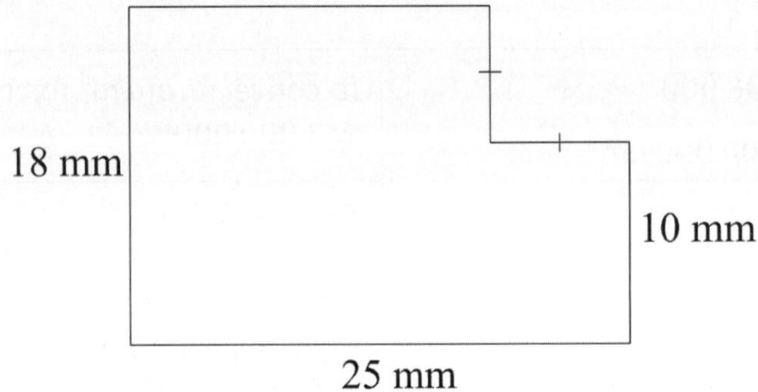

✓ Solution

Working	Explanation
18 mm 10 mm 25 mm $P = 2 \times 18 + 2 \times 25$ $= 36 + 50$ $= 86\text{ mm}$	This shape will have the same perimeter as a rectangle with sides of 18 mm and 25 mm. The perimeter of a rectangle is found by doubling the length and doubling the width, and then adding these results. Include units with your final answer.

Exercise 4.2

Calculate the perimeter of each of the following shapes:

a.

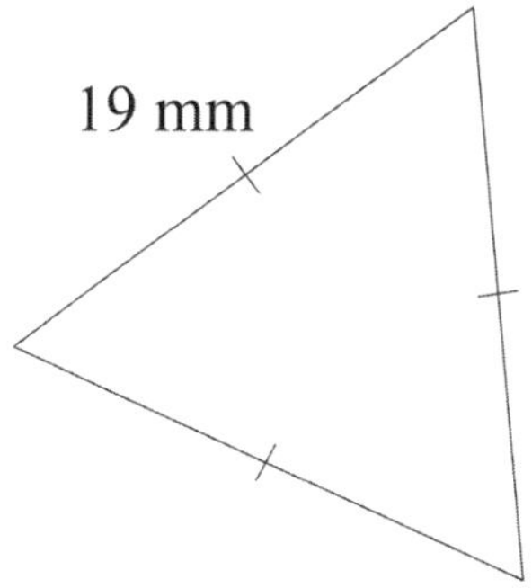

b.

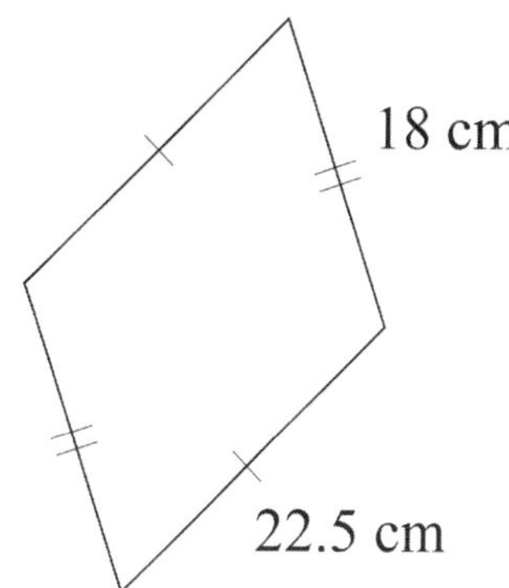

c.

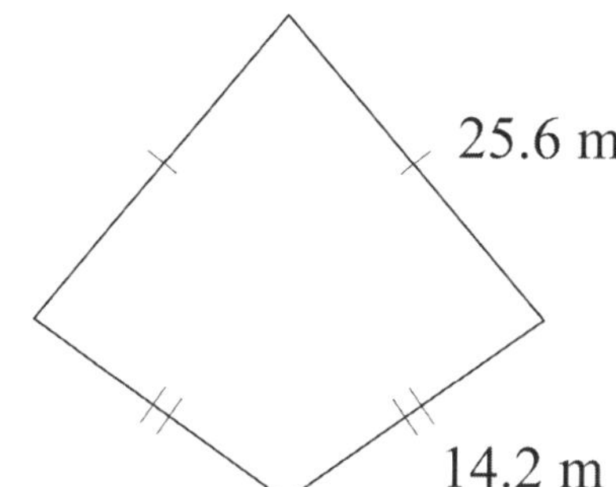

d.

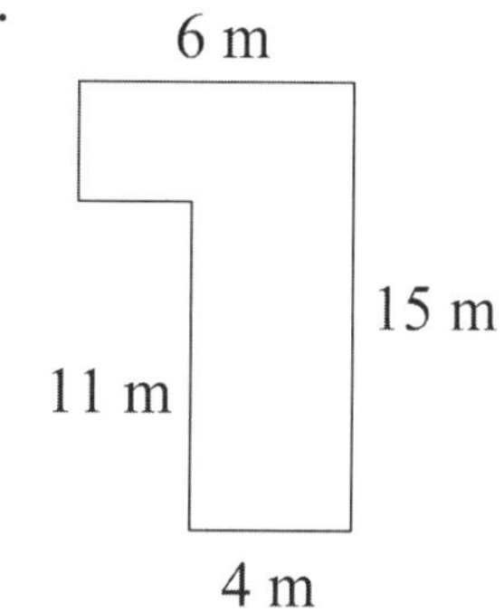

4.3 Area

Area is a measure of the space contained within a two-dimensional figure. It is measured in square units.

The following table gives the formulas for the areas of some common shapes.

Name of shape	Diagram	Area
Triangle		$A = \frac{bh}{2}$ where b is the length of the base of the triangle and h is the height of the triangle measured perpendicular to the base. The base can be any side of the triangle.
Rectangle		$A = lw$ where l and w are the length and width.

Parallelogram		$$A = bh$$ where b is the length of the base of the parallelogram and h is the height of the parallelogram measured perpendicular to the base. The base can be any side of the parallelogram but the height must be measured perpendicular to this side.
Rhombus		$$A = \frac{xy}{2}$$ where x and y are the lengths of the diagonals of the rhombus.
Kite		$$A = \frac{xy}{2}$$ where x and y are the lengths of the diagonals of the kite.
Trapezium		$$A = \frac{1}{2}(a + b)h$$ where a and b are the lengths of the parallel sides and h is the perpendicular height.

Example

Find the area of the following shape.

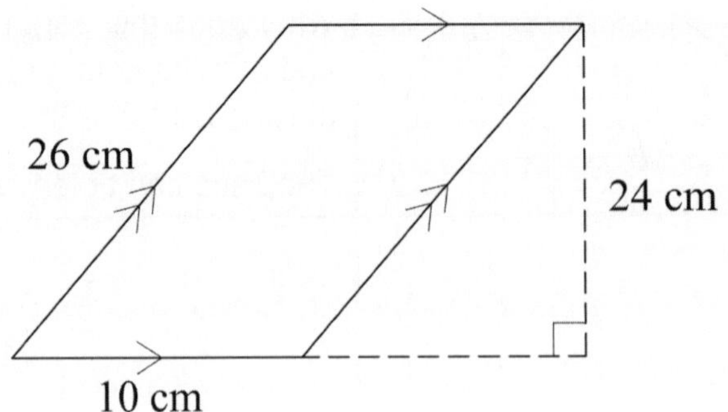

✓ Solution

Working	Explanation
$A = bh$	Use the formula for the area of a parallelogram.
$= 10 \times 24$	The height is measured perpendicular to the base, so $b = 10$ and $h = 24$.
$= 240 \text{ cm}^2$	Add units to the final answer.

Example

Find the area of the following shape.

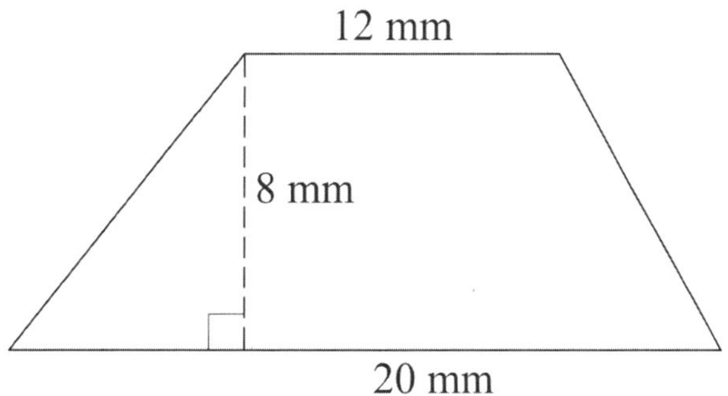

✓ Solution

Working	Explanation
$A = \frac{1}{2}(a + b)h$	Use the formula for the area of a trapezium.
$= \frac{1}{2} \times (20 + 12) \times 8$	The parallel side lengths, a and b, are 20 and 12, and the perpendicular height is 8.
$= \frac{1}{2} \times 32 \times 8$	Remember the order of operations: brackets first.
$= 16 \times 8$	Add units to the final answer.
$= 128 \text{ mm}^2$	

Example

Find the area of the following shape.

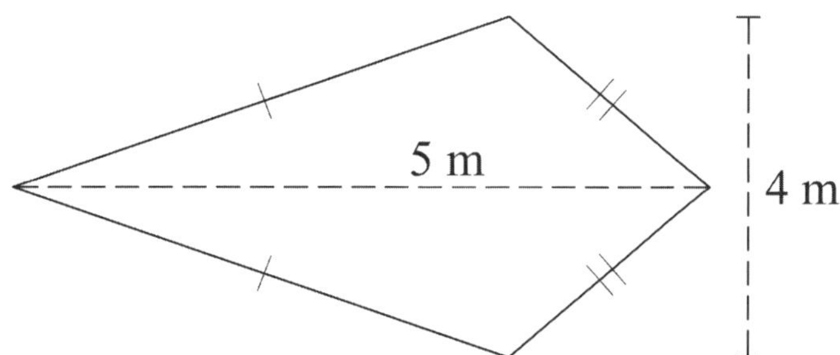

✓ Solution

Working	Explanation
$A = \frac{xy}{2}$ $= \frac{5 \times 4}{2}$ $= \frac{20}{2}$ $= 10 \text{ m}^2$	Use the formula for the area of a kite. The lengths of the diagonals, x and y, are 5 and 4. Add units to the final answer.

A composite shape is created from two or more basic shapes.

Example

Find the area of the following composite shape.

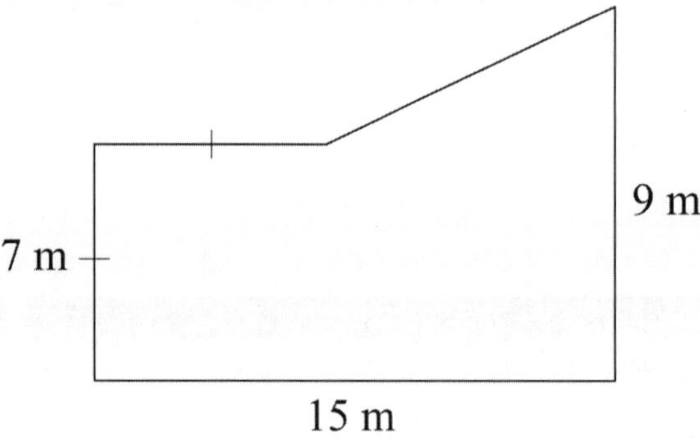

✓ Solution

Working	Explanation
7 m 15 m $A = lw$ $= 15 \times 7$ $= 105 \text{ m}^2$	The area is found by adding the area of a rectangle to the area of a triangle. Calculate the area of the rectangle. The rectangle has sides of length 15 and 7.

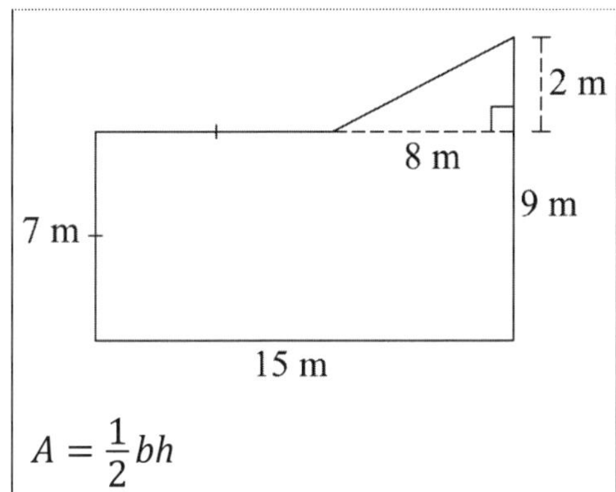 $A = \frac{1}{2}bh$ $= \frac{1}{2} \times 8 \times 2$ $= 8\ \text{m}^2$	The triangle has a base length of $15 - 7 = 8$ m. The height of the triangle is $9 - 7 = 2$ m.
$A = 105 + 8$ $= 113\ \text{m}^2$	Add the areas of the two component shapes to give the area of the composite shape.

Exercise 4.3.1

Calculate the area of each of the following shapes.

a.

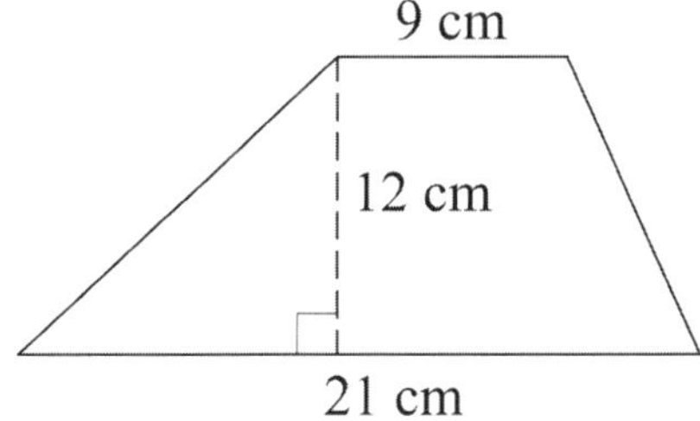

b.

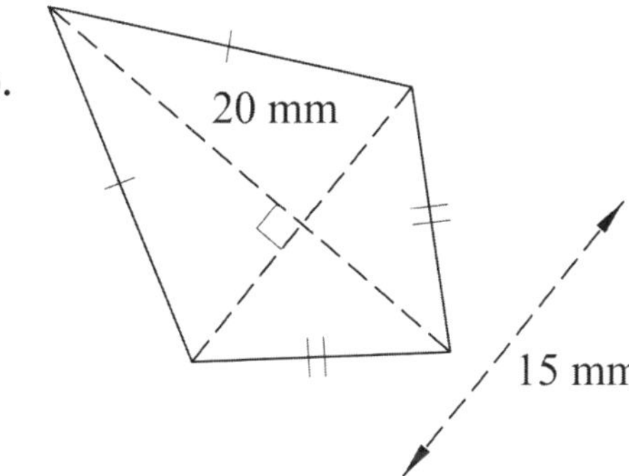

c.

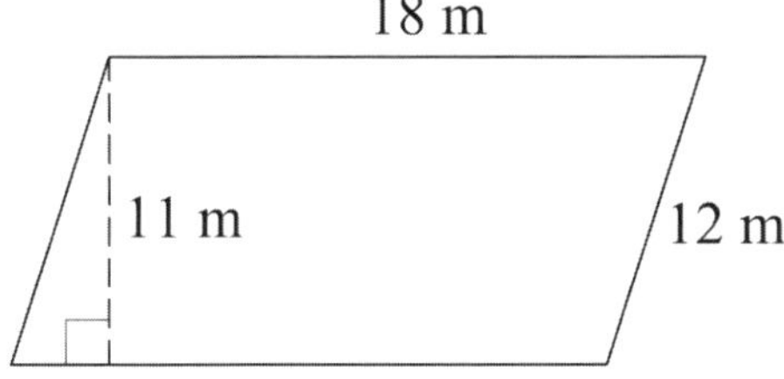

d.

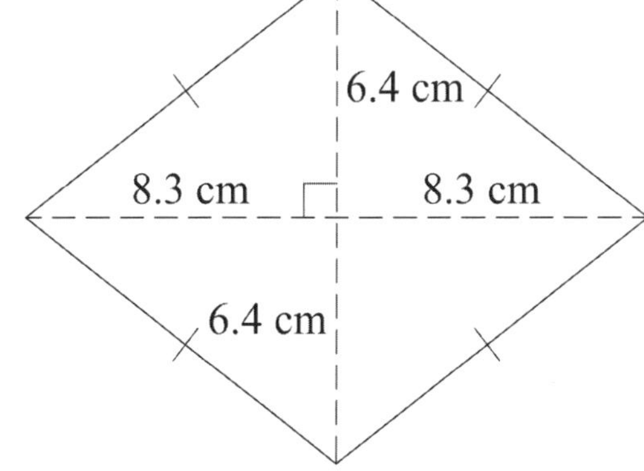

Exercise 4.3.2

Calculate the area of the shaded region in the diagram below.

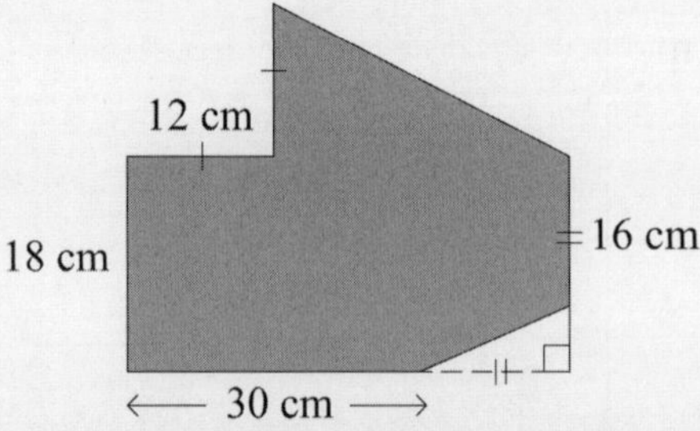

4.4 Circles

All points on a circle are the same distance from its centre. The **radius** of a circle is the distance from the centre to any point on the circle. The **diameter** of a circle is the length of a line that passes through the centre and extends to opposite ends of the circle. The diameter is double the length of the radius. The **circumference** is the distance around the circle.

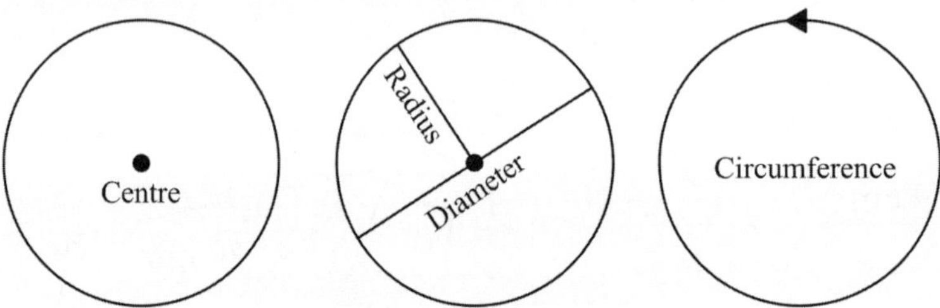

$$2 \times radius = diameter$$

The circumference (C) of a circle can be found using either:

- $C = 2\pi r$ where r is the radius, or
- $C = \pi d$ where d is the diameter.

$\pi = 3.14159265358979323846264338327950288419716939937510582097494459 23\ldots$

π is a very interesting number because it goes on without end, with the decimal places following no repeating pattern. For this reason, π cannot be written as a fraction. Any number that cannot be written as a fraction is called an **irrational number**.

Luckily for us, calculators have an inbuilt π button that we can use for calculations. If we cannot use a calculator, we leave our answer as a multiple of π.

Example

Calculate the exact circumference of the following circle.

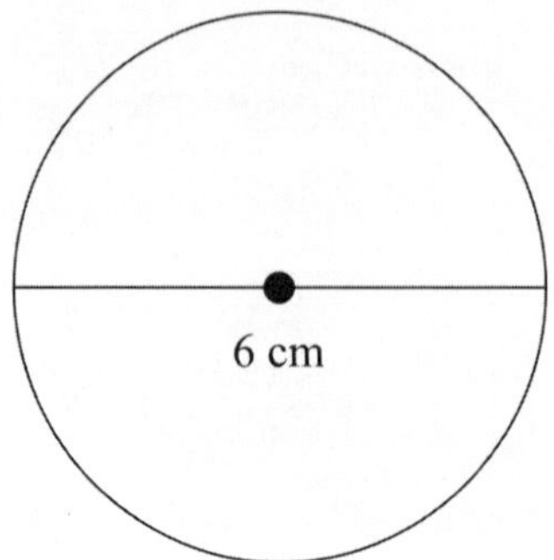

✓ Solution

Working	Explanation
$C = \pi d$ $= \pi \times 6$ $= 6\pi$ cm	We are given the diameter of the circle, so use the circumference formula that includes the diameter, d. Include units with your answer. (The circumference will have the same units as the diameter.)

Example

Calculate the circumference of the following circle. Give your answer correct to 2 decimal places.

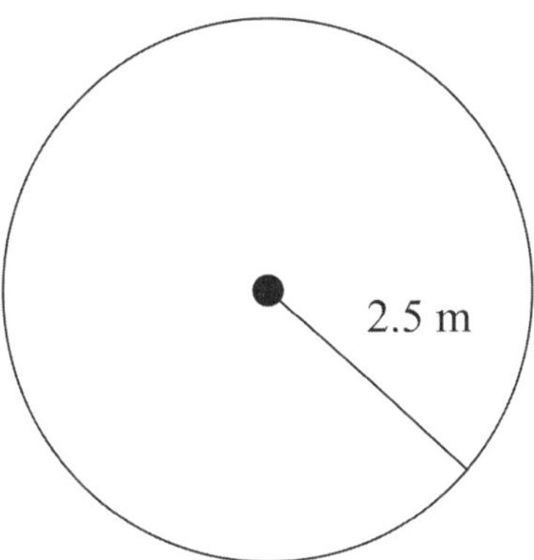

✓ Solution

Working	Explanation
$C = 2\pi r$ $= 2 \times \pi \times 2.5$ $= 15.7079\ldots$ $= 15.71$ m	We are given the radius of this circle, so use the circumference formula that includes the radius, r. Enter $2 \times \pi \times 2.5$ into a calculator and round the answer to 2 decimal places. Include units with your answer. (The circumference will have the same units as the radius.)

Example

Find the perimeter of this shape, giving your answer correct to 2 decimal places.

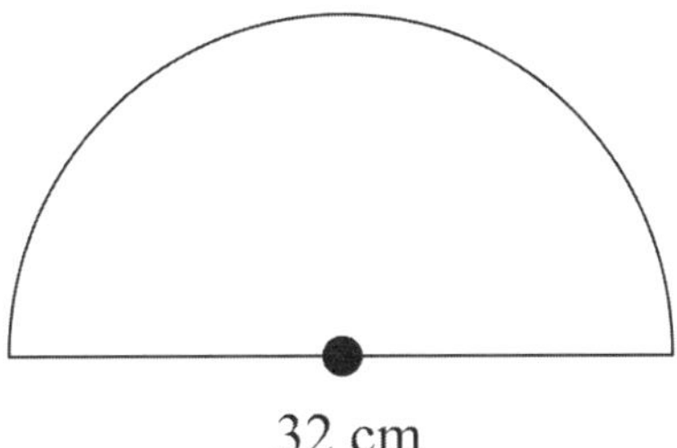

✓ Solution

Working	Explanation
Curve length $= \pi d \div 2$ $= \pi \times 32 \div 2$ $= 16\pi$	The curved length is half the circumference of a circle with diameter 32 cm.
Perimeter $= 16\pi + 32$ $= 82.26548...$ $= 82.27$ cm	Add the diameter to the curved length to obtain the perimeter of the shape. Enter $16 \times \pi + 32$ into a calculator to obtain the answer correct to 2 decimal places.

We can also use π to calculate the area of a circle.

The area of a circle is

$$A = \pi r^2$$

where r is the radius of the circle.

Example

Find the area of a circle with a radius of 3 m. Express your answer as an exact value.

✓ Solution

Working	Explanation
$A = \pi r^2$ $= \pi \times 3^2$ $= 9\pi$ m^2	Substitute 3 for r in the rule for calculating the area of a circle. πr^2 means $\pi \times r^2$ Include units with your answer. If the radius is measured in m, then the area will be measured in m^2.

Example

Find the area of a circle with a diameter of 46 mm. Give your answer correct to one decimal place.

✓ Solution

Working	Explanation
$r = 46 \div 2$ $= 23$ mm	First find the radius of the circle (which is the length of the diameter divided by 2).
$A = \pi r^2$ $= \pi \times 23^2$ $= 1661.9025\ldots$ $= 1661.9$ mm^2	Substitute 23 for r in the rule for calculating the area of a circle. Enter $\pi \times 23^2$ into a calculator to obtain an answer correct to 1 decimal place. Include units with your answer. If the radius is measured in mm then the area will be measured in mm^2.

Exercise 4.4

a. Find the exact circumference of a circle with radius 14 cm.

b. Find the circumference of a circle with diameter 12 mm correct to 2 decimal places.

c. Find the perimeter of the following figure correct to one decimal place.

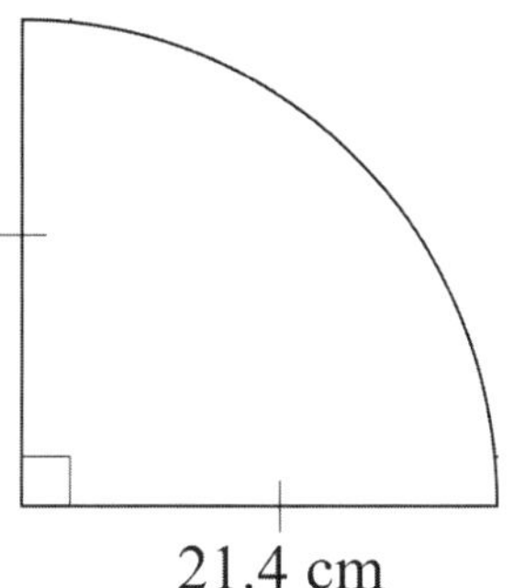

d. Find the area of the following circle correct to one decimal place.

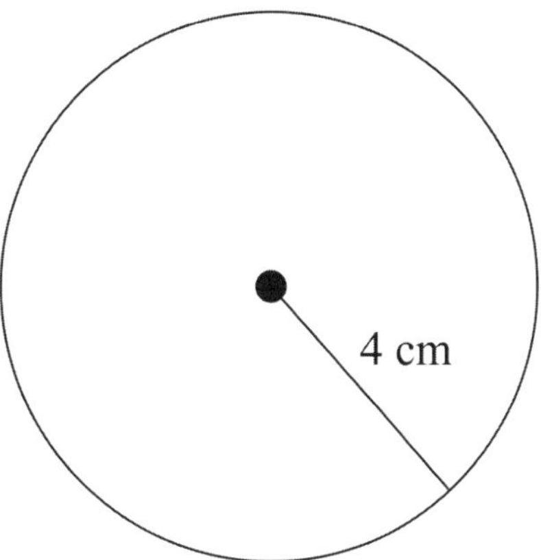

e. Find the area of the following circle correct to one decimal place.

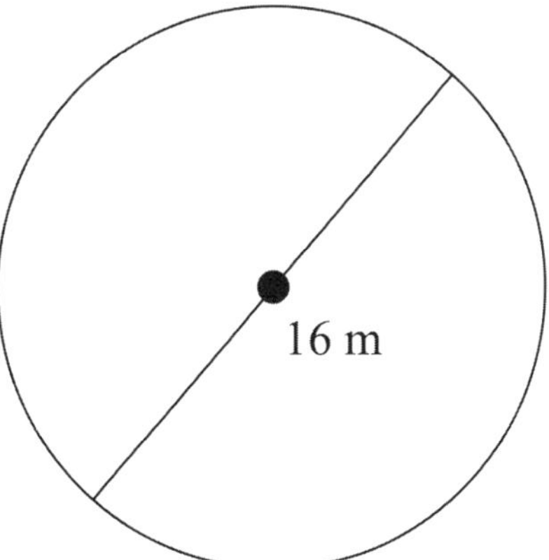

4.5 Volume

Volume measures the space occupied by a three-dimensional object. Volume is measured using cubic units, such as cm^3 or m^3. When we measure the volume of liquids, the standard unit is the litre (L). When we refer to the volume of liquid that a three-dimensional object can hold, we use the term **capacity**.

In general the volume, V, of an object is

$$V = Ah$$

where A is the area of the object's base and h is the object's height.

The formulas for calculating the volume of some common three-dimensional objects are listed below.

Name	Diagram	Formula
Cube	l	$V = l^3$
Rectangular prism	h, w, l	$V = lwh$
Cylinder	r, h	$V = \pi r^2 h$

Example

Find the volume of the following three-dimensional object.

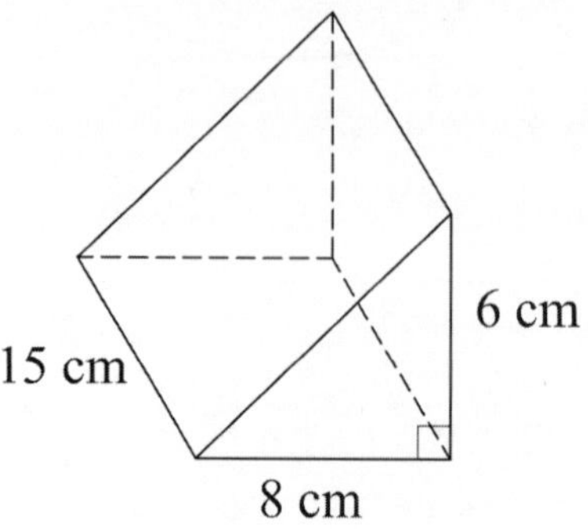

✓ Solution

Working	Explanation
$A = \frac{1}{2}bh$ $= \frac{1}{2} \times 8 \times 6$ $= 4 \times 6$ $= 24 \text{ cm}^2$	The volume of an object is found by multiplying the area of its base by its height. The base of the prism shown is a triangle with a base of 8 cm and a height of 6 cm. Calculate this area.
$V = Ah$ $= 24 \times 15$ $= 360 \text{ cm}^3$	Now multiply the area of the prism's base by its height, which is 15 cm. Include units with your answer.

Example

Find the volume of the following rectangular prism.

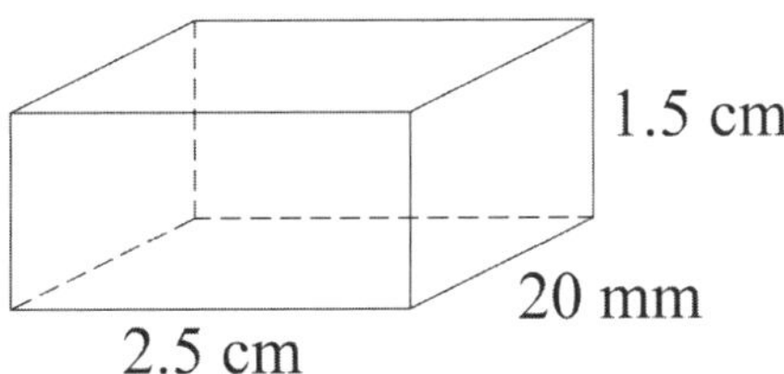

✓ Solution

Working	Explanation
20 mm = 2 cm	Convert all measurements to the same units.
$V = lwh$ $= 2.5 \times 2 \times 1.5$ $= 5 \times 1.5$ $= 7.5 \text{ cm}^3$	The volume of a rectangular prism is found by multiplying the length, width and height. Include units with your answer.

Example

Calculate the capacity of the following cylinder correct to the nearest litre.

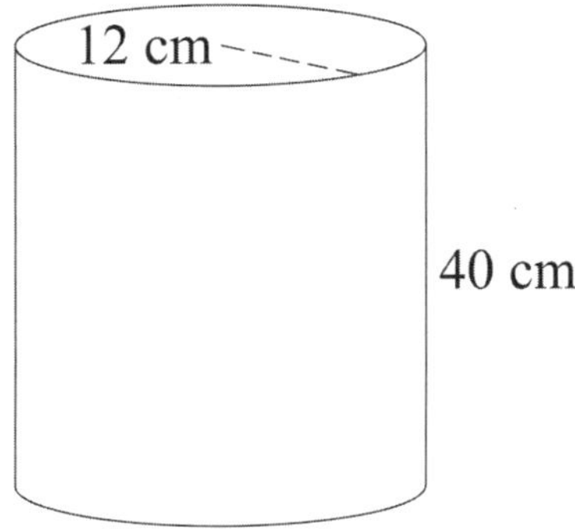

✓ *Solution*

Working	Explanation
$V = \pi r^2 h$ $= \pi \times 144 \times 40$ $= 18095.573\ldots$ cm^3	Calculate the volume in cm^3 using the formula for volume of a cylinder. The radius is 12 and height is 40. Enter this into a calculator.
$V = 18095.573\ldots$ mL $= 18.095573\ldots$ L $= 18$ L	1 cm^3 = 1 mL Divide by 1000 to convert to L. Round to the nearest whole number.

Exercise 4.5.1

Find the volume of each of the following three-dimensional objects.

a.

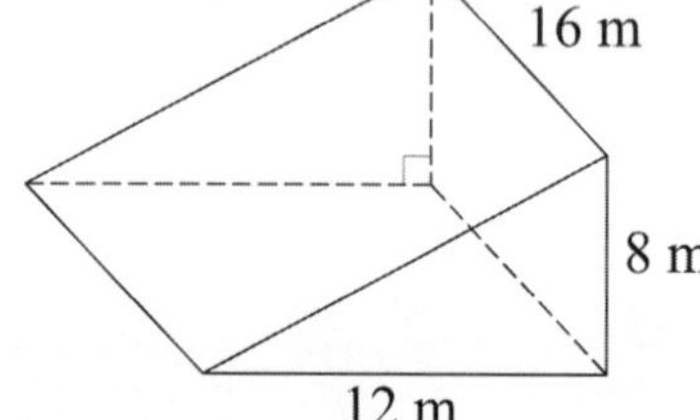

b.

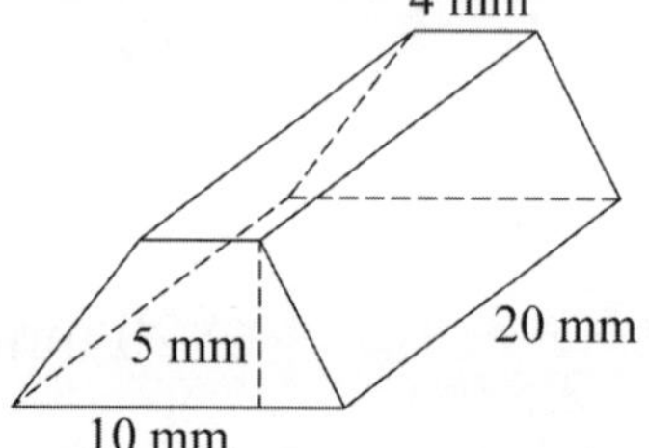

c.

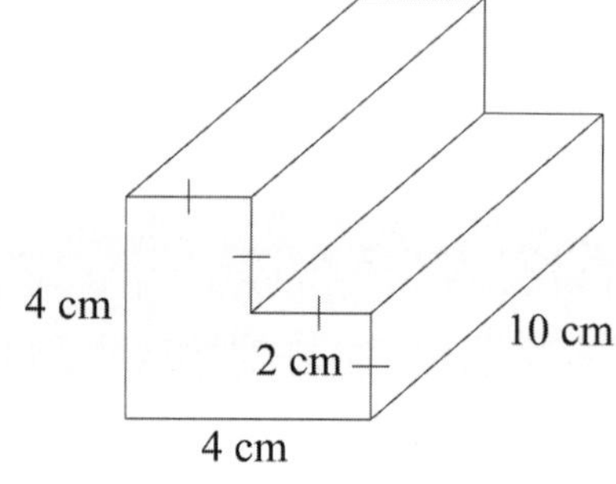

Exercise 4.5.2

Find the capacity of the following rectangular prism correct to the nearest litre.

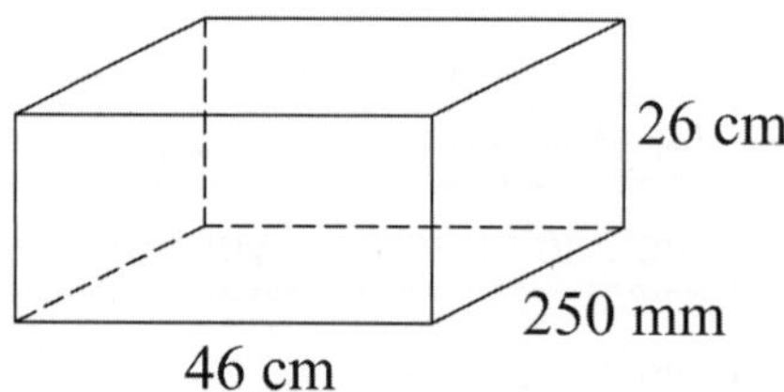

Exercise 4.5.3

Find the volume of the following cylinder correct to one decimal place.

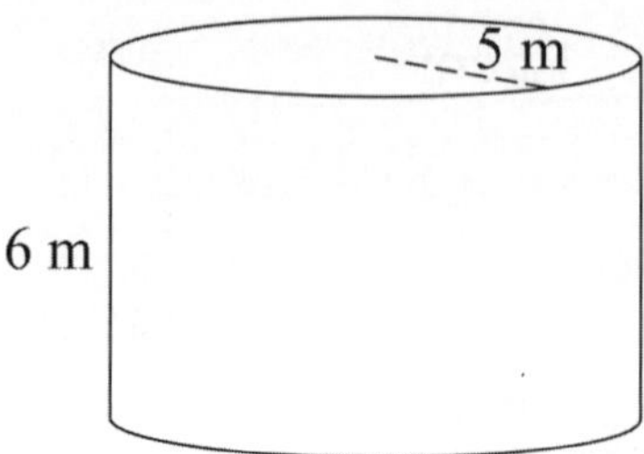

4.6 Pythagoras' theorem

Pythagoras' theorem describes how the sides of a right-angled triangle are related to each other.

In a right-angled triangle, the longest side is the side opposite the right-angle. This side is called the hypotenuse.

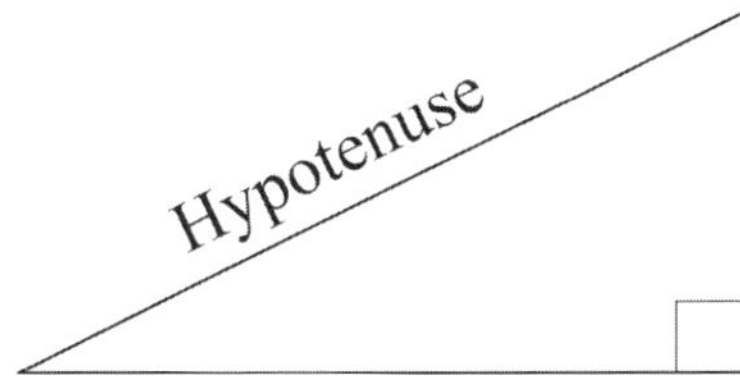

Pythagoras' theorem tells us that in any right-angled triangle, the square of the hypotenuse is equal to the sum of the squares of the other two sides.

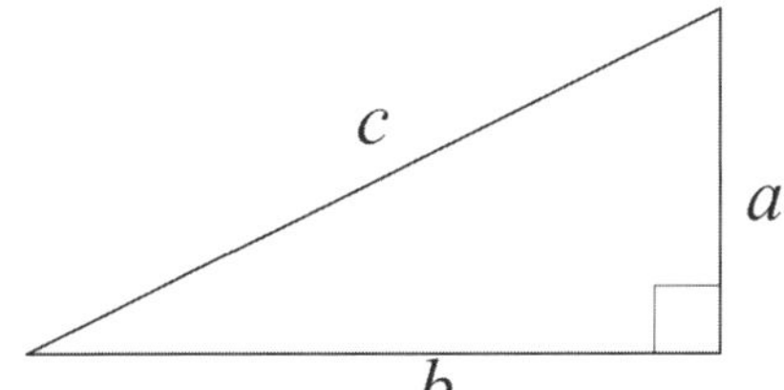

$$c^2 = a^2 + b^2$$

where c is the length of the hypotenuse, and a and b are the lengths of the other two sides.

Example

Find the length of the hypotenuse, labelled x, in the following triangle.

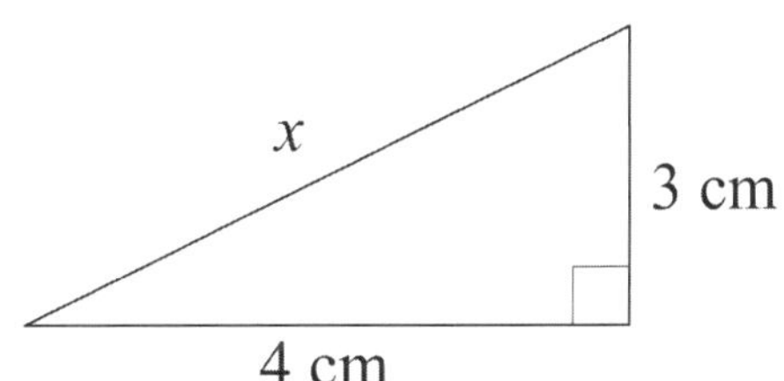

✓ *Solution*

Working	Explanation
$c^2 = a^2 + b^2$ $x^2 = 3^2 + 4^2$ $x^2 = 9 + 16$ $x^2 = 25$ $x = \sqrt{25}$ $x = 5$ cm	x is the hypotenuse, so this takes the place of c in the rule. The lengths of the other two sides are a and b. It does not matter which you call a and which you call b. Substitute 3 and 4 for a and b. To find x, take the square root of the result when you add 9 and 16. Include units with the answer.

When we calculate the length of the hypotenuse, we sometimes end up with a number whose square root cannot be given as an exact number. An example is $\sqrt{2}$, which is $1.41421356\ldots$ We cannot write this number as a fraction because, like π, its decimal version goes on without end, with the decimal places following no repeating pattern. Therefore, we need to leave the answer as the exact value of $\sqrt{2}$ or give a decimal approximation rounded to a specified number of decimal places.

Example

Find the exact length of the hypotenuse of the following triangle.

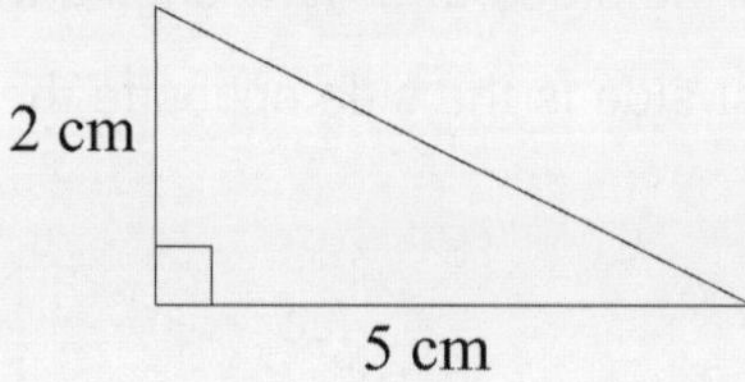

✓ *Solution*

Working	Explanation
$c^2 = a^2 + b^2$	In the rule, c represents the length of the hypotenuse.
$c^2 = 2^2 + 5^2$	Substitute the side lengths of 2 and 5 for a and b.
$c^2 = 4 + 25$	To find c, take the square root of the result when you add 4 and 25.
$c^2 = 29$	We cannot find the exact square root of 29, so leave the answer as $\sqrt{29}$.
$c = \sqrt{29}$ cm	Units must be included with the answer.

Example

Find the length of the hypotenuse of the following triangle correct to 2 decimal places.

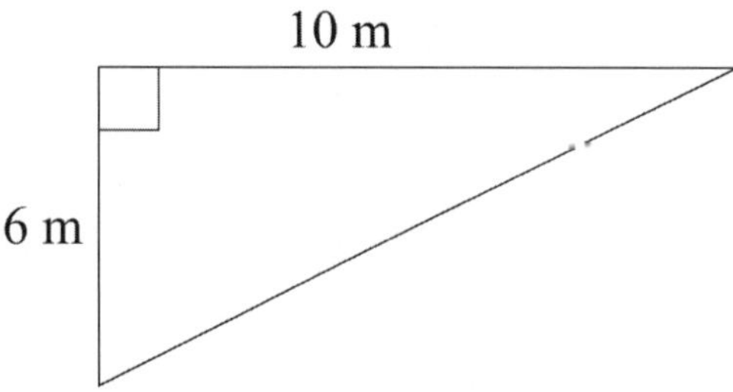

✓ *Solution*

Working	Explanation
$c^2 = a^2 + b^2$ $= 6^2 + 10^2$ $= 36 + 100$ $= 136$	In the rule, c represents the length of the hypotenuse. Substitute the side lengths of 6 and 10 for a and b and simplify.
$c = \sqrt{136}$ $= 11.6619\ldots$ $= 11.66$ m	To find c, take the square root of the result when you add 36 and 100. Use a calculator to find the square root of 136. Round this number to 2 decimal places and include units with your answer.

Exercise 4.6.1

Find the exact length of the hypotenuse of each of the following triangles.

a.

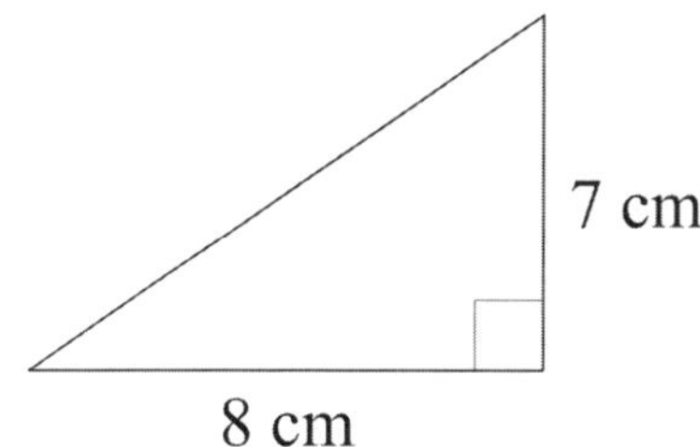

b.

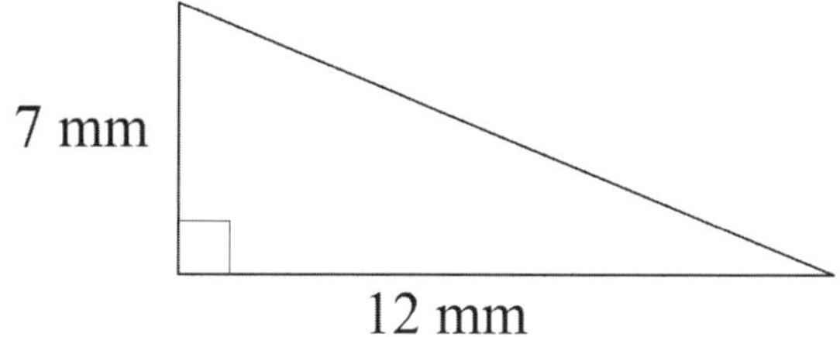

Exercise 4.6.2

Find the length of the hypotenuse of each of the following triangles correct to 1 decimal place.

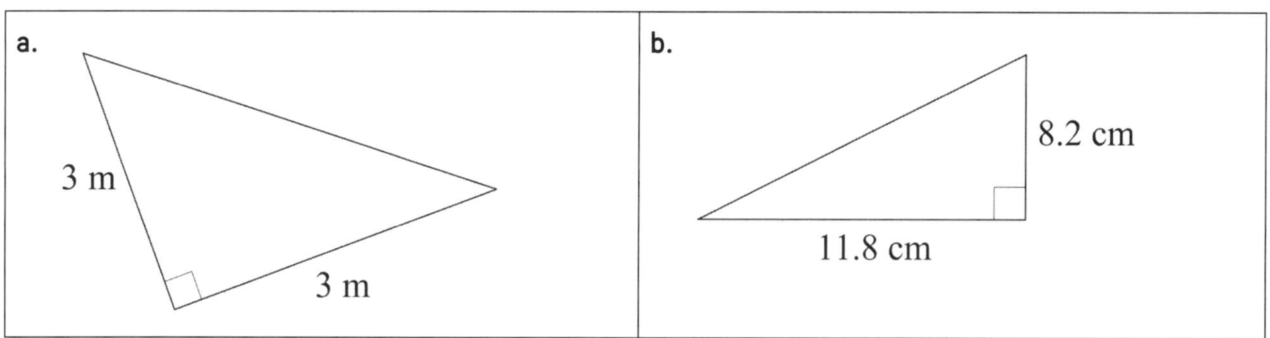

4.7 Time

The most common units for measuring time are days, hours, minutes and seconds. The following diagram shows how you can convert between these units.

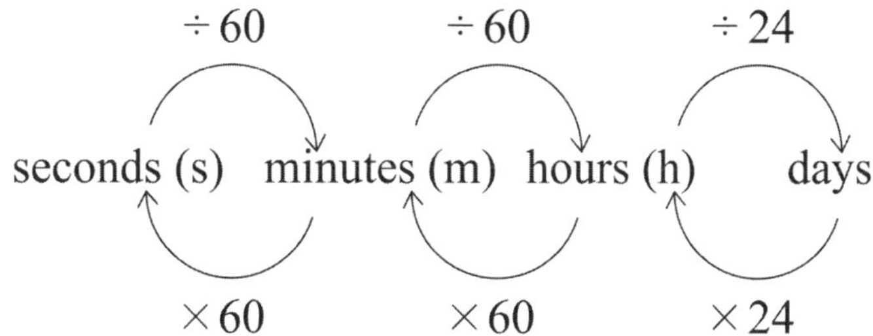

Example

Convert 4 days to hours.

✓ Solution

Working	Explanation
$4 \times 24 = 96$ 4 days = 96 h	To convert days to hours, multiply by 24.

Example

Convert 9 minutes to seconds.

✓ *Solution*

Working	Explanation
$9 \times 60 = 540$	To convert minutes to seconds, multiply by 60.
9 min = 540 s	A common abbreviation for minutes is min.

Example

Convert 140 minutes to hours and minutes.

✓ *Solution*

Working	Explanation
$140 = 120 + 20$ 120 minutes = 2 hours 140 minutes = 2 h 20 min	Each 60 minutes is 1 hour.

Times in the morning (before noon) are identified by am after the time. Times in the afternoon (after noon) are identified by pm after the time.

12 midnight is 12 am and 12 noon is 12 pm.

Example

Determine the time difference between 2.10 am on Tuesday and 4.40 pm on the same day.

✓ *Solution*

Working	Explanation
2.10 am until 12.10 pm is 10 h 12.10 pm until 4.10 pm is 4 h 2.10 am until 4.10 pm is $10 + 4 = 14$ h 4.10 pm to 4.40 pm is 30 minutes Time difference = 14 h 30 min	First count the hours from 2.10 am to 12.10 pm. Then count the hours between 12.10 pm and 4.10 pm. When added to the previous result, this gives the hours between 2.10 am and 4.10 pm. Finally, determine the number of minutes between 4.10 pm and 4.40 pm.

Example

Determine the time difference between 7.30 pm on Friday and 3.00 am on the following Sunday.

✓ Solution

Working	Explanation
7.30 pm until midnight is 4 h 30 minutes. Midnight until 3 am is 3 h. Time difference = 4 h 30 min + 24 h + 3 h = 31 h 30 min	First find the number of hours and minutes between 7.30 pm Friday and midnight Friday. Then find the time between midnight Saturday and 3.00 am Sunday. The time difference is the sum of these two values plus 24 hours for the whole of Saturday.

24-hour time gives time as the number of hours and minutes after midnight, rather than as am (before noon) and pm (after noon). 12 midnight is 0000 and 12 noon is 1200. Times before 10 am are given with a zero before the first digit. For example, 6.45 am is written as 0645 in 24-hour time.

Example

Convert 11.24 am to 24-hour time.

✓ Solution

Working	Explanation
11.24 am is 1124	Any time before 1 pm remains the same when written as a 24-hour time.

Example

Convert 8.15 pm to 24-hour time.

✓ Solution

Working	Explanation
8 + 12 = 20 8:15 pm is 2015	Any pm time must have 12 hours added when writing it as a 24-hour time.

Example

Convert 1024 to an am or pm time.

✓ Solution

Working	Explanation
1024 is 10.24 am	Any 24-hour time before 1200 is an am time.

Example

Convert 1625 to an am or pm time.

✓ *Solution*

Working	Explanation
1625 − 1200 = 4 h 25 min after midday 1625 is 4.25 pm	Any 24-hour time after 1200 is a pm time. Subtract 1200 to find the number of hours and minutes after midday.

Because of the rotation of the Earth, the world is divided into time zones. A particular location on the Earth will rotate into and out of sunlight over a 24-hour period. The time zones mean that 12 noon is the middle of the day and 12 midnight is the middle of the night regardless of where you are on the planet.

Traditionally, time is referenced from Greenwich, a district in London, England. The time in Greenwich is referred to as Greenwich Mean Time (GMT) or Coordinated Universal Time (UTC). When you move east from Greenwich you add time to the UTC. When you move west from Greenwich you subtract time from the UTC.

Example

In winter, the time in Melbourne is UTC + 10 hours. Find the time in Melbourne when the UTC time is 7.00 am.

✓ *Solution*

Working	Explanation
7.00 am + 10 hours is 5.00 pm	Add 10 hours to the UTC time to find the time in Melbourne.

Example

The time in Vancouver, Canada is UTC − 8 hours. Find the time in Vancouver when the UTC time is 0614 on Tuesday.

✓ *Solution*

Working	Explanation
0614 hours − 8 hours is 2214 on Monday	Subtract 8 hours from the UTC time to find the time in Vancouver.

Exercise 4.7.1

Find the length of time between:

a. 4.30 am and 6.40 am

b. 11.30 am and 5.50 pm

c. 9.15 pm on Saturday and 10.30 am on the following Monday.

Exercise 4.7.2

Convert the following am or pm times to 24-hour time.

a. 7.20 am

b. 5.32 pm

c. 8.40 pm

Exercise 4.7.3

Convert the following 24-hour times to an am or pm time.

a. 0900

b. 1825

c. 1934

d. 1109

Exercise 4.7.4

a. The time in Adelaide is UTC + 9 hours and 30 minutes. Find the time in Adelaide when the UTC time is 7.30 am.

b. The time in Colombia is UTC − 5 hours. Find the time in Colombia when the UTC time is 0130 on Monday.

Answers

Exercise 4.1

a. 2.16

b. 24000

c. 3000

d. 12000

e. 0.027

f. 22

g. 0.0035

h. 0.22435

Exercise 4.2

a. 57 mm

b. 81 cm

c. 79.6 m

d. 42 m

Exercise 4.3.1

a. 180 cm^2

b. 150 mm^2

c. 198 m^2

d. 106.24 cm^2

Exercise 4.3.2

1016 cm^2

Exercise 4.4

a. 28π cm

b. 37.70 mm

c. 76.4 cm

d. 50.3 cm^2

e. 201.1 m^2

Exercise 4.5.1

a. $768\ m^3$ b. $700\ mm^3$ c. $120\ cm^3$

Exercise 4.5.2

30 L

Exercise 4.5.3

$471.2\ m^3$

Exercise 4.6.1

a. $\sqrt{113}$ cm b. $\sqrt{193}$ mm

Exercise 4.6.2

a. 4.2 m b. 14.4 cm

Exercise 4.7.1

a. 2 h 10 min b. 6 h 20 min c. 37 h 15 min

Exercise 4.7.2

a. 0720 b. 1732 c. 2040

Exercise 4.7.3

a. 9.00 am b. 6.25 pm c. 7.34 pm d. 11.09 am

Exercise 4.7.4

a. 5.00 pm b. 2030 Sunday

Chapter 5 – Algebraic techniques

5.1 Basic algebra review

The following table defines some of the language of algebra.

Language	Meaning	Example
Pronumeral	A letter or symbol that represents a number.	a or x or y or π
Variable	A pronumeral that can take more than one value.	a or x or y
Term	A single pronumeral, a pronumeral multiplied by a number, pronumerals multiplied together or a number.	p or $-3k$ or $4xy$ or $-5x^2y$
Coefficient	The number by which a pronumeral or product of pronumerals is multiplied.	3 is the coefficient of $3x$ -2 is the coefficient of $-2y$ $\frac{1}{2}$ is the coefficient of $\frac{x^2y}{2}$ (since it is equal to $\frac{1}{2}x^2y$)
Expression	A combination of terms.	$2p - 3q + 4pq$
Constant	A term that does not contain a variable.	9 or -15 or $\frac{3}{4}$
Substitution	Replacing a pronumeral with a numerical value.	Substituting $g = 5$ in the expression $4g - 8$ gives $4 \times 5 - 8$

Example

Consider the expression $5x - 2y + 8z - 15$. State:

a. the number of terms

b. the coefficient of z

c. the coefficient of y

d. the constant term.

✓ Solution

Working	Explanation
a. The number of terms is 4.	Each of $5x$, $-2y$, $8z$ and -15 is a term.
b. The coefficient of z is 8.	The coefficient is the number in front of the pronumeral.
c. The coefficient of y is -2.	The coefficient is the number in front of the pronumeral.
d. The constant term is -15.	The constant term is the term that does not contain a variable.

When writing algebraic expressions, it is important to be familiar with the following language.

The **sum** of x and y means $x + y$.

The **difference** between x and y means $y - x$.

The **product** of x and y means $x \times y$, which we write as xy.

The **quotient** of x and y means $\frac{x}{y}$.

Example

Write an expression for each of the following.

a. the product of 7 and c

b. the sum of $3a$ and $2b$

c. the difference between 5 and $\frac{1}{4}$ of k

✓ *Solution*

Working	Explanation
a. $7c$	The product of 7 and c means $7 \times c$. In algebra we do not put a multiplication sign between numbers and pronumerals.
b. $3a + 2b$	Sum means 'addition'.
c. $\frac{1}{4}k - 5 = \frac{k}{4} - 5$	The difference between 5 and $\frac{1}{4}$ of k means $\frac{1}{4}$ of k minus 5. Multiplying by $\frac{1}{4}$ is the same as dividing by 4.

Exercise 5.1.1

For the expression $5a - 4b + 12 + 3ab$ state:

a. the coefficient of a

b. the coefficient of b

c. the coefficient of ab

d. the constant term.

Exercise 5.1.2

Write an expression for each of the following.

a. the sum of x and $3y$

b. the quotient of $5r$ and $7s$

c. the difference between $6x^2$ and $3x$

d. the product of 3 and g

e. the sum of $\frac{1}{2}$ of y and $\frac{1}{4}$ of x

5.2 Substitution

Substitution is when we replace a pronumeral with a number.

Example

If $m = 10$, evaluate:

a. $3m - 5$

b. $\frac{m}{2} + 4$

✓ *Solution*

Working	Explanation
a. $3m - 5 = 3 \times 10 - 5$ $= 30 - 5$ $= 25$	Substitute 10 for m. $3m$ means $3 \times m$. Carry out multiplication before subtraction.
b. $\frac{m}{2} + 4 = \frac{10}{2} + 4$ $= 5 + 4$ $= 9$	Substitute 10 for m. Carry out division before addition.

Example

Evaluate $3x^2 + 2xy$ if $x = 4$ and $y = -2$.

✓ *Solution*

Working	Explanation
$3x^2 + 2xy = 3 \times 4^2 + 2 \times 4 \times -2$ $= 3 \times 16 + 2 \times 4 \times -2$ $= 48 + (-16)$ $= 32$	Substitute 4 for x and -2 for y. $3x^2$ means $3 \times x^2$ and $2xy$ means $2 \times x \times y$. Square 4 first. Carry out multiplication next. Then subtract 16 from 48.

Exercise 5.2.1

If $a = 4$, evaluate:

a. $5a - 3$

b. $\frac{a}{2}$

c. $a^2 + a$

d. $40 - 6a$

Exercise 5.2.2

If $m = 5$ and $n = 9$, evaluate:

a. $2m + 3n$

b. $4m - 2n$

c. $m^2 + n^2$

d. $10mn$

Exercise 5.2.3

If $x = -2$ and $y = 3$, evaluate:

a. $2x + 5y$ b. $3y - 4x$ c. $5xy$

5.3 Simplifying algebraic expressions

Like terms are terms that contain the same pronumeral part.

Like terms	Unlike terms
$3y$, $-12y$ and $\frac{y}{2}$ $5ab$ and $-4ba$ $11d^2e^3$ and $11e^3d^2$	$2x$ and x^2 $-2p^2q$ and $5pq^2$

We can add or subtract like terms by adding or subtracting their coefficients.

Example

Simplify $5p + 8p - 4p$.

✓ *Solution*

Working	Explanation
$5p + 8p - 4p = 9p$	Add the coefficients of p. $5 + 8 - 4 = 9$

Example

Simplify $5x^2 - 3x + 9x^2 - 6x$.

✓ *Solution*

Working	Explanation
$5x^2 - 3x + 9x^2 - 6x$ $= 5x^2 + 9x^2 - 3x - 6x$ $= 14x^2 - 9x$	Rewrite the expression with the like terms grouped together. • $5x^2$ and $9x^2$ are like terms. • $-3x$ and $-6x$ are like terms. Add the coefficients of the x^2 terms and add the coefficients of the x terms.

Example

Simplify $4ab - 5b + 7b + 9ba$.

✓ ***Solution***

Working	Explanation
$4ab - 5b + 7b + 9ba$ $= 4ab + 9ba - 5b + 7b$ $= 13ab + 2b$	Rewrite the expression with the like terms grouped together. • $4ab$ and $9ba$ are like terms. • $-5b$ and $7b$ are like terms. Add the coefficients of the ab terms and the b terms.

When multiplying terms, we multiply the numbers and then multiply any pronumerals. We do not leave multiplication signs between numbers and pronumerals, or between pronumerals. When we multiply a pronumeral by itself, we use powers. For example, $a \times a$ is written as a^2, $a \times a \times a$ is written as a^3, $a \times a \times a \times a$ is written as a^4 and so on.

Example

Simplify $3x \times 2y$.

✓ ***Solution***

Working	Explanation
$3x \times 2y = 3 \times x \times 2 \times y$ $= 6 \times x \times y$ $= 6xy$	Rewrite the expression with multiplication signs included. Multiply the numbers and pronumerals. Rewrite the expression without multiplication signs.

Example

Simplify $5ab \times -4bc$.

✓ ***Solution***

Working	Explanation
$5ab \times -4bc = 5 \times a \times b \times -4 \times b \times c$ $= -20 \times a \times b \times b \times c$ $= -20 \times a \times b^2 \times c$ $= -20ab^2c$	Rewrite the expression with multiplication signs included. Multiply the numbers and pronumerals. Note that $b \times b = b^2$. Rewrite the expression without multiplication signs.

When we divide terms, we cancel any common factors in the numerator and denominator.

Example

Simplify $4xy \div 2x$.

✓ *Solution*

Working	Explanation
$4xy \div 2x = \frac{4xy}{2x}$	First write the expression as a fraction.
$= \frac{4 \times x \times y}{2 \times x}$	Insert multiplication signs into both numerator and denominator.
$= \frac{{}^{2}\not{4} \times \not{x} \times y}{\not{2} \times \not{x}}$	Cancel any common factors between numerator and denominator.
$= 2 \times y$	Multiply the remaining terms.
$= 2y$	Remove the multiplication sign in the final answer.

Example

Simplify $\frac{6p^2q}{12pr}$.

✓ *Solution*

Working	Explanation
$\frac{6p^2q}{12pr} = \frac{6 \times p \times p \times q}{12 \times p \times r}$	Write the numerator and denominator with multiplication signs included. Remember that p^2 is $p \times p$.
$= \frac{\not{6} \times p \times \not{p} \times q}{{}_{2}\not{12} \times \not{p} \times r}$	Cancel any common factors in the numerator and the denominator.
$= \frac{p \times q}{2 \times r}$	Multiply the remaining terms in the numerator and the denominator.
$= \frac{pq}{2r}$	Remove any multiplication signs in the final answer.

Exercise 5.3.1

Simplify each of the following expressions.

a. $5r + 8r - 2r$

b. $5b - 7c + 16b - 8c$

c. $5xy^2 + 6xy + 4x^2y - 2xy$

d. $4gh + 5g - 6hg + 4g$

 **Exercise 5.3.2**

Simplify each of the following expressions.

a. $4a \times 5c$ b. $-5m \times -3m$ c. $6x \times 5x$ d. $3xz \times -2xy$

 **Exercise 5.3.3**

Simplify each of the following expressions.

a. $6ab \div 3b$ b. $\dfrac{8xy^2}{2xy}$ c. $\dfrac{3r}{18s}$ d. $\dfrac{10x^2}{25x}$

5.4 Expanding brackets

When we expand an expression that contains brackets, we multiply each term inside the brackets by the term in front of the brackets.

Example

Expand $3(x - 5)$.

✓ *Solution*

Working	Explanation
$3(x - 5) = 3 \times x - 3 \times 5$ $= 3x - 15$	$3(x - 5)$ means $3 \times (x + 5)$. Multiply each term in the brackets by 3.

Example

Expand $2a(a + 3)$.

✓ *Solution*

Working	Explanation
$2a(a + 3) = 2a \times a + 2a \times 3$ $= 2a^2 + 6a$	$2a(a + 3)$ means $2a \times (a + 3)$. Multiply each term in the brackets by $2a$.

Example

Expand $-y(8-3y)$.

✓ ***Solution***

Working	Explanation
$-y(8-3y) = -y \times 8 - -y \times 3y$ $= -8y + 3y^2$	$-y(8-3y)$ means $-y \times (8-3y)$. Multiply each term in the brackets by $-y$.

It may be necessary to simplify expressions after expanding brackets.

Example

Expand and simplify $2(x+1) + 4x - 2$.

✓ ***Solution***

Working	Explanation
$2(x+1) + 4x - 2$ $= 2 \times x + 2 \times 1 + 4x - 2$	Expand the brackets by multiplying both x and 1 by 2.
$= 2x + 2 + 4x - 2$ $= 2x + 4x + 2 - 2$ $= 6x$	Add the like terms: • $2x + 4x = 6x$ and • $2 + (-2) = 0$

Example

Expand and simplify $3a(a-4) + 5(2a-1)$.

✓ ***Solution***

Working	Explanation
$3a(a-4) + 5(2a-1)$ $= 3a \times a + 3a \times -4 + 5 \times 2a + 5 \times -1$	Expand the brackets by multiplying a and -4 by $3a$, and multiplying $2a$ and -1 by 5.
$= 3a^2 - 12a + 10a - 5$ $= 3a^2 - 2a - 5$	Add the like terms: $-12a + 10a = -2a$.

Example

Expand and simplify $8(x + 3) - 4(x - 2)$.

✓ *Solution*

Working	Explanation
$8(x + 3) - 4(x - 2)$ $= 8 \times x + 8 \times 3 - 4 \times x - 4 \times -2$	Expand the brackets by multiplying x and 3 by 8, and multiplying x and -2 by -4.
$= 8x + 24 - 4x + 8$ $= 8x - 4x + 24 + 8$ $= 4x + 32$	Add the like terms: • $8x - 4x = 4x$ and • $24 + 8 = 32$.

Exercise 5.4.1

Expand the following expressions.

a. $5(a + b)$ **b.** $3(2m - n)$ **c.** $2(p - pq + 2q)$

d. $-3(a + 6)$ **e.** $-x(3x - 2)$ **f.** $-(3x + 2y)$

Exercise 5.4.2

Expand and simplify the following expressions.

a. $5(y + 4) + 3(y - 3)$ **b.** $3(x + 1) + 4(2x + 1)$

c. $6(x + 1) - 4(x + 2)$ **d.** $5(a - 3) - 7(3a - 4)$

5.5 Factorising expressions

We have seen that $3(x - 5) = 3x - 15$. The factorised form of the expression is $3(x - 5)$ since it is the product of the factors 3 and $x - 5$. The expanded form of the expression is $3x - 15$.

The process of going from the factorised form to the expanded form is referred to as **expanding**.

The process of going from the expanded form to the factorised form is referred to as **factorising**.

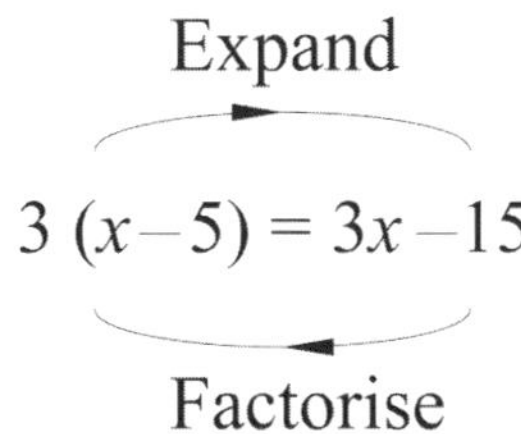

To factorise an expression:

1. Find the **highest common factor** of the terms in the expression.
2. Write the highest common factor in front of a pair of brackets.
3. Divide each term in the expression by the highest common factor and place the result inside the brackets.

Example

Factorise $2x + 4$.

✓ ***Solution***

Working	Explanation
$2x + 4 = 2(x + 2)$	The highest common factor of $2x$ and 4 is 2. This common factor goes outside a pair of brackets and then we divide each term of the expression by the common factor: $2x \div 2 = x$ $4 \div 2 = 2$.

Example

Factorise $10x - 25y$.

✓ ***Solution***

Working	Explanation
$10x - 25y = 5(2x - 5y)$	The highest common factor of $10x$ and $25y$ is 5. This common factor goes outside the brackets and we then divide each term by the common factor: $10x \div 5 = 2x$ and $25y \div 5 = 5y$.

Example

Factorise $4xy - 6xy^2$.

✓ ***Solution***

Working	Explanation
$4xy - 6xy^2 = 2xy(2 - 3y)$	The highest common factor of $4xy$ and $6xy^2$ is $2xy$. This common factor goes outside the brackets and then we divide each term by the common factor: $4xy \div 2xy = 2$ and $6xy^2 \div 2xy = 3y$.

We can also take out negative factors. This is usually done if the first term in the expression being factorised is negative.

Example

Factorise $-5p + 10$.

✓ Solution

Working	Explanation
$-5p + 10 = -5(p - 2)$	Take out the common factor of -5. $-5p \div -5 = p$ and $10 \div -5 = -2$.

Example

Factorise $-4xy - 6xz$.

✓ Solution

Working	Explanation
$-4xy - 6xz = -2x(2y + 3z)$	Take out the common factor of $-2x$. $-4xy \div -2x = 2y$ and $-6xz \div -2x = 3z$.

 **Exercise 5.5.1**

Factorise each of the following expressions.

a. $4r + 16$
b. $2w - 14z$
c. $9t - 3$
d. $5a - ab$
e. $15 - 6c$
f. $m^2 + 2m$

 **Exercise 5.5.2**

Factorise each of the following expressions.

a. $-2y - 6$
b. $-2t + 8$
c. $-2x^2 + 4xy$
d. $-3t - 12w$
e. $-3x^2 - 12xz$
f. $-8h + 4h^2$

5.6 Applications of algebra

Algebra has applications in all areas of mathematics, including measurement and geometry.

Example

Find an expression for the perimeter of the quadrilateral shown below.

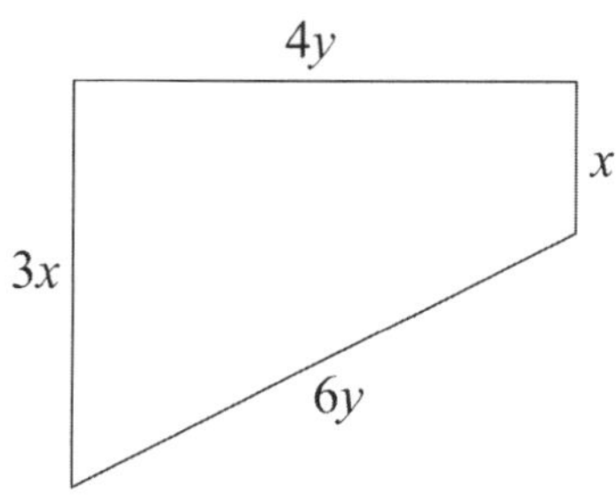

✓ Solution

Working	Explanation
Perimeter $= 3x + 4y + x + 6y$ $= 4x + 10y$	Add the lengths of the sides to find the perimeter. Add the like terms: • $3x + x = 4x$ and • $4y + 6y = 10y$.

Example

What is the perimeter of the quadrilateral shown on the previous page if $x = 2$ and $y = 3$?

✓ Solution

Working	Explanation
Perimeter $= 4x + 10y$ $= 4 \times 2 + 10 \times 3$ $= 8 + 30$ $= 38$	Substitute $x = 2$ and $y = 3$ into the expression for the perimeter. Remember that multiplication is done before addition when evaluating.

Example

Find an expression for the sum of the two angles labelled in the following triangle.

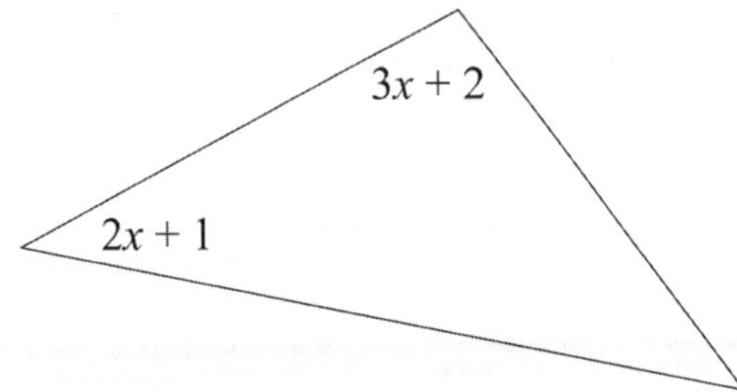

✓ Solution

Working	Explanation
Angle sum $= 3x + 2 + 2x + 1$ $= 5x + 3$	Add the like terms: • $3x + 2x = 5x$ and • $2 + 1 = 3$.

Example

If $x = 30°$ find the size of the third angle in the triangle shown above.

✓ ***Solution***

Working	Explanation
Angle sum $= 5x + 3$ $= 5 \times 30 + 3$ $= 150 + 3$ $= 153°$	Substitute 30 for x. Remember that multiplication is done before addition when evaluating.
Third angle $= 180 - 153$ $= 27°$	The angle sum in a triangle is 180°, so the third angle is equal to 180° minus the sum of the other two angles. It is usual to include the degrees symbol at the end of calculations involving angles.

Exercise 5.6.1

Find an expression for the perimeter of each of the following shapes.

a.

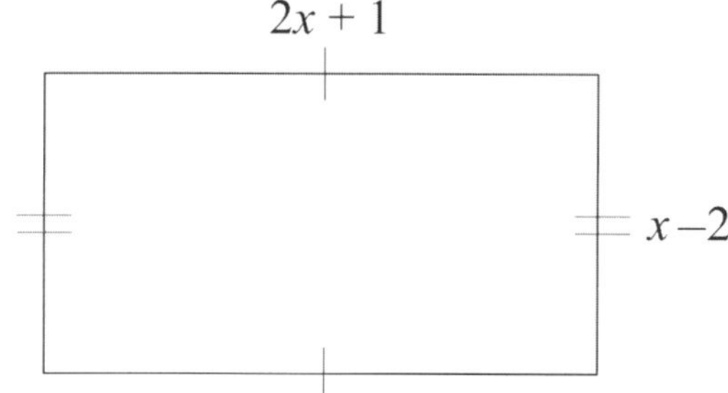

b.

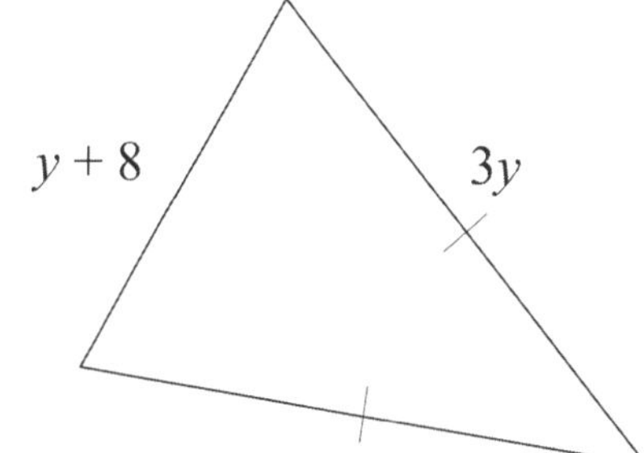

Exercise 5.6.2

Find an expression for the area of each of the following shapes in expanded form.

a.

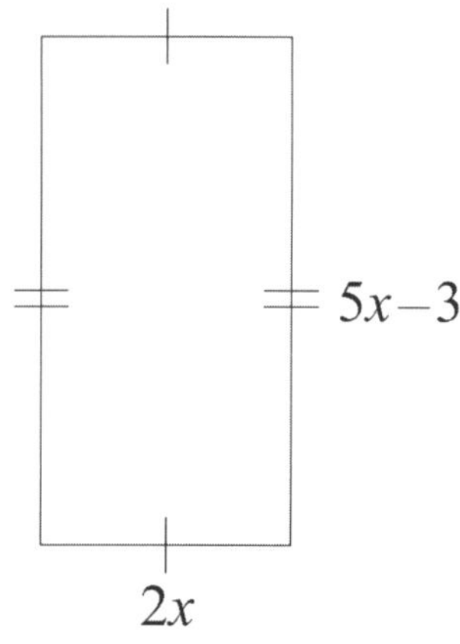

b.

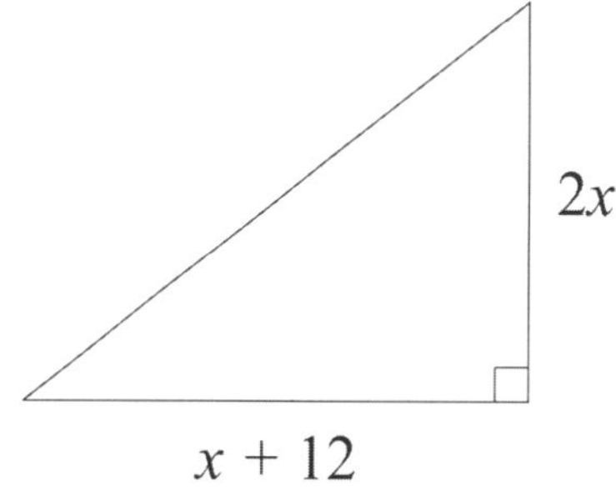

Exercise 5.6.3

a. Find an expression for the sum of the two angles labelled in the following triangle.

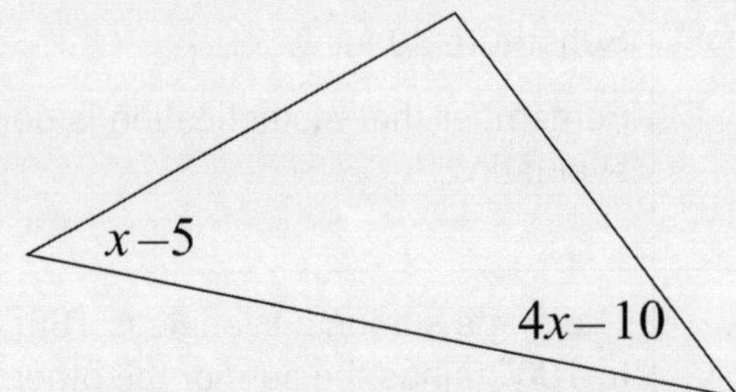

b. If $x = 20^{\circ}$, find the size of the third angle.

Answers

Exercise 5.1.1

a. 5 **b.** -4 **c.** 3 **d.** 12

Exercise 5.1.2

a. $x + 3y$ **b.** $\frac{5r}{7s}$ **c.** $3x - 6x^2$ **d.** $3g$ **e.** $\frac{y}{2} + \frac{x}{4}$

Exercise 5.2.1

a. 17 **b.** 2 **c.** 20 **d.** 16

Exercise 5.2.2

a. 37 **b.** 2 **c.** 106 **d.** 450

Exercise 5.2.3

a. 11 **b.** 17 **c.** -30

Exercise 5.3.1

a. $11r$ **b.** $21b - 15c$ **c.** $5xy^2 + 4x^2y + 4xy$ **d.** $-2gh + 9g$

Exercise 5.3.2

a. $20ac$ **b.** $15m^2$ **c.** $30x^2$ **d.** $-6x^2yz$

Exercise 5.3.3

a. $2a$ **b.** $4y$ **c.** $\frac{r}{6s}$ **d.** $\frac{2x}{5}$

Exercise 5.4.1

a. $5a + 5b$ b. $6m - 3n$ c. $2p - 2pq + 4q$ d. $-3a - 18$

e. $-3x^2 + 2x$ f. $-3x - 2y$

Exercise 5.4.2

a. $8y + 11$ b. $11x + 7$ c. $2x - 2$ d. $-16a + 13$

Exercise 5.5.1

a. $4(r + 4)$ b. $2(w - 7z)$ c. $3(3t - 1)$ d. $a(5 - b)$

e. $3(5 - 2c)$ f. $m(m + 2)$

Exercise 5.5.2

a. $-2(y + 3)$ b. $-2(t - 4)$ c. $-2x(x - 2y)$ d. $-3(t + 4w)$

e. $-3x(x + 4z)$ f. $-4h(2 - h)$

Exercise 5.6.1

a. $6x - 2$ b. $7y + 8$

Exercise 5.6.2

a. $10x^2 - 6x$ b. $x^2 + 12x$

Exercise 5.6.3

a. $5x - 15$ b. 95°

Chapter 6 – Indices

6.1 Index notation

Consider the expression $5 \times 5 \times 5 \times 5 \times 5 \times 5$. We can write this in index notation as 5^6. This is read as 5 to the power 6. In index notation, 5 is called the base and 6 is called the index, power or exponent.

Base → 5^{6} ← Index

Example

Write each of the following in index notation.

a. $4 \times 4 \times 4 \times 4 \times 4 \times 4 \times 4$

b. $2 \times 2 \times 2 \times 5 \times 5 \times 5 \times 5 \times 13 \times 13$

✓ Solution

Working	Explanation
a. $4 \times 4 \times 4 \times 4 \times 4 \times 4 \times 4 = 4^7$	Count the number of times each number is multiplied by itself. 4 is multiplied by itself 7 times, so 4 is the base and 7 is the index.
b. $2 \times 2 \times 2 \times 5 \times 5 \times 5 \times 5 \times 13 \times 13$ $= 2^3 \times 5^4 \times 13^2$	Count the number of times each number is multiplied by itself. • $2 \times 2 \times 2 = 2^3$ • $5 \times 5 \times 5 \times 5 = 5^4$ • $13 \times 13 = 13^2$ In this example three numbers can be written in index notation.

Example

Evaluate:

a. 3^4

b. $2^3 \times 3^2$

✓ Solution

Working	Explanation
a. $3^4 = 3 \times 3 \times 3 \times 3$ $= 81$	Write 3^4 in expanded form: $3 \times 3 \times 3 \times 3 = 9 \times 3 \times 3$ $= 9 \times 9$ $= 81.$
b. $2^3 \times 3^2 = 2 \times 2 \times 2 \times 3 \times 3$ $= 8 \times 9$ $= 72$	Write $2^3 \times 3^2$ in expanded form: $2 \times 2 \times 2 = 8$ and $3 \times 3 = 9$.

We can also use index notation for expressions involving pronumerals.

Example

Write each of the following expressions in index notation.

a. $a \times a \times a \times b \times b \times b \times b$

b. $2 \times x \times y \times 3 \times x \times y \times y \times y$

✓ Solution

Working	Explanation
a. $a \times a \times a \times b \times b \times b \times b = a^3 \times b^4$ $= a^3b^4$	$a \times a \times a = a^3$ and $b \times b \times b \times b = b^4$ In an algebraic expression, we do not place a multiplication sign between pronumerals.
b. $2 \times x \times y \times 3 \times x \times y \times y \times y$ $= 2 \times 3 \times x \times x \times y \times y \times y \times y$ $= 6 \times x^2 \times y^4$ $= 6x^2y^4$	$2 \times 3 = 6$, $x \times x = x^2$ and $y \times y \times y \times y = y^4$

Exercise 6.1.1

Write each of the following expressions using index notation.

a. $7 \times 7 \times 7 \times 7 \times 7 \times 7 \times 7 \times 7 \times 7$

b. $3 \times 3 \times 3 \times 5 \times 5 \times 7 \times 7 \times 7$

c. $p \times p \times p \times p \times q \times q$

d. $5 \times g \times g \times 7 \times h \times h \times h$

Exercise 6.1.2

Evaluate:

a. 2^5

b. 4^3

c. $2^3 \times 5^2$

Exercise 6.1.3

Copy and complete the following table. These values will come in handy in the future. Try to commit them to memory.

Powers of 2	Powers of 3	Powers of 4	Powers of 5	Powers of 6	Powers of 7	Powers of 8
$2^2 =$	$3^2 =$	$4^2 =$	$5^2 =$	$6^2 =$	$7^2 =$	$8^2 =$
$2^3 =$	$3^3 =$	$4^3 =$	$5^3 =$	$6^3 =$	$7^3 =$	$8^3 =$
$2^4 =$	$3^4 =$	$4^4 =$	$5^4 =$			
$2^5 =$	$3^5 =$					

6.2 The product of powers law

Consider the following calculation:

$$a^4 \times a^5 = a \times a \times a \times a \times a \times a \times a \times a \times a = a^9$$

The result could be obtained simply by adding the indices: $5 + 4 = 9$.

When we multiply numbers written in index notation that share the same base, we can add the indices.

$$a^m \times a^n = a^{m+n}$$

Example

Simplify the expression $x^5 \times x^6$.

✓ Solution

Working	Explanation
$x^5 \times x^6 = x^{5+6} = x^{11}$	x^5 and x^6 have the same base, so we can add the indices.

Example

Simplify the expression $x^3y^2 \times x^5y$.

✓ Solution

Working	Explanation
$x^3y^2 \times x^5y = x^3 \times x^5 \times y^2 \times y$ $= x^{3+5}y^{2+1}$ $= x^8y^3$	x^3 and x^5 have the same base, so we can add the indices. y^2 and y have the same base so we can add the indices. (**Note**: y is the same as y^1.)

Example

Simplify the expression $4m^5 \times 3m^2$.

✓ ***Solution***

Working	Explanation
$4m^5 \times 3m^2 = 4 \times 3 \times m^5 \times m^2$ $= 12m^{5+2}$ $= 12m^7$	Multiply the numbers 4 and 3. m^5 and m^2 have the same base, so we can add the indices.

Example

Simplify he expression $2pq^2 \times 9p^3q^6$.

✓ ***Solution***

Working	Explanation
$2pq^2 \times 9p^3q^6 = 2 \times 9 \times p \times p^3 \times q^2 \times q^6$ $= 18p^{1+3}q^{2+6}$ $= 18p^4q^8$	Multiply the numbers 2 and 9. p and p^3 have the same base, so we can add the indices. (p is the same as p^1.) q^2 and q^6 have the same base, so we can add the indices.

Exercise 6.2

Simplify each of the following expressions.

a. $b^2 \times b^5$ **b.** $x^3 \times x \times x^4$ **c.** $2c^2 \times 5c^4$ **d.** $x^2z^4 \times xz^7$

e. $a^3b^4 \times ab$ **f.** $5x^2y^2 \times xy^4$ **g.** $9c^2d \times 4cd^2$ **h.** $f^2g^3 \times g^5h^2$

6.3 The quotient of powers law

Consider the expression $a^8 \div a^3$. We can write this expression as a fraction: $\frac{a^8}{a^3}$. In expanded form, $\frac{a^8}{a^3} = \frac{a \times a \times a \times a \times a \times a \times a \times a}{a \times a \times a}$.

This can be simplified by cancelling common factors in the numerator and the denominator.

$$\frac{a^8}{a^3} = \frac{\cancel{a} \times \cancel{a} \times \cancel{a} \times a \times a \times a \times a \times a}{\cancel{a} \times \cancel{a} \times \cancel{a}} = a \times a \times a \times a \times a = a^5$$

We can see now that $a^8 \div a^3 = a^{8-3} = a^5$.

When we divide numbers written in index notation that share the same base, we can subtract the indices.

$$a^m \div a^n = a^{m-n}$$

Example

Simplify $w^7 \div w^2$.

✓ *Solution*

Working	Explanation
$w^7 \div w^2 = w^{7-2} = w^5$	w^7 and w^2 share the same base, so we can subtract the indices.

Example

Simplify $\frac{m^9}{m^5}$.

✓ *Solution*

Working	Explanation
$\frac{m^9}{m^5} = m^9 \div m^5 = m^{9-5} = m^4$	m^9 and m^5 share the same base, so we can subtract the indices.

Example

Simplify $\frac{12x^5}{3x^2}$.

✓ *Solution*

Working	Explanation
$\frac{12x^5}{3x^2} = 12x^5 \div 3x^2 = 4x^{5-2} = 4x^3$	$12 \div 3 = 4$ x^5 and x^2 share the same base, so we can subtract the indices.

Example

Simplify $\frac{3x^4y^2}{6x^2y}$.

✓ ***Solution***

Working	Explanation
$\frac{3x^4y^2}{6x^2y} = \frac{x^{4-2}y^{2-1}}{2} = \frac{x^2y}{2}$	$3 \div 6 = \frac{1}{2}$ x^4 and x^2 share the same base, so we can subtract the indices. y^2 and y share the same base, so we can subtract the indices.

Exercise 6.3

Simplify each of the following expressions.

a. $p^7 \div p^3$

b. $\frac{m^{12}}{m^9}$

c. $\frac{8y^7}{2y^4}$

d. $\frac{6x^4y^5}{12x^2y^3}$

6.4 The power of a power law

Consider the expression $(a^5)^3$. In expanded form

$$\begin{aligned}(a^5)^3 &= a^5 \times a^5 \times a^5 \\ &= a \times a \times a \times a \times a \times a \times a \times a \times a \times a \times a \times a \times a \times a \times a \\ &= a^{15}\end{aligned}$$

When a number written in index form is raised to a power, we can multiply the powers.

$$(a^m)^n = a^{mn}$$

Example

Simplify $(y^4)^2$.

✓ ***Solution***

Working	Explanation
$(y^4)^2 = y^{4\times2}$ $= y^8$	When we have a number in index form raised to a power, we can multiply the powers.

Example

Simplify $(2a)^3$.

✓ *Solution*

Working	Explanation
$(2a)^3 = 2^3 \times a^3$ $= 8a^3$	Both the coefficient of a and a are raised to the power of 3. $2^3 = 2 \times 2 \times 2 = 8$.

Example

Simplify $\left(3p^2q^3\right)^3$.

✓ *Solution*

Working	Explanation
$\left(3p^2q^3\right)^3 = 3^3 \times \left(p^2\right)^3 \times \left(q^3\right)^3$ $= 27p^{2\times3}q^{3\times3}$ $= 27p^6q^9$	Raise each term in the brackets to the power of 3. $3^3 = 3 \times 3 \times 3 = 27$. Simplify $\left(p^2\right)^3$ and $\left(q^3\right)^3$ by multiplying the indices in each case.

Example

Simplify $(-5x^4)^2$.

✓ *Solution*

Working	Explanation
$(-5x^4)^2 = (-5)^2 \times (x^4)^2$ $= 25x^{4\times2}$ $= 25x^8$	Both the coefficient of x^4 and x^4 are raised to the power of 2. $(-5)^2 = -5 \times -5 = 25$. Multiplying two minus values gives a positive result. Simplify $(x^4)^2$ by multiplying the indices.

Exercise 6.4

Simplify each of the following expressions.

a. $\left(p^5\right)^3$ b. $(a^7)^2$ c. $(2m)^5$ d. $(-3y)^3$

e. $(ab^4)^3$ f. $\left(p^2q^4r^3\right)^5$ g. $(2a^2b^3)^3$ h. $\left(8x^3y^2\right)^3$

6.5 The zero exponent law

Consider the expression $\frac{a^7}{a^7}$. This is equal to 1 since when you divide a number by itself, the result is always 1.

Now apply the second index law (the quotient of powers law) to the expression.

$$\frac{a^7}{a^7} = a^{7-7} = a^0$$

It follows that

$$\boldsymbol{a^0 = 1}$$

Example

Simplify m^0.

✓ ***Solution***

Working	Explanation
$m^0 = 1$	Any number or pronumeral raised to the power of 0 equals 1.

Example

Simplify $(5p)^0$.

✓ ***Solution***

Working	Explanation
$(5p)^0 = 1$	Any number or pronumeral raised to the power of 0 equals 1.

Example

Simplify $5p^0$.

✓ ***Solution***

Working	Explanation
$5p^0 = 5 \times p^0$ $= 5 \times 1$ $= 5$	Only p is raised to the power of zero in this expression.

Example

Simplify $4a^2b^0 + 5a^0b$.

✓ *Solution*

Working	Explanation
$4a^2b^0 + 5a^0b = 4 \times a^2 \times b^0 + 5 \times a^0 \times b$ $= 4a^2 \times 1 + 5 \times 1 \times b$ $= 4a^2 + 5b$	$b^0 = 1$ and $a^0 = 1$ $4a^2$ and $5b$ are not like terms, so they cannot be added.

Exercise 6.5

Simplify each of the following expressions.

a. p^0 **b.** $(2q)^0$ **c.** $(x^2y)^0$ **d.** $7t^0$

e. $-3k^0$ **f.** $8a^0 + 5b^0$ **g.** $5y^0z^4$ **h.** $3x^0y^5 + 5y^0z^2$

6.6 Using index laws to simplify expressions

Sometimes it is necessary to use more than one index law to simplify an expression.

Example

Simplify $\dfrac{a^4 \times a^5}{a^3 \times a}$.

✓ *Solution*

Working	Explanation
$\dfrac{a^4 \times a^5}{a^3 \times a} = \dfrac{a^{4+5}}{a^{3+1}}$ $= \dfrac{a^9}{a^4}$ $= a^{9-4}$ $= a^5$	All terms have the same base. Simplify the numerator by adding the indices. Simplify the denominator by adding the indices. When dividing, subtract the indices.

Example

Simplify $\dfrac{2m^2 \times 8m^6}{4m^3}$.

✓ ***Solution***

Working	Explanation
$\dfrac{2m^2 \times 8m^6}{4m^3} = \dfrac{(2 \times 8 \times m^2 \times m^6)}{4m^3}$	Simplify the numerator and multiply the numbers in it.
$= \dfrac{16m^{2+6}}{4m^3}$	Since m^2 and m^6 have the same base, add the indices.
$= \dfrac{16m^8}{4m^3}$	Divide the numbers: $16 \div 4 = 4$.
$= 4m^{8-3}$	Since m^8 and m^3 have the same base, subtract the indices.
$= 4m^5$	

Example

Simplify $3x^4 \times (2x^2)^3$.

✓ ***Solution***

Working	Explanation
$3x^4 \times (2x^2)^3 = 3x^4 \times 2^3 \times (x^2)^3$	Raise each term in the brackets to the power of 3.
$= 3x^4 \times 8 \times x^{2 \times 3}$	$2^3 = 2 \times 2 \times 2 = 8$ and multiply the indices in $(x^2)^3$.
$= 3 \times x^4 \times 8 \times x^6$	Multiply the numbers: $3 \times 8 = 24$.
$= 24x^{4+6}$	Since x^4 and x^6 have the same base, add the indices.
$= 24x^{10}$	

Exercise 6.6

Simplify each of the following expressions.

a. $\dfrac{k^5 \times k^7}{k^4}$

b. $\dfrac{y^2 \times y^3}{(y^2)^2}$

c. $\dfrac{(2x^2)^6}{(4x^3)^2}$

d. $\dfrac{3d^2 \times 8d^5}{(2d)^3}$

e. $\dfrac{5p^0}{(15p)^0}$

f. $\dfrac{t^5}{t^2} \times \dfrac{t^9}{t^6}$

g. $5x^5 \times (2x^3)^4$

h. $(3a^2b^4)^2 \times 2a^3b$

Answers

Exercise 6.1.1

a. 7^9　　b. $3^3 \times 5^2 \times 7^3$　　c. p^4q^2　　d. $35g^2h^3$

Exercise 6.1.2

a. 32　　b. 64　　c. 200

Exercise 6.1.3

Powers of 2	Powers of 3	Powers of 4	Powers of 5	Powers of 6	Powers of 7	Powers of 8
$2^2 = 4$	$3^2 = 9$	$4^2 = 16$	$5^2 = 25$	$6^2 = 36$	$7^2 = 49$	$8^2 = 64$
$2^3 = 8$	$3^3 = 27$	$4^3 = 64$	$5^3 = 125$	$6^3 = 216$	$7^3 = 343$	$8^3 = 512$
$2^4 = 16$	$3^4 = 81$	$4^4 = 256$	$5^4 = 625$			
$2^5 = 32$	$3^5 = 243$					

Exercise 6.2

a. b^7　　b. x^8　　c. $10c^6$　　d. x^3z^{11}

e. a^4b^5　　f. $5x^3y^6$　　g. $36c^3d^3$　　h. $f^2g^8h^2$

Exercise 6.3

a. p^4　　b. m^3　　c. $4y^3$　　d. $\frac{x^2y^2}{2}$

Exercise 6.4

a. p^{15}　　b. a^{14}　　c. $32m^5$　　d. $-27y^3$

e. a^3b^{12}　　f. $p^{10}q^{20}r^{15}$　　g. $8a^6b^9$　　h. $512x^9y^6$

Exercise 6.5

a. 1　　b. 1　　c. 1　　d. 7

e. -3　　f. 13　　g. $5z^4$　　h. $3y^5 + 5z^2$

Exercise 6.6

a. k^8　　b. y　　c. $4x^6$　　d. $3d^4$

e. 5　　f. t^6　　g. $80x^{17}$　　h. $18a^7b^9$

Chapter 7 – Ratios

7.1 Writing ratios

Ratios can be used to compare quantities.

In the picture below there are three triangles and two stars.

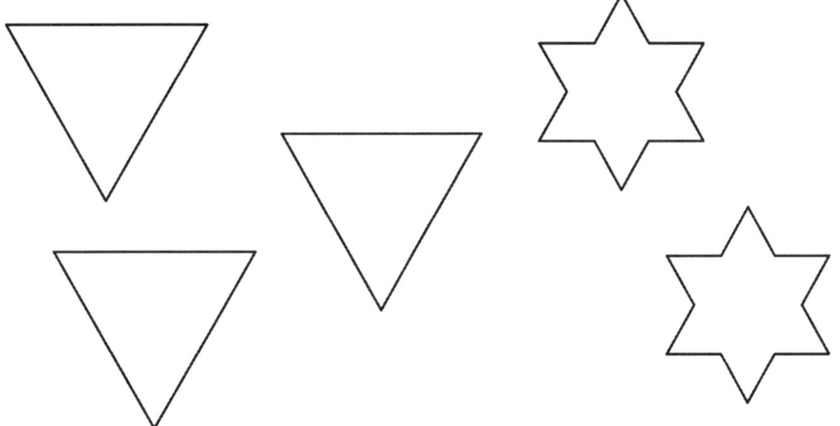

We can compare the triangles and stars in the form of a ratio: the ratio of triangles to stars is $3:2$ and the ratio of stars to triangles is $2:3$. In a ratio, ':' is read as 'to'.

Example

In a bag there are 6 red marbles and 5 green marbles. Determine the ratio of:

a. red marbles to green marbles

b. green marbles to red marbles

c. red marbles to all marbles in the bag.

✓ *Solution*

Working	Explanation
a. $6:5$	The ratio is written as **red marbles : green marbles**
b. $5:6$	The ratio is written as **green marbles : red marbles**
c. $6:11$	The ratio is written as **red marbles : total marbles**

Exercise 7.1.1

There are 15 dogs and 8 cats at a boarding kennel. Determine the ratio of:

a. dogs to cats

b. cats to dogs

c. cats to all the animals at the kennel.

Exercise 7.1.2

A cutlery drawer contains 16 knives, 13 forks and 21 spoons. Determine the ratio of:

a. knives to forks

b. forks to spoons

c. knives to forks to spoons

d. forks to all cutlery in the drawer.

7.2 Simplifying ratios

A ratio can be simplified by dividing it or multiplying it by the highest common factor.

When working with fractions in a ratio, begin by giving all numbers in the ratio the same denominator.

Example

Simplify $4:10$.

✓ Solution

Working	Explanation
$4:10 = 2:5$	4 and 10 have a highest common factor of 2, so we divide each term by 2 to simplify the ratio.

Example

Simplify $6:27:18$.

✓ Solution

Working	Explanation
$6:27:18 = 2:9:6$	6, 27 and 18 have a highest common factor of 3, so we divide each term by 3 to simplify the ratio.

Example

Simplify $\frac{1}{5}:\frac{3}{10}$.

✓ Solution

Working	Explanation
$\frac{1}{5}:\frac{3}{10} = \frac{2}{10}:\frac{3}{10}$ $\frac{2}{10}:\frac{3}{10} = 2:3$	Both fractions can be written with a common denominator of 10. Write the ratio so that both fractions have a denominator of 10. The simplified ratio is the ratio of the numerators.

Example

Simplify $3.5:5$.

✓ ***Solution***

Working	Explanation
$3.5:5 = 7:10$	Multiply both numbers by 2 so that the numbers in the ratio are whole numbers.

Exercise 7.2.1

Simplify each of the following ratios.

a. $6:16$ **b.** $45:10$ **c.** $30:1000$ **d.** $8:12:24$

e. $90:18:36$ **f.** $\frac{1}{3}:\frac{5}{6}$ **g.** $\frac{2}{16}:\frac{1}{9}$ **h.** $\frac{2}{9}:\frac{1}{6}$

i. $\frac{1}{5}:\frac{1}{2}:\frac{7}{10}$ **j.** $2.5:4.5$ **k.** $1.2:5.1$ **l.** $70:3.5$

When comparing quantities with units, it is important that the quantities have the same units. However, the ratios do not have units.

Example

Write 600 g to 1 kg as a simplified ratio.

✓ ***Solution***

Working	Explanation
$600:1000$	Write each quantity with the same units (in this case grams).
$600:1000 = 6:10$	1 kg is 1000 g.
$6:10 \quad = 3:5$	Divide both terms by the common factor: 100.
	Simplify by dividing the resulting terms by the highest common factor: 2.

Example

Write 45 c to \$5 as a simplified ratio.

✓ Solution

Working	Explanation
$45:500$ $45:500 = 9:100$	Write each quantity with the same units. \$5 is 500 c. Divide both terms by the highest common factor: 5.

Example

Write 1.5 m to 50 cm as a simplified ratio.

✓ Solution

Working	Explanation
$150:50$ $150:50 = 15:5$ $15:5 \quad = \quad 3:1$	Write each quantity with the same units. 1.5 m is 150 cm. Divide both terms by the common factor: 10. Simplify by dividing the resulting terms by the common factor: 5.

Exercise 7.2.2

Write each of the following as a simplified ratio.

a. 2 kg to 500 g
b. \$3 to 60 c
c. 15 mm to 20 cm
d. 0.3 L to 250 mL
e. 210 g to 4.2 kg
f. 2 t to 600 kg
g. 6 m to 48 cm
h. 15 g to 30 mg

7.3 Ratios, percentages and fractions

Example

A fruit cake recipe uses sultanas, currants and raisins in the ratio of $3:2:5$.

a. What fraction of the fruit used in this recipe is currants?

b. What percentage of the fruit is raisins?

c. If the total mass of fruit used in this recipe is 500 g, how many grams of sultanas are used?

✓ ***Solution***

Working	Explanation
a. Total parts $= 3 + 2 + 5 = 10$ Current fraction $= \frac{2}{10}$ $= \frac{1}{5}$	Calculate the total number of parts in the ratio. The required fraction is the number of current parts divided by the total parts. Simplify the fraction by cancelling the common factor of 2.
b. Raisin fraction $= \frac{5}{10}$ $= \frac{1}{2}$ Raisin percentage $= \frac{1}{2} \times 100\%$ $= 50\%$	The fraction of raisins is the number of raisin parts divided by the total number of parts. Simplify the fraction by cancelling the common factor of 5. Multiply by 100 to convert the result to a percentage.
c. Sultana fraction $= \frac{3}{10}$ Sultana mass $= \frac{3}{10} \times 500$ $= 3 \times 50$ $= 150$ g	The fraction of sultanas is the number of sultana parts divided by the total number of parts. The mass of sultanas is $\frac{3}{10}$ of the mass of fruit.

Exercise 7.3.1

A jug of cordial is made of 1 part cordial concentrate to 4 parts water.

a. Write this as a ratio.

b. What fraction of a jug of this cordial is cordial concentrate?

c. What percentage of a jug of this cordial is water?

Exercise 7.3.2

A bag contains only pink, purple and white balls in the ratio of $4:5:1$.

a. What fraction of the balls in the bag are pink?

b. What percentage of the balls in the bag are white?

c. If there are 60 balls in the bag, how many of them are purple?

7.4 Dividing a quantity according to a given ratio

A quantity can be divided according to a ratio by considering each part of the ratio as a fraction of the total number of parts.

Example

Divide 480 according to the ratio $7:5$.

✓ Solution

Working	Explanation
$7+5=12$	Calculate the total number of parts by adding the terms in the ratio.
$480 \div 12 = 40$	Find the size of one part by dividing 480 by 12.
$7 \times 40 = 280$ $5 \times 40 = 200$	Find 7 parts and 5 parts: • Multiply the size of one part by 7. • Multiply the size of one part by 5. So 480 should be divided into parts of 280 and 200.

Example

A merchandise store at a concert has 600 T-shirts in sizes small, medium and large in the ratio of $1:2:3$. How many of each size T-shirt are available at the store?

✓ Solution

Working	Explanation
$1+2+3=6$	Calculate the total number of parts by adding the terms in the ratio.
$600 \div 6 = 100$	Find the size of one part by dividing 600 by 6.
Number of small $= 1 \times 100 = 100$ Number of medium $= 2 \times 100 = 200$ Number of large $= 3 \times 100 = 300$	The number of small T-shirts is 1 part. The number of medium T-shirts is 2 parts. The number of large T-shirts is 3 parts. Multiply the number of parts by the size of 1 part.

Sometimes it is easier to use a calculator.

Example

$2500 is shared between Ari, Shiya and Fatima in the ratio of $1:2:10$. Determine how much each person receives.

✓ ***Solution***

Working	Explanation
$1 + 2 + 10 = 13$	Calculate the total number of parts in the ratio.
$2500 \div 13 = 192.30769...$	Determine the size of one part by dividing 2500 by 13.
Ari's share is $192.31.	Ari's share is 1 part. Since this is money, round the amount to 2 decimal places.
$2500 \div 13 \times 2 = 384.61538...$ Shiya's share is $384.62	Shiya's share is 2 parts, so multiply 1 part by 2. Round the amount to 2 decimal places.
$2500 \div 13 \times 10 = 1923.0769...$ Fatima's share is $1923.08.	Fatima's share is 10 parts, so multiply 1 part by 10. Round the amount to 2 decimal places.

Exercise 7.4

a. Divide 450 in the ratio of $7:2$.

b. Divide 5500 in the ratio of $4:7$.

c. A cruise ship carries crew and passengers in the ratio of $1:7$. If there are 864 people in total on the ship, how many are crew and how many are passengers?

d. Divide $5200 in the ratio of $1:2:10$.

e. An amount of $9250 is divided in the ratio of $3:5$ between Minny and Mo. Determine how much each person receives. Use a calculator.

7.5 Equivalent ratios

Ratios that are in the same proportion are equivalent ratios.

For example, the ratios $5:6$ and $15:18$ are equivalent since the number that is multiplied by the first number in the first ratio to get the first number in the second ratio is the same as the number that is multiplied by the second number in the first ratio to get the second number in the second ratio. That number is 3. We can write this as a proportion statement: $5:6 = 15:18$.

Finding unknowns in equivalent ratios

Example

Find the unknown in the proportion statement $8:9 = 16:y$.

✓ Solution

Working	Explanation
$8:9 = 16:y$ $\times 2 \left(\begin{matrix} 8:9 \\ 16:y \end{matrix} \right) \times 2$ $y = 9 \times 2 = 18$	8 and 16 are corresponding numbers in the proportion statement. Use this to determine what the first ratio is multiplied by to obtain the second ratio. The ratios are in proportion, so multiply 9 by 2 to find y.

Example

Find the unknown in the proportion statement $x:5 = 12:20$.

✓ Solution

Working	Explanation
$x:5 = 12:20$ $\div 4 \left(\begin{matrix} 12:20 \\ x:5 \end{matrix} \right) \div 4$ $x = 12 \div 4 = 3$	5 and 20 are corresponding numbers in the proportion statement. Use this to determine what the second ratio is divided by to obtain the first ratio. The ratios are in proportion, so divide 12 by 4 to find x.

Exercise 7.5.1

Find the value of the pronumeral in each of the following proportion equations.

a. $a:7 = 15:35$ **b.** $4:b = 24:54$ **c.** $c:28 = 3:4$ **d.** $4:5 = 44:d$

Equivalent fractions

Sometimes a proportion statement will involve fractions. If fractions are equivalent, then the numerator and denominator of one fraction can be multiplied or divided by the same number to obtain the other fraction.

Example

Find the value of the pronumeral in the proportion statement $\frac{2}{5} = \frac{8}{q}$.

✓ Solution

Working	Explanation
$\frac{2}{5} = \frac{8}{q}$ $2 \times 4 = 8$ $q = 5 \times 4$ $q = 20$	Determine the factor that the first fraction has been multiplied by to obtain the second fraction by examining the numerator of each fraction. The numerator in the second fraction is 4 times the numerator in the first fraction. Since the numerator in the first fraction is multiplied by 4 to obtain the second, multiply the denominator of the first fraction by 4 to obtain q.

Example

Find the value of the pronumeral in the proportion statement $\frac{p}{3} = \frac{18}{27}$.

✓ Solution

Working	Explanation
$\frac{p}{3} = \frac{18}{27}$ $3 \times 9 = 27$ $p = 18 \div 9$ $p = 2$	Determine the factor that the first fraction has been multiplied by to obtain the second fraction by examining the denominator of each fraction. The denominator in the second fraction is 9 times the denominator in the first fraction. Since the first denominator is multiplied by 9 to obtain the second, divide the numerator of the second fraction by 9 to obtain the first.

Exercise 7.5.2

Find the value of the pronumeral in each of the following proportion statements.

a. $\frac{r}{6} = \frac{24}{36}$ b. $\frac{24}{27} = \frac{8}{s}$ c. $\frac{3}{8} = \frac{t}{32}$ d. $\frac{200}{160} = \frac{5}{v}$

Using equations to find unknowns in equivalent ratios

Equation-solving techniques can be used to find an unknown in a proportion statement.

Example

Find k if $3:8 = k:28$.

✓ Solution

Working	Explanation
$\frac{3}{8} = \frac{k}{28}$ $\frac{3}{8} \times 28 = k$ $k = \frac{3}{8} \times \frac{28}{1}$ $k = \frac{3}{2} \times \frac{7}{1}$ $k = \frac{21}{2}$ or $k = 10.5$	Rewrite each ratio as a fraction. Multiply both sides by 28 and simplify to find the value of k.

Exercise 7.5.3

Find the value of x in each of the following proportion statements.

a. $x:5 = 3:2$ b. $x:11 = 4:5$ c. $7:3 = x:4$ d. $x:3 = 6:5$

Applications of equivalent ratios

Equivalent ratios are useful in many real-life situations.

Example

An orchard has trees that produce green apples and trees that produce red apples in the ratio of $3:10$. If 150 trees produce green apples, how many trees produce red apples?

✓ Solution

Working	Explanation
Let r be the number of trees that produce red apples.	Assign a pronumeral to the unknown quantity.
$3:10 = 150:r$	Write a proportion statement.
$r = 10 \times 50 = 500$ 500 trees produce red apples in the orchard.	3 is multiplied by 50 to obtain 150, so multiply 10 by 50 to find r.

Exercise 7.5.4.

a. The ratio of the temperature at 8 am one day to 2 pm on the same day is $4:9$. If the temperature at 8 am was 12°C, what was the temperature at 2 pm?

b. The ratio of cats to dogs at a kennel is $4:5$. If there are 25 dogs at the kennel, how many cats are there?

7.6 Scales

Scales with units

To draw something to scale is to use a small distance to represent a larger distance. A map is an example of something drawn to scale. Most maps display a ratio that indicates what larger distance is represented by a smaller distance. Units are often included with the ratio.

Example

A map is drawn to scale so that 1 cm on the map represents 5 km.

Calculate:

a. the distance represented by 4 cm on the map

b. the distance on the map that represents 35 km.

✓ Solution

Working	Explanation
a. $\times 4 \left(\begin{array}{c} 1\text{ cm} : 5\text{ km} \\ 4\text{ cm} : 20\text{ km} \end{array} \right) \times 4$ 4 cm on the map represents 20 km.	Write the scale as a ratio. 1 cm is multiplied by 4 to give 4 cm, so 5 km also needs to be multiplied by 4.
b. $\times 7 \left(\begin{array}{c} 1\text{ cm} : 5\text{ km} \\ 7\text{ cm} : 35\text{ km} \end{array} \right) \times 7$ 35 km is represented by 7 cm on the map.	Write the scale as a ratio. 5 km is multiplied by 7, so 1 cm also needs to be multiplied by 7.

Exercise 7.6.1

For the given distances listed below, find the actual distances represented on a map according to the scale $1\text{ cm} : 8\text{ km}$.

a. 5 cm

b. 12 cm

Exercise 7.6.2

A scale drawing has the scale $1\text{ cm} : 10\text{ m}$. Find the actual length of an object with a length of 3.6 cm on the drawing.

Converting scaled distances to actual distances

When units are not included in the ratio for a scale, both quantities will have the same units when the scale ratio is applied. It is often necessary to convert the result to more appropriate units for the final answer.

A scale ratio of 1 : 25 000 means that the actual distances are 25 000 times the scaled distances.

The scale on a diagram or map is written as

scaled distance : actual distance

Example

A map has a scale of 1 : 25 000. Calculate the actual distance represented on the map by a distance of 2 cm.

✓ *Solution*

Working	Explanation
$\times 2 \left(\begin{array}{c} 1 : 25\,000 \\ 2 : 50\,000 \end{array} \right) \times 2$ Actual distance $= 50\ 000$ cm $= 50\ 000 \div 100$ m $= 500$ m	The ratio gives **scaled distance : actual distance**. Multiply the ratio by 2 to calculate the actual distance in cm. Write the actual distance with appropriate units (for example, metres). Divide by 100 to convert centimetres to metres.

Example

A map has a scale of 1 : 25 000. Calculate the actual distance represented on the map by a distance of 4 mm.

✓ *Solution*

Working	Explanation
$\times 4 \left(\begin{array}{c} 1 : 25\,000 \\ 4 : 100\,000 \end{array} \right) \times 4$ Actual distance $= 100\ 000$ mm $= 100\ 000 \div 1\ 000$ m $= 100$ m	The ratio gives **scaled distance : actual distance**. Multiply the ratio by 4 to calculate the actual length in mm. Write the actual distance with appropriate units (such as metres). Divide by 1000 to convert millimetres to metres.

Exercise 7.6.3

A map has a scale of 1 : 20 000. Calculate the actual distance represented on the map by:

a. 5 cm

b. 12 cm.

Exercise 7.6.4

Find the actual distance represented by 14 mm on a map with a scale of $1:50\,000$.

Converting actual distances to scaled distances

Example

A map has a scale of $1:500\,000$. Find the scaled distance that represents an actual distance of 15 km.

✓ *Solution*

Working	Explanation
$15 \text{ km} = 15 \times 100\,000 \text{ cm}$ $= 1\,500\,000 \text{ cm}$	Convert the actual distance of 15 km to cm. The ratio gives **scaled distance : actual distance**.
$\times 3$ ($1:500\,000$ → $3:1\,500\,000$) $\times 3$	Multiply the ratio by 3 to find the scaled distance. The scaled distance will also be measured in cm.
A distance of 3 cm on the map represents an actual distance of 15 km.	

Example

A scale drawing of a plane uses a scale of $1:50$. If the plane is 16 m long, how long is it on the scale drawing?

✓ *Solution*

Working	Explanation
$1:50$ $x:16$	The ratio gives **scaled distance : actual distance**. The drawing distance is unknown, and the actual distance is 16 m.
$\frac{x}{16} = \frac{1}{50}$ $x = \frac{1}{50} \times 16$ $x = 0.32$	Write an equation. To solve for the unknown (x) multiply both sides by 16.
Drawing length $= 0.32$ m $= 0.32 \times 100$ cm $= 32$ cm	Write the answer with appropriate units.

Exercise 7.6.5

a. Find the scaled distance representing an actual distance of 600 m using a scale of 1 : 2000.

b. A scale diagram of an aeroplane uses a scale of 1 : 80. What length on the diagram would represent the plane's actual wingspan of 25 m?

Determining a scale ratio

Example

On a map, 2 cm represents 5 km. Express this as a scale.

✓ ***Solution***

Working	Explanation
2 cm:5 km = 2 cm:500 000 cm = 1:250 000	Write the ratio as **scaled distance : actual distance.** Write both quantities with the same units. Simplify the ratio by dividing by 2. Do not include units with the scale.

Exercise 7.6.6

a. A scale plan of a barn is drawn so that the actual length of the barn, which is 32 m, is represented by 64 cm on the plan. Determine the scale used for the plan.

b. Determine the scale used on a map where 5 cm represents 2 km.

Answers

Exercise 7.1.1

a. $15:8$ b. $8:15$ c. $8:23$

Exercise 7.1.2

a. $16:13$ b. $13:21$ c. $16:13:21$ d. $13:50$

Exercise 7.2.1

a. $3:8$ b. $9:2$ c. $3:100$
d. $2:3:6$ e. $5:1:2$ f. $2:5$
g. $9:8$ h. $4:3$ i. $2:5:7$
j. $5:9$ k. $12:51$ l. $20:1$

Exercise 7.2.2

a. $4:1$ b. $5:1$ c. $3:40$
d. $6:5$ e. $1:20$ f. $10:3$
g. $25:2$ h. $500:1$

Exercise 7.3.1

a. $1:4$ b. $\frac{1}{5}$ c. 80%

Exercise 7.3.2

a. $\frac{2}{5}$ b. 10% c. 30

Exercise 7.4

a. 7 parts is 350 and 2 parts is 100.
b. 4 parts is 2000 and 7 parts is 3500.
c. 108 crew and 756 passengers
d. 1 part is \$400, 2 parts is \$800 and 10 parts is \$4000.
e. Minny: \$3468.75 and Mo: \$5781.25

Exercise 7.5.1

a. $a = 3$ b. $b = 9$ c. $c = 21$ d. $d = 55$

Exercise 7.5.2

a. $r = 4$ b. $s = 9$ c. $t = 12$ d. $v = 4$

Exercise 7.5.3

a. $x = \frac{15}{2}$ or 7.5 b. $x = \frac{44}{5}$ or 8.8 c. $x = \frac{28}{3}$ d. $x = \frac{18}{5}$ or 3.6

Exercise 7.5.4

a. 27°C b. 20

Exercise 7.6.1

a. 40 km b. 96 km

Exercise 7.6.2

36 m

Exercise 7.6.3

a. 1 km b. 2.4 km

Exercise 7.6.4

700 m

Exercise 7.6.5

a. 30 cm b. 31.25 cm

Exercise 7.6.6

a. 1:50 b. 1:40 000

Chapter 8 – Rates

A rate gives a measure of how one quantity changes when another quantity changes. Rates compare two quantities that have units, so a rate must also have units.

A rate is indicated by the word **per** or the symbol '/'.

Some examples of rates are given below.

Cost rate	$5 per kg or $5/kg
Run rate	4.2 runs per over or 4.2 runs/over
Growth rate	5.2 cm per year or 5.2 cm/year
Speed	60 km per hour or 60 km/h

8.1 Calculating rates

To calculate a rate, we divide the first quantity in the rate by the second quantity in the rate.

$$\textit{rate} = \frac{\textit{quantity } X}{\textit{quantity } Y}$$

For example, if we are interested in the run rate (i.e. the runs/over) we divide the number of runs (the first quantity) by the number of overs (the second quantity).

Example

Gemma earns $364.50 for working 15 hours at a supermarket. Calculate her hourly rate of pay in dollars per hour.

✓ *Solution*

Working	Explanation
$\text{Hourly rate} = \frac{\text{amount earned}}{\text{number of hours}}$ $= \frac{364.50}{15}$ $= \$24.30/\text{h}$	Divide the amount earned by the number of hours worked. Include units in your answer. In this case the units are dollars per hour.

Exercise 8.1

a. Lucas earns $195.30 for working 9 hours in his part-time job. Calculate his hourly rate of pay.

b. A car uses 64.39 litres of petrol to travel 685 km. Calculate the petrol consumption for this trip in litres per km.

c. 5 kilograms of potatoes cost $16. Calculate the price per kilogram.

8.2 Calculating quantities from rates

The following diagrams may help you calculate quantities from rates. The relative position of the items in a triangle indicates their relationship with the highlighted item when the highlighted item is to be calculated. For example, when **Rate** is highlighted, x is above y, indicating that rate is calculated by dividing x by y. Another example: when $\boldsymbol{x}$ is highlighted, Rate and y are beside each other, indicating that when x is to be calculated, Rate and y should be multiplied.

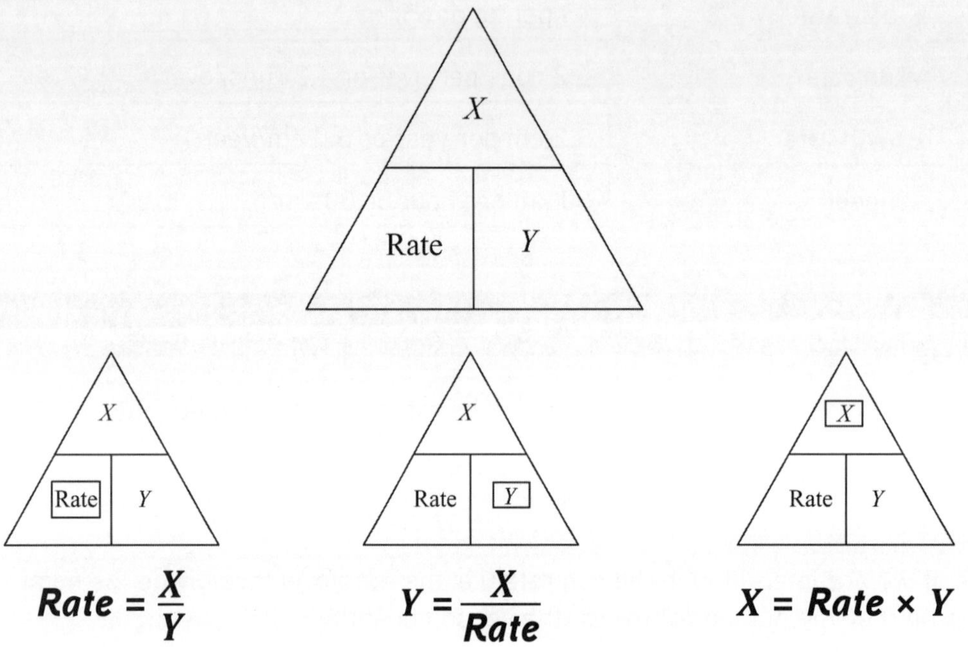

$$\textbf{Rate} = \frac{X}{Y} \qquad Y = \frac{X}{\textbf{Rate}} \qquad X = \textbf{Rate} \times Y$$

Example

Lucien types at a rate of 48 words/minute. How many words can he type in 12 minutes?

✓ Solution

Working	Explanation
Number of words $= 48 \times 12$ $= 576$	Multiply the rate (words/minute) by the number of minutes to get the number of words.

Exercise 8.2.1

a. A butcher charges 9 dollars per kilogram for minced lamb. What is the cost of 3 kg?

b. A mobile phone plan offers unlimited international calls for an additional \$5 per month. What is the annual (i.e. yearly) cost for international calls on this plan?

c. Water is leaking from a tank at a rate of 50 L/h. How many litres of water will leak from the tank in 6 hours?

Example

Meg's run rate in a cricket innings was 6.4 runs/over. She made a total of 96 runs. For how many overs did she bat?

✓ ***Solution***

Working	Explanation
Number of overs $= \frac{\text{runs}}{\text{run rate}}$ $= \frac{96}{6.4}$ $= 15$	Divide the number of runs by the run rate to find the number of overs.

Exercise 8.2.2

a. The growth rate of a tree is 5.4 cm/year. How many years will it take the tree to grow 37.8 cm?

b. Cherries are sold for $24 per kg. How many kilograms of cherries can be purchased for $30?

c. Kiah earns $17.40 per hour in her part-time job. How many hours will it take her to earn $435?

8.3 Speed

Speed is a rate that measures the distance travelled in a certain unit of time. Speed is usually measured in kilometres per hour (km/h) or metres per second (m/s).

Average speed gives the speed over a whole journey rather than the speed at any time during the journey.

$$\textit{average speed} = \frac{\textit{distance}}{\textit{time}}$$

which we abbreviate to the rule $s = \frac{d}{t}$.

The relationship between speed, distance and time is illustrated in the following diagrams.

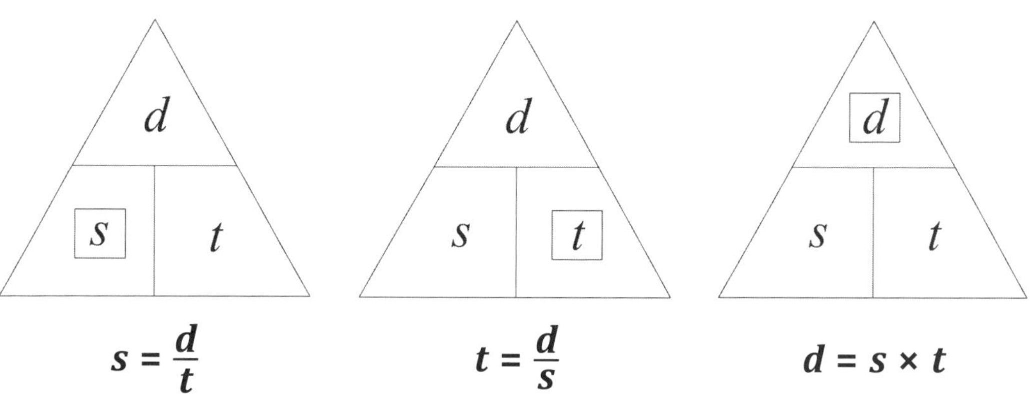

Example

A truck travels 800 km in 10 hours. What is the average speed for the journey?

✓ Solution

Working	Explanation
$s = \frac{d}{t}$ $= \frac{800}{10}$ $= 80$ km/h	Average speed $= \frac{\text{distance}}{\text{time}}$ Include appropriate units with the answer (in this case km/h).

Example

Khan cycles at an average speed of 16 km/h for 2.5 hours. How far does she cycle?

✓ Solution

Working	Explanation
$d = s \times t$ $= 16 \times 2.5$ $= 40$ km	Distance = average speed × time Include units with the answer. In this example, distance is measured in km.

Example

How long would it take a bug to walk 84 cm if it is walking at an average speed of 7 cm/s?

✓ Solution

Working	Explanation
$t = \frac{d}{s}$ $= \frac{84}{7}$ $= 12$ s	time $= \frac{\text{distance}}{\text{average speed}}$ Include appropriate units with the answer. In this example, time is being measured in seconds.

Exercise 8.3

a. A train takes 3 hours to travel 270 km. What is its average speed?

b. How long would it take to complete a journey of 720 km travelling at an average speed of 80 km/h?

c. Nick travels for 3 hours at an average speed of 75 km/h. He then travels for another 2 hours at an average speed of 80 km/h. How far does he travel in total?

8.4 Exchange rates

Exchange rates enable you to convert between different currencies. Some examples of exchange rates on a particular day are shown below. (Exchange rates usually change each day.)

1 Australian Dollar (AUD) equals 0.685 US Dollar (USD)	AUD to USD: multiply by 0.685 USD to AUD: divide by 0.685
1 Australian Dollar (AUD) equals 0.536 British Pound Sterling (GBP)	AUD to GBP: multiply by 0.536 GBP to AUD: divide by 0.536
1 Australian Dollar equals 96.814 Japanese Yen (JPY)	AUD to JPY: multiply by 96.814 JPY to AUD: divide by 96.814
1 Australian Dollar equals 10 528.900 Indonesian Rupiah (IDR)	AUD to IDR: multiply by 10 528.900 IDR to AUD: divide by 10 528.900

Example

Using the exchange rates in the table above, find the value of \$2000 AUD in British pound sterling (GBP).

✓ Solution

Working	Explanation
$2000 \times 0.536 = 1072$ 2000 AUD = 1072 GBP	Multiply by 0.536 to convert AUD to GBP.

Example

Using the exchange rates in the table above, find the value of 15 000 Japanese yen in Australian dollars.

✓ Solution

Working	Explanation
$15\,000 \div 96.814 = 154.936...$ 15 000 JPY = 154.94 AUD	Divide by 96.814 to convert JPY to AUD. Round to two decimal places for AUD.

Exercise 8.4

a. Using the exchange rates in the table on the previous page, find the value of:

i. \$5000 AUD in USD

ii. 60 000 IDR in AUD.

b. Given that 1 AUD = 4.622 Chinese yen (CNY) find the value of:

i. \$500 AUD in CNY

ii. 1000 CNY in AUD.

8.5 Simple interest

With a simple interest investment or loan, interest is calculated on the amount invested or the amount borrowed.

The simple interest formula is

$$I = \frac{Prt}{100}$$

where I is the simple interest

P is the principal (i.e. the amount invested or borrowed)

r is the % interest rate p.a. (p.a. stands for 'per annum', which means per year)

t is the time of the investment or loan in years.

Calculating simple interest

Example

Steph invests \$3000 at a simple interest rate of 5.2% p.a. for 4 years.

Calculate:

a. the interest Steph will receive on her investment

b. the total amount of money Steph will have after 4 years.

✓ Solution

Working	Explanation
a. $I = \frac{Prt}{100}$ $I = \frac{3000 \times 5.2 \times 4}{100}$ $I = \$624$	\$3000 is the principal, P. 5.2% p.a. is the rate, r. 4 years is the time, t. Substitute these values into the simple interest formula and evaluate.
b. Total amount $= 3000 + 624$ $= \$3624$	Total amount = principal + interest

Exercise 8.5.1

a. Vlad invests $\$8000$ at a simple interest rate of 4.8% p.a. for 2 years. Calculate:

  i. the interest Vlad will receive on his investment

  ii. the total amount of money Vlad will have after 4 years.

b. Hasanya borrows $\$6000$ at a simple interest rate of 7.2% p.a. for 18 months. Calculate the total amount Hasanya will owe at the end of 18 months.

Finding the principal, rate or time

If the principal, rate or time is unknown, we need to set up an equation and solve it for the unknown quantity.

Example

Determine the principal investment required to earn $\$705$ interest at a simple interest rate of 4.7% p.a. over 3 years.

✓ *Solution*

Working	Explanation
$I = \frac{Prt}{100}$ $705 = \frac{P \times 4.7 \times 3}{100}$ $705 = \frac{P \times 14.1}{100}$ $705 \times 100 = P \times 14.1$ $70\,500 = P \times 14.1$ $\frac{70\,500}{14.1} = P$ $P = \$5000$	$\$705$ is the interest, I. 4.7% p.a. is the rate, r. 3 years is the time, t. Substitute these values into the simple interest formula. Solve for P. Multiply by 100. Divide by 14.1.

Example

Marcus invests \$5000 at 4% p.a. simple interest and receives \$800 interest. For how long, in years, did he invest his money?

✓ ***Solution***

Working	Explanation
$I = \frac{Prt}{100}$ $800 = \frac{5000 \times 4 \times t}{100}$ $800 = \frac{20\,000 \times t}{100}$ $800 \times 100 = 20\,000 \times t$ $80\,000 = 20\,000 \times t$ $\frac{80\,000}{20\,000} = t$ $t = 4$ years	\$800 is the interest, I. 4% p.a. is the rate, r. \$5000 is the principal, P. Substitute these values into the simple interest formula. Solve for t. Multiply by 100. Divide by 20 000.

Example

Sally has \$2000 and wishes to double her money in 5 years. What simple interest rate per annum is required for her to achieve her goal?

✓ ***Solution***

Working	Explanation
$I = \frac{Prt}{100}$ $2000 = \frac{2000 \times r \times 5}{100}$ $2000 = \frac{10\,000 \times r}{100}$ $2000 \times 100 = 10\,000 \times r$ $200\,000 = 10\,000 \times t$ $\frac{200\,000}{10\,000} = r$ $r = 20\%$	To double her money, the interest Sally earns must be the same as the amount she invests. \$2000 is the interest, I. 5 years is the time, t. \$2000 is the principal, P. Substitute these values into the simple interest formula. Solve for r. Multiply by 100. Divide by 10 000.

Exercise 8.5.2

a. Determine the principal investment required to earn \$2625 interest at a simple interest rate of 3.5% p.a. over 6 years.

b. Cindy invests \$18 000 over 5 years and receives \$5670 interest. What is the simple interest rate for her investment?

c. Qian Yi invests \$10 000 at a simple interest rate of 5% p.a. How many years will it take for her investment to double in value?

8.6 Income tax

The table below shows how income tax was calculated on taxable incomes in Australia in the 2023–2024 financial year.

Resident tax rates 2023–2024	
Taxable income	**Income tax on this income**
0 – \$18 200	Nil
\$18 201 – \$45 000	19 c for each \$1 over \$18 200
\$45 001 – \$120 000	\$5092 plus 32.5 c for each \$1 over \$45 000
\$120 001 – \$180 000	\$29 467 plus 37 c for each \$1 over \$120 000
\$180 001 and over	\$51 667 plus 45 c for each \$1 over \$180 000

Source: ATO.gov.au

Example

Using the table above, calculate the income tax on a taxable income of \$60 000.

✓ ***Solution***

Working	Explanation
\$60 000 lies between \$45 001 and \$120 000 on the tax scales. Tax = \$5092 plus 32.5 c for each \$1 over \$45 000	Identify the taxable income bracket within which \$60 000 falls. Follow the instructions in the table to calculate the tax.
$\$60\,000 - \$45\,000 = \$15\,000$ $0.325 \times \$15\,000 = \$4875$	Subtract \$45 000 to find the amount over \$45 000. 32.5 c for each dollar is the same as \$0.325 per dollar, so multiply \$15 000 by 0.325.
$\text{Tax} = 5092 + 4875$ $= \$9967$	Add \$5092 to calculate the total tax.

Gross income refers to the amount earned before tax and **net income** refers to the amount earned after tax is deducted.

net income = gross income – tax

Example

Xanthe earns a gross income of \$22 500 from her part-time job. Determine her net income.

✓ ***Solution***

Working	Explanation
\$22 500 lies between \$18 201 and \$45 000 on the tax scales. Tax = 19 c for each dollar over \$18 200	Identify the taxable income bracket within which \$22 500 falls. Follow the instructions in the table on the previous page to calculate the tax.
$\$22\,500 - \$18\,200 = \$4300$	Subtract \$18 200 from Xanthe's income to find the amount over \$18 200.
Tax $= 0.19 \times \$4300$ $= \$817$	19 c for each dollar is the same as \$0.19 per dollar, so multiply \$4300 by 0.19.
Net income $= 22\,500 - 817$ $= \$21\,683$	Net income = gross income – tax.

Exercise 8.6

a. Calculate the tax payable on a taxable income of \$78 560.

b. Calculate the tax payable on a gross income of \$135 000.

c. Erika has a gross income of \$56 400. Calculate her net income.

Answers

Exercise 8.1

a. 21.70 \$/h
b. 0.094 L/km
c. 3.20 \$/kg

Exercise 8.2.1

a. \$27
b. \$60
c. 300 L

Exercise 8.2.2

a. 7 years
b. 1.25 kg
c. 25 hours

Exercise 8.3

a. 90 km/h
b. 9 hours
c. 385 km

Exercise 8.4a

i. 3425 USD
ii. \$5.70 AUD

Exercise 8.4b

i. 2311 CNY
ii. \$216.36 AUD

Exercise 8.5.1a

i. \$768
ii. \$8768

Exercise 8.5.1b

\$6648

Exercise 8.5.2

a. \$12 500
b. 6.3%
c. 20 years

Exercise 8.6

a. \$15 999
b. \$35 017
c. \$47 603

Chapter 9 – Solving equations and inequalities

9.1 Equations and inverse operations

An equation is a statement of arithmetic that has a left-hand side and a right-hand side connected by an equals sign. An equation is a true statement.

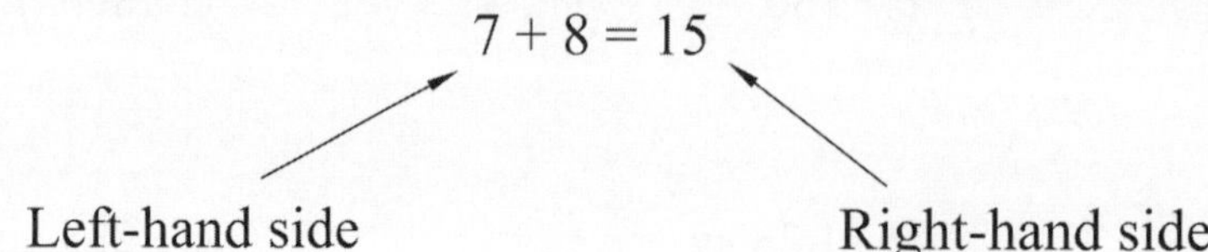

For an equation to be balanced, both sides must be equal. To keep an equation balanced, if we do something to one side we must do the same thing to the other side.

For example, if we add 3 to one side of the equation above, we must add 3 to the other side of the equation. The statement is balanced and it remains true.

$$7 + 8 + 3 = 15 + 3$$

The left-hand side is equal to 18 and the right-hand side is also equal to 18.

When an equation contains an unknown pronumeral (as in $x + 3 = 8$), we solve the equation by rearranging it so that the pronumeral is on its own on one side of the equation. We do this using **inverse operations**.

Operation	Inverse operation
$+$	$-$
$-$	$+$
$\times$	$\div$
$\div$	$\times$

When we find the solution to an equation, we are finding the value of the pronumeral that makes the equation true.

Example

Solve the equation $x + 3 = 8$.

✓ *Solution*

Working	Explanation
$x + 3 = 8$ $x + 3 - 3 = 8 - 3$ $x = 8 - 3$ $x = 5$	Our goal is to get the unknown pronumeral (x) on its own on one side of the equation. The equation involves addition and the inverse of addition is subtraction. So subtract 3 from both sides and simplify. This leaves the pronumeral on its own and gives the solution.

Example

Solve the equation $x - 2 = -5$.

✓ *Solution*

Working	Explanation
$x - 2 = -5$ $x - 2 + 2 = -5 + 2$ $x = -5 + 2$ $x = -3$	The equation involves subtraction and the inverse of subtraction is addition. So add 2 to both sides and simplify.

Example

Solve the equation $5x = 17$.

✓ *Solution*

Working	Explanation
$5x = 17$ $\frac{5x}{5} = \frac{17}{5}$ $x = \frac{17}{5}$ or $3\frac{2}{5}$	The equation involves multiplication and the inverse of multiplication is division. So divide both sides by 5. 17 is not divisible by 5, so leave the answer as an improper fraction or convert it to a mixed number.

Example

Solve the equation $\frac{x}{4} = -2$.

✓ *Solution*

Working	Explanation
$\frac{x}{4} = -2$ $\frac{x}{4} \times 4 = -2 \times 4$ $x = -2 \times 4$ $x = -8$	The equation involves division and the inverse operation of division is multiplication. So multiply both sides by 4.

Exercise 9.1

Solve each of the following equations for the unknown pronumeral.

a. $m - 7 = -12$ **b.** $4m = 18$ **c.** $\frac{m}{3} = 10$ **d.** $m - 8 = -3$

9.2 Multi-step equations

To solve some equations we may need to apply more than one inverse operation. One approach to this is to draw a flowchart of the operations in the equation.

For example, consider the equation $\frac{2x}{3} - 4 = 2$. We can draw a flowchart that shows the order in which operations are carried out on the left-hand side of the equation to obtain the result on the right-hand side.

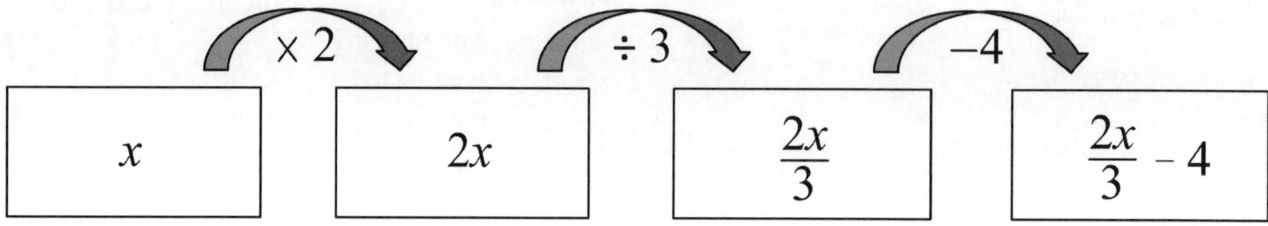

We can then reverse each step using inverse operations to find the solution to the equation.

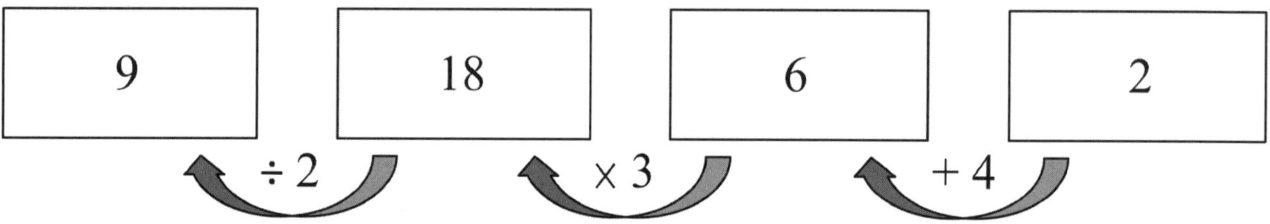

The solution to the equation is $x = 9$.

We can also work through the same steps algebraically, beginning with the addition of 4 and ending with division by 2.

$$\frac{2x}{3} - 4 = 2$$

$$\frac{2x}{3} = 2 + 4$$

$$\frac{2x}{3} = 6$$

$$2x = 6 \times 3$$

$$2x = 18$$

$$x = \frac{18}{2}$$

$$x = 9$$

Example

Solve $2p - 5 = 25$ for the unknown pronumeral.

✓ ***Solution***

Working	Explanation
$2p - 5 = 25$ $2p = 25 + 5$ $2p = 30$ $p = \frac{30}{2}$ $p = 15$	Two steps involving inverse operations are required: • Add 5 to both sides. • Divide both sides by 2.

Example

Solve $\frac{3x + 4}{2} = 11$ for the unknown pronumeral.

✓ ***Solution***

Working	Explanation
$\frac{3x + 4}{2} = 11$ $3x + 4 = 11 \times 2$ $3x + 4 = 22$ $3x = 22 - 4$ $3x = 18$ $x = 6$	Three steps involving inverse operations are required: • Multiply both sides by 2. • Subtract 4 from both sides. • Divide both sides by 3.

Example

Solve $5 - \frac{3x}{8} = -1$ for the unknown pronumeral.

✓ ***Solution***

Working	Explanation
$5 - \frac{3x}{8} = -1$ $-\frac{3x}{8} + 5 = -1$ $-\frac{3x}{8} = -1 - 5$ $-\frac{3x}{8} = -6$ $-3x = -6 \times 8$ $-3x = -48$ $x = \frac{-48}{-3}$ $x = 16$	Rewrite the equation so that the term containing x comes first. Now apply three steps of inverse operations: • Subtract 5 from both sides. • Multiply both sides by 8. • Divide both sides by -3.

Exercise 9.2

Solve each of the following equations for the unknown pronumeral.

a. $5a - 7 = 13$ **b.** $\frac{b}{4} + 2 = -5$ **c.** $5 - 2c = 3$

d. $\frac{4d}{5} = -8$ **e.** $\frac{5e + 1}{3} = 7$ **f.** $\frac{2f - 3}{3} + 4 = 11$

9.3 Equations with brackets

Equations with brackets can be solved by first expanding the brackets. If the coefficient of the bracketed terms is a factor of the number on the other side of the equation, then it is easier to divide first. This cancels the coefficient. Two examples are:

- For the equation $3(2x - 1) = 30$, the coefficient, 3, is a factor of 30, so we begin by dividing both sides by 3. This gives $(2x - 1) = 10$.
- For the equation $2(x - 5) = 13$, the coefficient, 2, is not a factor of 13, so we begin by expanding the bracket. This gives $2x - 10 = 13$.

Example

Solve $6(x+3)=24$ for x.

✓ *Solution*

Working	Explanation
$6(x+3)=24$ $x+3=\frac{24}{6}$ $x+3=4$ $x=4-3$ $x=1$	24 is divisible by 6, so divide both sides by 6. Subtract 3 from both sides and simplify.

Example

Solve $3(2-7x)=-29$ for x.

✓ *Solution*

Working	Explanation
$3(2-7x)=-29$	-29 is not divisible by 3, so expand the brackets.
$6-21x=-29$	Rewrite the equation so that the term containing x comes first.
$-21x+6=-29$ $-21x=-29-6$ $-21x=-35$ $x=\frac{-35}{-21}$ $x=\frac{5}{3}$	Subtract 6 from both sides. Divide both sides by -21. Simplify the fraction by dividing numerator and denominator by -7.

Exercise 9.3

Solve each of the following equations for x.

a. $2(x+7)=30$ **b.** $-5(x-2)=15$ **c.** $4(2x-3)=16$

d. $3(x-8)=2$ **e.** $-4(x+3)=10$ **f.** $2(3x-1)=5$

9.4 Equations with pronumerals on both sides

When we solve equations with pronumerals on both sides, we collect like terms containing the pronumerals on one side of the equation. This is usually the first step in solving this type of equation. If the equation has brackets, then we expand these first.

Example

Solve $5x - 20 = 2x - 2$ for x.

✓ ***Solution***

Working	Explanation
$5x - 20 = 2x - 2$ $5x - 20 - 2x = -2$ $3x - 20 = -2$	Subtract $2x$ from both sides. Simplify: $5x - 2x = 3x$
$3x = -2 + 20$ $3x = 18$	Add 20 to both sides and simplify.
$x = \frac{18}{3}$ $x = 6$	Divide both sides by 3.

Example

Solve $3 - 4x = 15 + 2x$ for x.

✓ ***Solution***

Working	Explanation
$3 - 4x = 15 + 2x$ $3 - 4x - 2x = 15$ $-6x + 3 = 15$	Subtract $2x$ from both sides. Simplify: $-4x - 2x = -6x$
$-6x = 15 - 3$ $-6x = 12$ $x = \frac{12}{-6}$ $x = -2$	Subtract 3 from both sides. Divide both sides by -6.

Example

Solve $2(2x-1)=3(x-5)$ for x.

✓ Solution

Working	Explanation
$2(2x-1)=3(x-5)$ $4x-2=3x-15$	Expand the brackets on both sides.
$4x-2-3x=-15$ $x-2=-15$ $x=-15+2$ $x=-13$	Subtract $3x$ from both sides. Simplify: $4x-3x=x$ Add 2 to both sides.

Exercise 9.4

Solve the following equations for x.

a. $5x+3=2x+9$ **b.** $2x-7=5-3x$ **c.** $2(x-5)=3(x-7)$

9.5 Applications of equations

Example

An electrician charges an \$80 call-out fee and then \$120 per hour. If they charged \$680 for a job, how many hours did they work on the job?

✓ Solution

Working	Explanation
Let h be the number of hours worked. $80+120h=680$	Assign a pronumeral to represent the unknown quantity. Write a suitable equation: 80 plus 120 × the number of hours worked must equal 680.
$120h=680-80$ $120h=600$ $h=\frac{600}{120}$ $h=5$ The electrician worked for 5 hours.	Subtract 80 from both sides and simplify. Divide both sides by 120.

Example

Find the value of x in the following diagram.

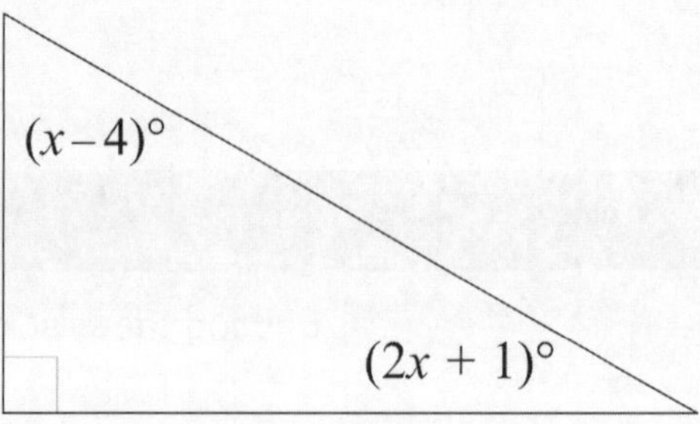

✓ ***Solution***

Working	Explanation
$x - 4 + 2x + 1 + 90 = 180$	The angle sum in a triangle is 180°.
$3x + 87 = 180$	$x + 2x = 3x$ and $-4 + 1 + 90 = 87$.
$3x = 180 - 87$	Subtract 87 from both sides.
$3x = 93$	Divide both sides by 3 and simplify.
$x = \frac{93}{3}$	
$x = 31$	

Exercise 9.5

a. The length of a rectangle is 3 cm more than twice its width. If the perimeter of the rectangle is 42 cm, find its length and width.

b. A plumber charges a \$60 call-out fee and then \$130 per hour. If a job costs \$450, for how many hours did the plumber work?

c. The sum of three consecutive numbers is 138. Let the numbers be x, $x + 1$ and $x + 2$. Find the three numbers.

9.6 Solving inequalities

An inequality is an expression that **compares** two values. For example, it might state that one is greater than the other (written as $x > y$). Unlike equations, the equals sign is not used in inequalities. Instead, an inequality symbol is used.

The inequality symbols are listed in the following table.

Symbol	$>$	$<$	$\geq$	$\leq$
Meaning	greater than	less than	greater than or equal to	less than or equal to

We solve inequalities in the same way that we solve equations. However, if we multiply or divide by a negative number, we need to reverse the direction of the inequality (so that greater than becomes less than, less than becomes greater than, and so on).

Example

Solve $4p - 6 \geq 10$ for the pronumeral.

✓ ***Solution***

Working	Explanation
$4p - 6 \geq 10$ $4p \geq 10 + 6$ $4p \geq 16$ $p \geq \frac{16}{4}$ $p \geq 4$	Add 6 to both sides and simplify. Divide both sides by 4 and simplify.

Example

Solve $3 - \frac{2w}{5} \leq -1$ for the pronumeral.

✓ ***Solution***

Working	Explanation
$3 - \frac{2w}{5} \leq -1$ $-\frac{2w}{5} + 3 \leq -1$	Rewrite the inequality so that the term containing the pronumeral comes first.
$-\frac{2w}{5} \leq -1 - 3$ $-\frac{2w}{5} \leq -4$	Subtract 3 from both sides and simplify.
$-2w \leq -4 \times 5$ $-2w \leq -20$	Multiply both sides by 5 and simplify.
$w \geq \frac{-20}{-2}$ $w \geq 10$	Divide both sides by -2. When dividing by a negative number the inequality must be reversed (i.e. $\leq$ becomes $\geq$).

Example

Solve $3y - 1 < 2y + 6$ for the pronumeral.

✓ ***Solution***

Working	Explanation
$3y - 1 < 2y + 6$	Subtract $2y$ from both sides and simplify.
$3y - 1 - 2y < 6$	Add 1 to both sides and simplify.
$y - 1 < 6$	
$y < 6 + 1$	
$y < 7$	

Exercise 9.6

Solve each of the following inequalities for the pronumeral.

a. $3(k + 2) < 9$

b. $-\frac{2x}{3} > 6$

c. $4y + 5 \geq 2(y + 2)$

Answers

Exercise 9.1

a. $m = -5$ b. $m = \frac{9}{2}$ c. $m = 30$ d. $m = 5$

Exercise 9.2

a. $a = 4$ b. $b = -28$ c. $c = 1$ d. $d = -10$

e. $e = 4$ f. $f = 12$

Exercise 9.3

a. $x = 8$ b. $x = -1$ c. $x = \frac{7}{2}$ d. $x = \frac{26}{3}$

e. $x = -\frac{11}{2}$ f. $x = \frac{7}{6}$

Exercise 9.4

a. $x = 2$ b. $x = \frac{12}{5}$ c. $x = 11$

Exercise 9.5

a. width = 6 cm, length = 15 cm b. 3 hours c. 45, 46 and 47

Exercise 9.6

a. $k < 1$ b. $x < -9$ c. $y \geq -\frac{1}{2}$

Chapter 10 – Statistics

10.1 Data collection

Statistics is the analysis of data. There are two types of data: categorical data and numerical data.

Categorical data is data that represents characteristics or qualities of people or objects. Some examples are people's favourite colours, letter grades on a test or countries visited.

Numerical data is data that is counted or measured. Some examples are the heights of trees, the number of siblings people have or the times taken by a swimming team to swim 50 metres.

The characteristic being observed is referred to as a **variable**. We say that favourite colour is a **categorical variable** and height is a **numerical variable**.

Example

Classify each of the following statistical variables as categorical or numerical.

a. the hair colour of students in a Year 8 class

b. the number of windows in houses in a street

c. the weights of dogs boarding at a kennel

✓ *Solution*

Working	Explanation
a. categorical	Hair colour cannot be counted or measured.
b. numerical	The number of windows can be counted.
c. numerical	The weight of a dog can be measured.

Collecting data sometimes involves questioning or observing every member of a population. A **population** is the complete set of people or objects that the information is collected about. When data is collected about every member of a population, the survey is called a **census**.

Sometimes only part of the population is surveyed. The part of the population that is surveyed is referred to as a **sample**.

When collecting data it is important to select a sample that avoids bias. **Bias** occurs when the sample is not representative of the population.

One way to minimise bias is to select a large enough sample that is likely to represent the population.

Example

A survey is conducted to determine how many books each student in a school reads in a fortnight. Students who are reading in the library at a lunchtime are asked how many books they have read in the last fortnight.

Explain how this sample is likely to be biased.

✓ Solution

Working	Explanation
The sample is biased because students who read in the library at lunchtime are likely to read more books in a fortnight than other students. Hence the result is likely to overstate the number of books that students read in a fortnight.	A biased sample is one that is not representative of all members of the population. In this case the population is all students in the school.

There are different ways of selecting samples from a population.

- **Random sampling** is where every member of the population has an equal chance of being selected.
- **Systematic sampling** is where every member of the population is listed and then every n^{th} member from that list is selected.
- **Convenience sampling** is where a sample is selected based on a particular location, such as a shopping centre or railway station.
- **Stratified sampling** is where the population is first divided into different groups and then sampling proceeds by randomly selecting a number from each group that is proportional to the size of the group. More members are randomly selected for the sample from larger groups and fewer members are randomly selected for the sample from smaller groups.

Example

Name the sampling technique used when every third student is selected from an alphabetical list of all Year 7 students at a school.

✓ Solution

Working	Explanation
systematic sampling	The students are selected at regular intervals from a list of students (in this case, every third student).

Exercise 10.1.1

Classify each of the following variables as categorical or numerical.

a. the heights of doors in a building

b. your family's favourite animals

c. the price per litre of petrol at petrol stations in your neighbourhood

d. the suburbs in your city that receive higher than average rainfall

e. the makes of cars in a car yard

Exercise 10.1.2

Explain how each of the following samples is a biased sample.

a. A teacher conducts a survey to discover students' opinions on the quality of hot lunches sold in the school canteen. The teacher asks 8 students in a Year 7 class.

b. To determine how busy a city intersection is, the number of cars passing through the intersection between 11 am and 12 pm is counted each day for a week.

Exercise 10.1.3

Name the sampling technique used to create the sample in each of the following cases.

a. School leavers are assigned numbers and then 50 numbers are randomly drawn. The students whose number is drawn are interviewed about their experiences at school.

b. Thirty passengers on a platform waiting for a train are asked about their satisfaction with the public transport system.

c. There are 100 students in Year 12 and 120 students in Year 11 at a particular school. A sample of 44 students is taken by randomly selecting 20 students from Year 12 and 24 students from Year 11.

10.2 Frequency tables

Once data is collected it is useful to organise it in a way that makes it easier to understand and easier to observe any patterns. One way of doing this is to use a **frequency table**.

A frequency table has:

- a column for each data value
- a column to keep a tally as data is recorded in the table
- a column for the frequency of each data value (i.e. the number of times the data value occurs).

Example

A group of people in a gelato bar were asked their favourite flavour from those available on the day. Their answers are listed below.

chocolate	strawberry	lemon	vanilla	strawberry
chocolate	chocolate	vanilla	lemon	lemon
lemon	vanilla	chocolate	strawberry	vanilla
strawberry	chocolate	lemon	chocolate	chocolate

Organise this data using a frequency table.

✓ Solution

<table>
<tr><th>Working</th><th>Explanation</th></tr>
<tr><td>
<table>
<tr><th>Flavour</th><th>Tally</th><th>Frequency</th></tr>
<tr><td>chocolate</td><td>卌 II</td><td>7</td></tr>
<tr><td>strawberry</td><td>IIII</td><td>4</td></tr>
<tr><td>vanilla</td><td>IIII</td><td>4</td></tr>
<tr><td>lemon</td><td>卌</td><td>5</td></tr>
</table>
</td><td>
Create a frequency table with a column for the flavours (headed Flavour), a column to tally the flavours (headed Tally) and a column for the frequency with which a flavour is favoured (headed Frequency).

In the Flavour column enter each flavour mentioned in the survey.

Now work through the data provided, placing a stroke in the Tally column for each flavour you encounter.

Use 卌 to indicate groups of 5. This will make counting easier.

Count the tallies and add each total to the Frequency column.
</td></tr>
</table>

When collecting numerical data (such as times or heights), it is often convenient to group data into distinct intervals, known **class intervals**.

Example

The following frequency table shows the height of tomato plants in a vegetable garden. The heights are grouped into class intervals of 10 cm.

Height (cm)	Tally	Frequency
0 – <10	卌 卌 III	
10 – <20		17
20 – <30		19
30 – <40	卌 IIII	
40 – <50	卌 卌 卌 卌 I	

Complete the **Tally** column and the **Frequency** column.

✓ *Solution*

Working	Explanation
See table below	The frequency for the $10 - <20$ interval is 17. $17 = 3 \times 5 + 2$ so the tally is 卌 卌 卌 II. The frequency for the $20 - <30$ interval is 19. $19 = 3 \times 5 + 4$ so the tally is 卌 卌 卌 IIII. The tally for the $0 - <10$ interval is $2 \times 5 + 3 = 13$. The tally for $30 - <40$ interval is $5 + 4 = 9$. The tally for the $40 - <50$ interval is $4 \times 5 + 1 = 21$.

Height (cm)	Tally	Frequency
$0 - <10$	卌 卌 III	13
$10 - <20$	卌 卌 卌 II	17
$20 - <30$	卌 卌 卌 IIII	19
$30 - <40$	卌 IIII	9
$40 - <50$	卌 卌 卌 卌 I	21

Exercise 10.2.1

Complete the following frequency table for the colour of cars observed in a supermarket car park.

Colour	Tally	Frequency
blue	卌 卌 II	
red	卌 卌 卌 IIII	
green		9
white	卌 卌 卌 卌 卌 I	
silver		22
black	卌 卌 卌	
yellow		8

Exercise 10.2.2

The lengths of fish caught on a fishing trip are given below. The values are in centimetres.

52	63	57	41	32	17	36	53	64	25
38	34	42	23	44	35	54	50	36	29
27	48	33	38	18	45	32	28	52	33
36	42	18	26	24	60	54	33	47	37
42	45	38	28	25	30	44	37	32	41

Construct a frequency table for this data using class intervals of 10 starting at $10 - <20$.

10.3 Graphs from frequency tables

We can represent the data presented in frequency tables using graphs. The vertical axis is used to represent frequency.

Example

Construct a column graph to represent the data shown in the following frequency table.

Favourite colour	Frequency
red	14
yellow	12
blue	21
green	13
black	8
pink	15
purple	6
orange	2

✓ *Solution*

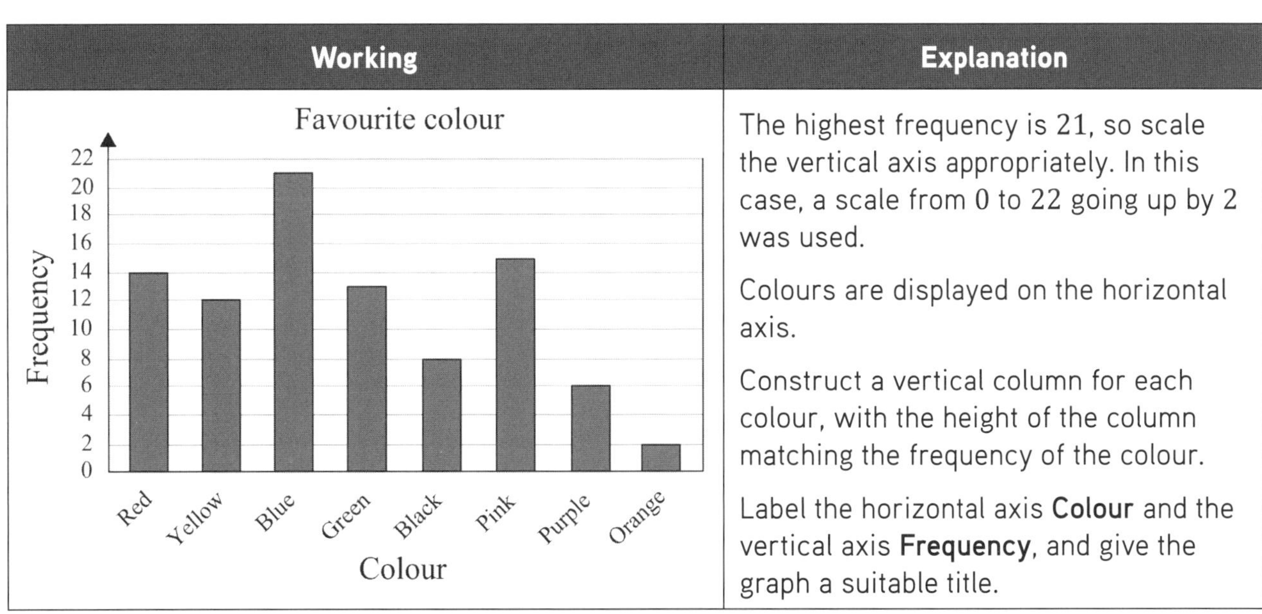

Working	Explanation
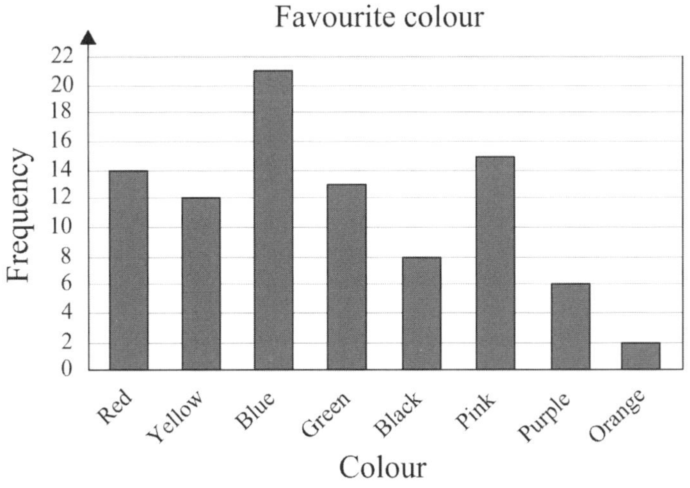	The highest frequency is 21, so scale the vertical axis appropriately. In this case, a scale from 0 to 22 going up by 2 was used. Colours are displayed on the horizontal axis. Construct a vertical column for each colour, with the height of the column matching the frequency of the colour. Label the horizontal axis **Colour** and the vertical axis **Frequency**, and give the graph a suitable title.

Example

The graph below shows the number of pet rabbits owned by children who attended a rabbit show.

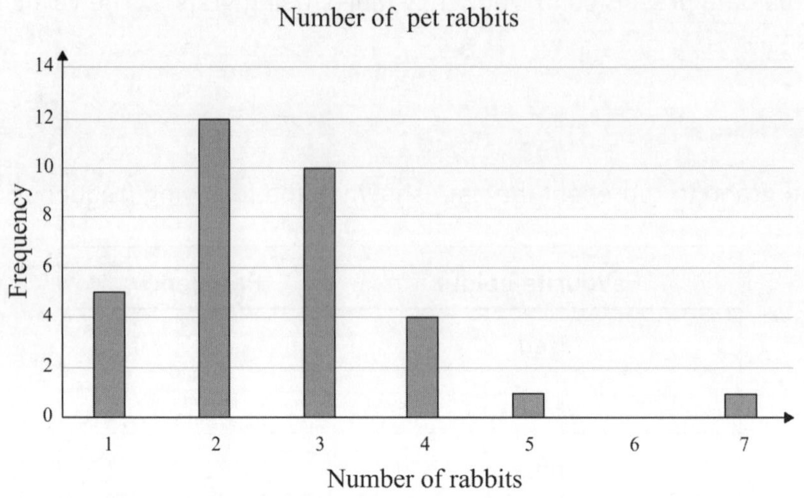

a. How many children were at the rabbit show?

b. What is the most common number of rabbits owned?

c. How many children owned 4 rabbits?

✓ Solution

Working	Explanation
a. $5 + 12 + 10 + 4 + 1 + 1 = 33$ children	Add the heights of all the columns.
b. 2 rabbits	This is the number of rabbits for the highest column.
c. 4 children	This is the frequency of owning 4 rabbits, so the height of the 4 column gives the number of children.

Exercise 10.3.1

A group of students were asked their favourite type of TV show. The results are shown in the following frequency table.

Type of show	Frequency
reality	22
comedy	30
drama	12
murder mystery	8
anime	9
documentary	7
other	13

Construct a column graph to display the data in this table.

Exercise 10.3.2

The following graph shows the number of hours spent practising music by a group of Year 8 students in a week.

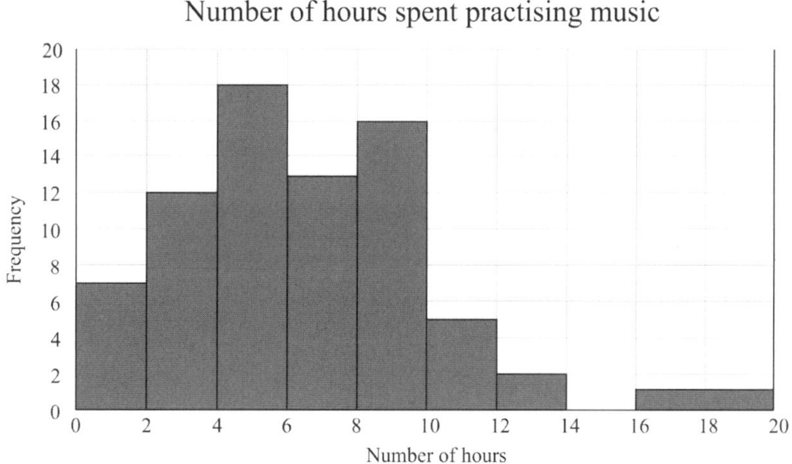

a. How many students spent between 2 and 4 hours practising?

b. What was the most common amount of time spent practising?

c. How many students practised for more than 10 hours?

10.4 Mean, median, mode and range

The middle of a set of data can be described in a number of ways. Three ways are the mean, the median and the mode.

Mean

The **mean** is the average value of the data. It is calculated by adding all the values in the data set and then dividing the result by the number of values in the set.

$$\textit{mean} = \frac{\textit{sum of all data values}}{\textit{number of data values}}$$

Example

Find the mean of 26, 31, 43, 56, 51, 29, 24, 59, 41, 22.

✓ ***Solution***

Working	Explanation
$\text{mean} = \frac{26+31+43+56+51+29+24+59+41+22}{10}$ $= \frac{382}{10}$ $= 38.2$	The mean $= \frac{\text{sum of all data values}}{\text{number of data values}}$, so add all the values and divide by the number of values.

The mean can also be calculated from data presented in a frequency table. The procedure is as follows.

1. Calculate the total frequency (i.e. the total number of data values).
2. Multiply each data value by its frequency.
3. Sum all the values obtained at step 2.
4. Divide the value obtained at step 3 by the value obtained at step 1.

Example

The scores out of 10 obtained by students on a science quiz are shown in the frequency table below.

Score	Frequency
5	2
6	6
7	5
8	7
9	9
10	1

Calculate the mean score for this quiz.

✓ Solution

Working	Explanation
total frequency $= 2 + 6 + 5 + 7 + 9 + 1$ $= 30$	Find the total frequency by adding the values in the frequency column.
mean $= \dfrac{5\times2+6\times6+7\times5+8\times7+9\times9+10\times1}{30}$ $= \dfrac{228}{30}$ $= 7.6$	Multiply each data value by its frequency and add all the results. Divide the result by the total frequency.

Median

The **median** of a set of data is the middle value when the data is ordered from smallest to largest or largest to smallest.

If there is an odd number of data values, then the median is the middle value in the ordered data set.

If there is an even number of data values, then the median lies halfway between the two middle values in the ordered data set.

The median can be found by calculating $\frac{n+1}{2}$, where n is the number of values in the data set. The $\frac{n+1}{2}$th value is the median.

For a data set with 15 values, the median is the $\frac{15+1}{2} = 8$th value in the ordered set.

For a data set with 20 values, the median is the $\frac{20+1}{2} = 10.5$th value, which is halfway between the 10th and 11th values in the ordered set. To find halfway between two numbers, add them together and then divide by 2.

Example

Find the median of 18, 32, 41, 16, 23, 55, 27, 19, 22.

✓ ***Solution***

Working	Explanation
16, 18, 19, 22, 23, 27, 32, 41, 55 16, 18, 19, 22, $\boxed{23}$, 27, 32, 41, 55 median = 23	Write the data in order (for example, from smallest to largest). There are 9 values in the data set, so the median is the $\frac{9+1}{2} = 5$th value.

Example

Find the median of 3, 14, 5, 5, 8, 10, 18, 16, 20, 19, 4, 7.

✓ ***Solution***

Working	Explanation
3, 4, 5, 5, 7, 8, 10, 14, 16, 18, 19, 20 3, 4, 5, 5, 7, $\boxed{8, 10,}$ 14, 16, 18, 19, 20 median = 9	Write the data in order. There are 12 data values, so the median is the $\frac{12+1}{2} = 6.5$th value. The median lies halfway between the sixth and seventh data values: 8 and 10. $\frac{8+10}{2} = 9$ 9 is halfway between 8 and 10, so 9 is the median.

Mode

The mode is the most frequently occurring value in a data set. Some data sets may have more than one mode.

Example

Find the mode of 3, 14, 5, 5, 8, 10, 18, 16, 20, 19, 4, 7.

✓ ***Solution***

Working	Explanation
3, 14, $\boxed{5}$, $\boxed{5}$, 8, 10, 18, 16, 20, 19, 4, 7 mode = 5	The value 5 occurs more than any other data value. Thus 5 is the mode.

Range

The range is a measure of the spread of the data in a data set. It is the difference between the highest and lowest data values.

range = highest value – lowest value

Example

Find the range for the following test scores.

18, 25, 32, 48, 36, 27, 39, 42, 49, 50, 43, 32, 35, 28, 29, 31, 40

✓ *Solution*

Working	Explanation
$\boxed{18}$, 25, 32, 48, 36, 27, 39, 42, 49, $\boxed{50}$, 43, 32, 35, 28, 29, 31, 40 Range $= 50 - 18$ $= 32$	The largest value is 50 and the smallest value is 18. The difference between these two is the range.

Exercise 10.4.1

Find the mean of the data set 35, 27, 83, 42, 59, 16, 24, 18.

Exercise 10.4.2

The scores out of 10 obtained by students in a history quiz are shown in the following frequency table.

Score	Frequency
5	1
6	8
7	3
8	5
9	6
10	2

Calculate the mean of the scores.

Exercise 10.4.3

Find the median, mode and range of each of the following data sets.

a. 16, 14, 15, 18, 19, 21, 23, 25, 18, 16, 31, 16, 27

b. 82, 60, 43, 67, 69, 81, 85, 64, 58, 67, 59, 84, 42, 56

Answers

Exercise 10.1.1

a. numerical
b. categorical
c. numerical
d. categorical
e. categorical

Exercise 10.1.2

a. The students are selected from only one class and the size of this sample is too small.
b. Only collecting data for the same one-hour period each day is not going to be indicative of the traffic flow through the intersection at all times of the day.

Exercise 10.1.3

a. random sampling
b. convenience sampling
c. stratified sampling

Exercise 10.2.1

Colour	Tally	Frequency
blue	𝍸 𝍸 II	12
red	𝍸 𝍸 𝍸 IIII	19
green	𝍸 IIII	9
white	𝍸 𝍸 𝍸 𝍸 𝍸 I	26
silver	𝍸 𝍸 𝍸 𝍸 II	22
black	𝍸 𝍸 𝍸	15
yellow	𝍸 III	8

Exercise 10.2.2

Length (cm)	Tally	Frequency
10 – <20	III	3
20 – <30	𝍸 IIII	9
30 – <40	𝍸 𝍸 𝍸 II	17
40 – <50	𝍸 𝍸 I	11
50 – <60	𝍸 II	7
60 – <70	III	3

Exercise 10.3.1

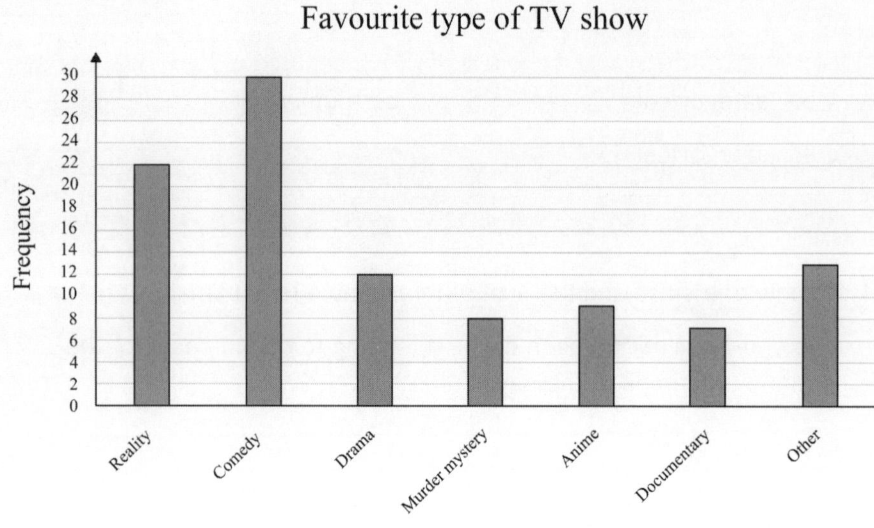

Exercise 10.3.2

a. 12 b. between 4 and 6 hours c. 9

Exercise 10.4.1

38

Exercise 10.4.2

7.52

Exercise 10.4.3

a. median = 18, mode = 16, range = 17 b. median = 65.5, mode = 67, range = 43

Chapter 11 – Probability

11.1 Introduction to probability

Probability is a measure of how likely something is to happen. It ranges from 0 (impossible) to 1 (certain).

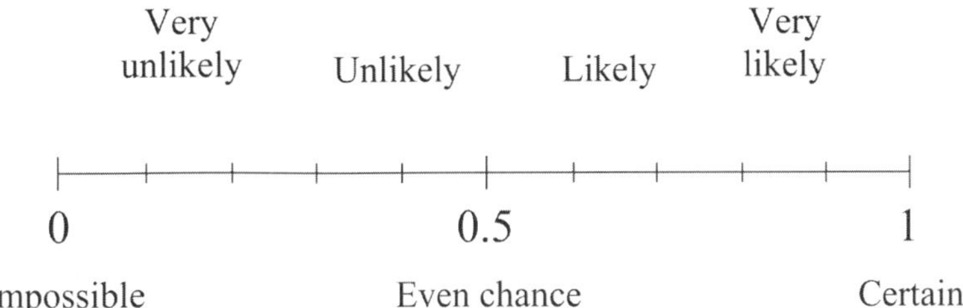

Example

Describe each of the following as either impossible, very unlikely, unlikely, even chance, likely, very likely or certain.

a. Tossing a head when a fair coin is tossed once.

b. Finding an ice block on the surface of the Sun.

c. Randomly selecting a weekday (Monday to Friday) from a particular week.

d. Randomly selecting a blue marble from a jar containing 20 blue marbles.

✓ *Solution*

Working	Explanation
a. even chance	A fair coin will either land heads up or tails up.
b. impossible	The temperature on the surface of the Sun is much greater than the boiling point of water.
c. very likely	Five out of the 7 days in each week are weekdays.
d. certain	All marbles in the jar are blue, so this is the only coloured marble that could be selected.

In situations where we calculate probabilities, we refer to each thing that can occur as an **outcome**.

In probability a **random experiment** is an experiment in which the outcome cannot be predicted.

An **event** is an outcome or set of outcomes that we are particularly interested in.

The **sample space** for a random experiment is the set of all possible outcomes. The sample space is written as a set using set brackets, $\{\}$. The elements of the set are separated by commas.

Example

List the sample space in each of the following probability experiments.

a. Selecting a letter at random from the word FIDGET.

b. Selecting a number at random from the prime numbers less than 50.

✓ *Solution*

Working	Explanation
a. {F, I, D, G, E, T}	The sample space is the letters from the word FIDGET, separated by commas.
b. $\{2, 3, 5, 7, 11, 13, 17, 19, 23, 29, 31, 37, 41, 43, 47\}$	Prime numbers have only two factors: the number itself and 1.

Equally likely events have the same chance of occurring. For example, if a ball is randomly selected from a bag containing 10 red balls and 10 green balls, then the events 'selecting a red ball' and 'selecting a green ball' are equally likely. However, if you randomly selected a ball from a bag containing 5 yellow balls and 4 blue balls, then the events 'selecting a yellow ball' and 'selecting a blue ball' are not equally likely.

Exercise 11.1.1

Describe each of the following as either impossible, very unlikely, unlikely, even chance, likely, very likely or certain.

a. Randomly selecting the letter K from the letters in the word FREEDOM.

b. Randomly selecting a black kitten from a litter with four black kittens and four tabby kittens.

c. Rolling a number that is less than 7 on a fair six-sided die.

d. Winning $1 000 000 in a lottery.

Exercise 11.1.2

List the sample space for each of the following probability experiments.

a. Spinning the spinner below and it stopping on the colour indicated by the arrow.

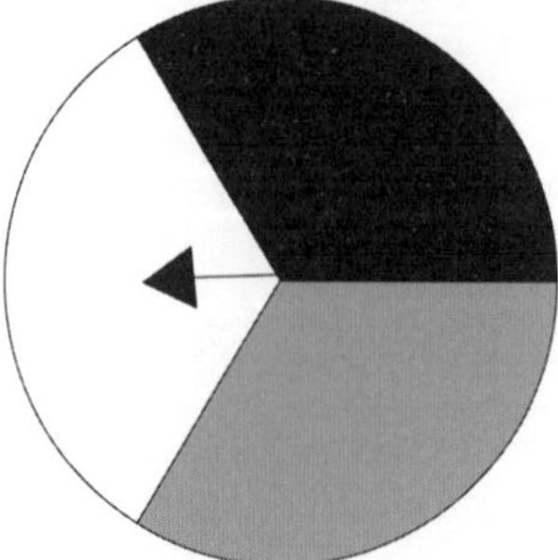

b. Randomly selecting a number from the even numbers between 1 and 19.

c. Randomly selecting a month of the year.

11.2 Calculating probabilities

In a probability experiment, the probability of an event is equal to the number of outcomes in the event divided by the total number of possible outcomes.

$$\textbf{Pr(event)} = \frac{\textbf{number of outcomes in the event}}{\textbf{total number of possible outcomes}}$$

Example

With one roll of a fair six-sided die, determine the probability of a number less than 6 appearing uppermost.

✓ Solution

Working	Explanation
Pr(number less than 6) $= \frac{5}{6}$	The outcomes in the event 'a number less than 6' are 1, 2, 3, 4 and 5. The total number of possible outcomes is 6, since you could roll 1, 2, 3, 4, 5 or 6. Hence the probability of the event is 5 divided by 6.

Example

One sweet is selected at random from a jar containing 5 red, 4 yellow and 3 orange sweets. What is the probability that the sweet selected is orange?

✓ Solution

Working	Explanation
Pr(orange) $= \frac{3}{12}$ $= \frac{1}{4}$	3 sweets are orange out of a total of 12 sweets: $5 + 4 + 3 = 12$. Hence the probability of the event is 3 divided by 12. Simplify the fraction.

Example

One number is selected at random from the whole numbers 1 to 20. What is the probability that it is greater than 12 or a multiple of 3?

✓ Solution

Working	Explanation
Pr(greater than 12 or multiple of 3) $=\frac{12}{20}$ $=\frac{3}{5}$	There are 8 numbers greater than 12: 13, 14, 15, 16, 17, 18, 19 and 20. The multiples of 3 are: 3, 6, 9, 12, 15 and 18. So there are 12 numbers that are greater than 12 or a multiple of 3: 3, 6, 9, 12, 13, 14, 15, 16, 17, 18, 19 and 20. (**Note**: we do not include 15 and 18 twice.) Hence the probability of the event is 12 divided by 20. Simplify the fraction.

Some special terminology is often used in probability questions. For example:

- **'at least'** means greater than or equal to ($\geq$)
- **'at most'** means less than or equal to ($\leq$).

Exercise 11.2.1

a. From a team of fifteen Year 7 and ten Year 8 students, one student is randomly selected to be the captain. What is the probability that the captain will be a Year 8 student?

b. One letter is randomly selected from the word HIPPOPOTAMUS. What is the probability that it is a P?

Exercise 11.2.2

A box contains 30 tickets numbered 1 to 30. If one ticket is selected at random from the box, what is the probability that the number on the ticket is:

a. 16 **b.** a multiple of 5 **c.** at least 24 **d.** at most 8.

11.3 Complementary events

In a random experiment:

- all probabilities are between 0 and 1 inclusive
- the sum of all the probabilities is equal to 1.

In an experiment where you spin the spinner shown below exactly once, the **complement** of the event 'spinning white' is 'not spinning white'.

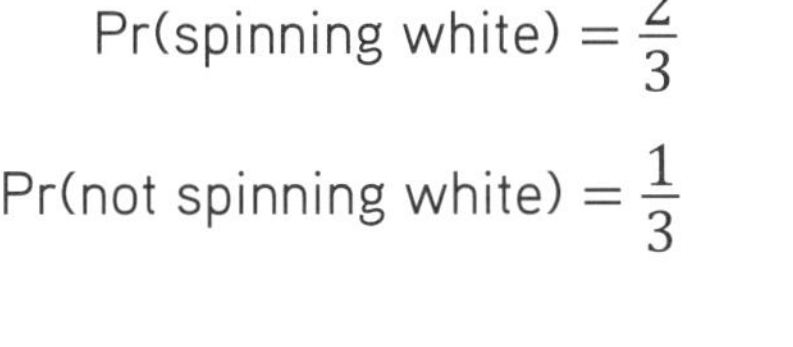

$$\text{Pr(spinning white)} = \frac{2}{3}$$

$$\text{Pr(not spinning white)} = \frac{1}{3}$$

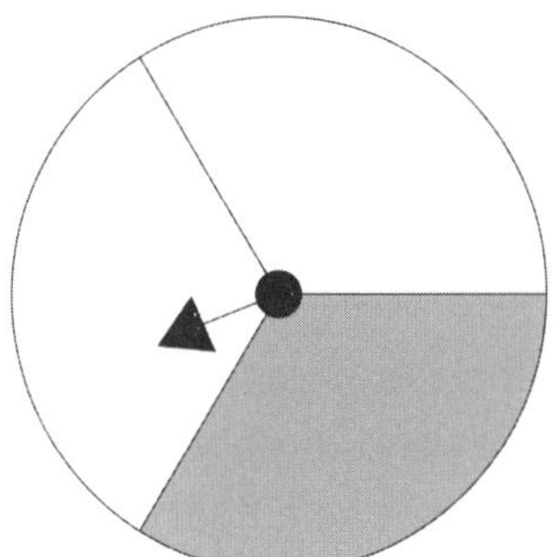

The events 'spinning white' and 'not spinning white' are complementary events and their probabilities add to 1. The complement of an event A is denoted by A'. Hence

$$Pr(A) + Pr(A') = 1$$

since an outcome will be either in A or not in A.

For any event A

$$Pr(A') = 1 - Pr(A)$$

Example

The probability that it rains on a particular day is 0.75. What is the probability that it does not rain?

✓ *Solution*

Working	Explanation
$\text{Pr(not rain)} = 1 - \text{Pr(rain)}$ $= 1 - 0.75$ $= 0.25$	The events 'rain' and 'not rain' are complementary events, so their probabilities add to 1.

Exercise 11.3

a. The probability that a train arrives on time at a station is 0.8. What is the probability that the train does not arrive on time?

b. A bookshelf contains 3 mathematics books, 5 biology books and 4 chemistry books. One book is selected at random from the shelf. What is the probability that the book is not a biology book?

11.4 Venn diagrams

A Venn diagram is a way of representing the possible outcomes and the sample space of a probability experiment. An example is shown below.

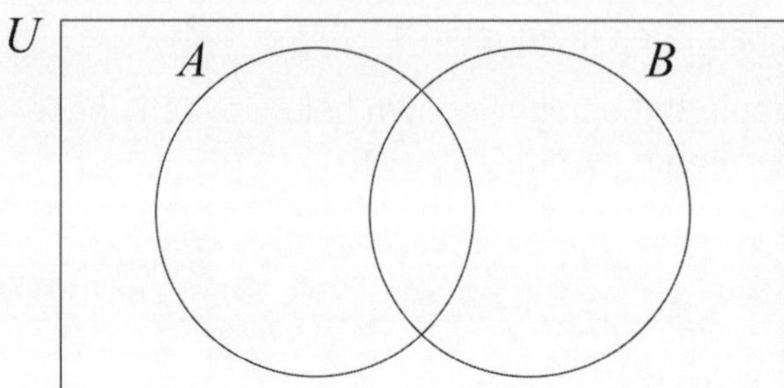

The rectangle contains the sample space for the probability experiment. The sample space is also called the **universal set** and is denoted by U. Each circle inside the rectangle represents a set of possible outcomes. If there are shared outcomes the circles will be shown as overlapping (as in the example above).

Example

A number is selected at random from the integers 1 to 10 inclusive. Let A be the event 'an odd number is selected' and B be the event 'a number greater than 5 is selected'.

a. Write down the sample space.

b. Write down the set that represents event A.

c. Write down the set that represents event B.

d. Represent all this information in Venn diagram.

✓ *Solution*

Working	Explanation
a. $U = \{1, 2, 3, 4, 5, 6, 7, 8, 9, 10\}$	The sample space is the universal set U, which contains the integers from 1 to 10 including 1 and 10.
b. $A = \{1, 3, 5, 7, 9\}$	A is the set of odd integers from the sample space.
c. $B = \{6, 7, 8, 9, 10\}$	B is the set of integers greater than 5 from the sample space.
d. 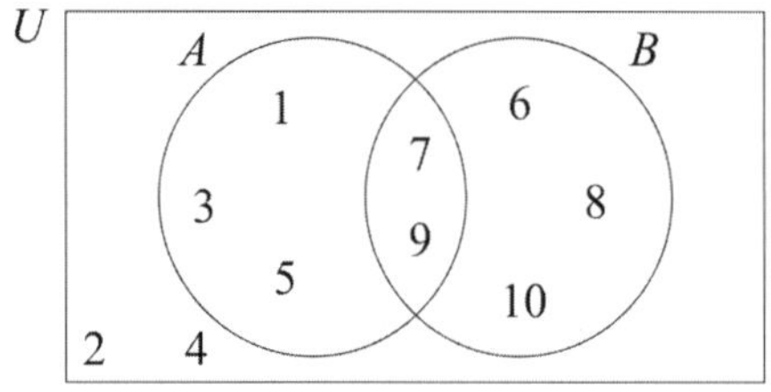 U: A only: 1, 3, 5; A and B: 7, 9; B only: 6, 8, 10; outside: 2, 4	7 and 9 are outcomes common to both A and B, so they are placed in the region where the two sets overlap. 1, 3 and 5 are in event A but not in event B, so they are placed in set A but outside the region where A and B overlap. 6, 8 and 10 are in event B but not in event A, so they are placed in set B but outside the region where A and B overlap. 2 and 4 are in neither set so are placed in the region outside the circles.

When using Venn diagrams for probability problems, it is more common to show the number of outcomes in each region rather than each individual outcome. For example, the information in the diagram in the example on the previous page could be summarised as follows.

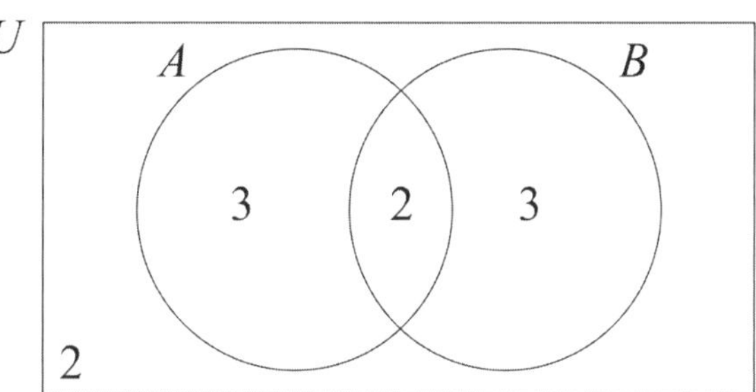

Example

In a class of 30 students, 10 play in the school band, 14 play in the school football team and 7 do neither activity. Represent this information using a Venn diagram.

✓ *Solution*

Working	Explanation
U B F	Construct a Venn diagram with a circle representing students in the band (B) and a circle representing students who play in the football team (F).
U B F 7	7 students do neither activity, so place this number in the region outside sets B and F.
U B F 1 7	This leaves $30 - 7 = 23$ students to be added to the circles in the Venn diagram. There are 10 students in the band and 14 who play football. This gives a total of 24. This is 1 more than the number of students to be added to the circles, so 1 student must play in the band and play football. Place the number 1 in the region where the two sets overlap.

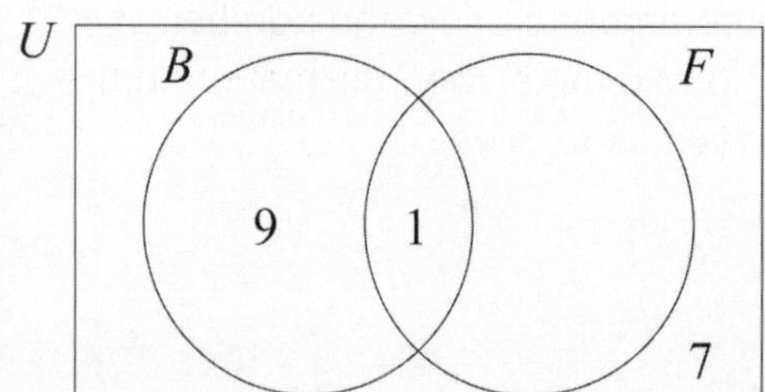	There are 10 students who play in the band but one has already been represented. So there are 9 students who only play in the band. Place the number 9 in the region of the B set that does not overlap the F set.
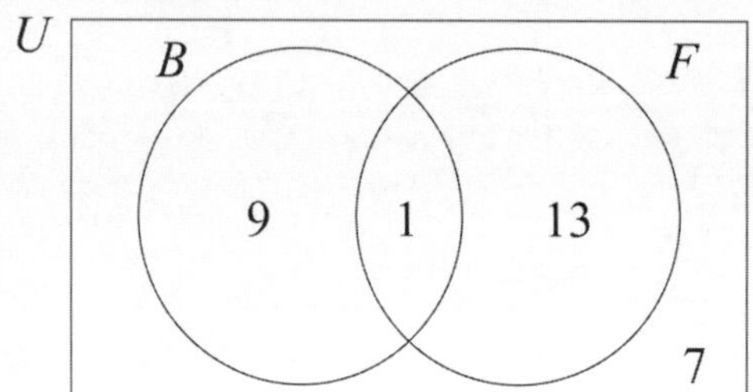	There are 14 students in the football team but one has already been represented. So there are 13 students who only play football. Place the number 13 in the region of the F set that does not overlap the B set. Check that the numbers in the Venn diagram add to 30, the total number of students. $9 + 1 + 13 + 7 = 30$.

Exercise 11.4.1

A number is selected at random from the odd positive integers less than 20. Let A be the event 'a multiple of 3 is selected' and B be the event 'a number greater than 12 is selected'.

a. Write down the sample space.

b. Write down the set that is event A.

c. Write down the set that is event B.

d. Represent this information in Venn diagram.

Exercise 11.4.2

In a small country town, 60 students attend the local primary school. 36 students catch the bus to school and 44 students walk to school. 32 students both walk and catch the bus. Represent this information using a Venn diagram.

11.5 Venn diagrams and probabilities

Probabilities can be calculated from Venn diagrams using the formula

$$Pr(event) = \frac{\text{number of elements in the region representing the event}}{\text{total number of elements}}$$

The regions that represent possible events are shaded in the Venn diagrams below.

A

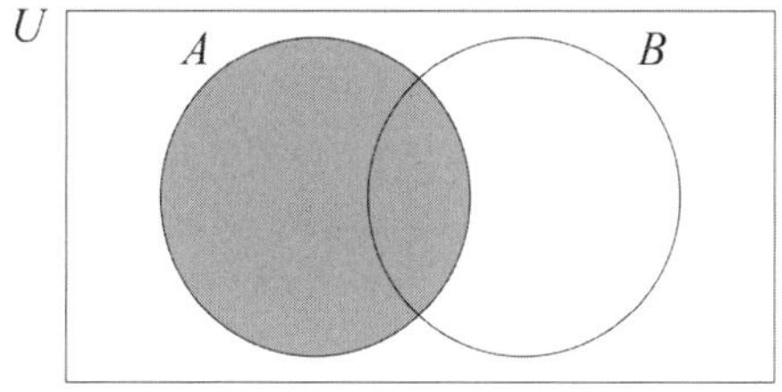

A' (not A)

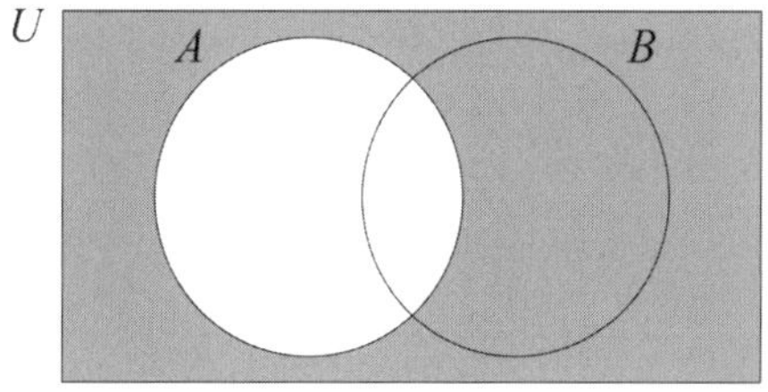

B

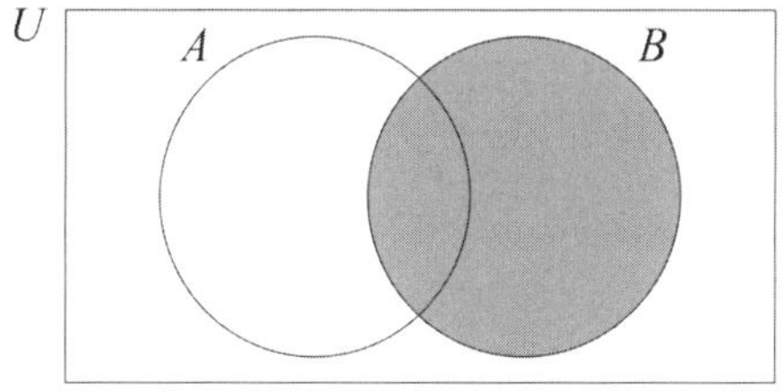

B' (not B)

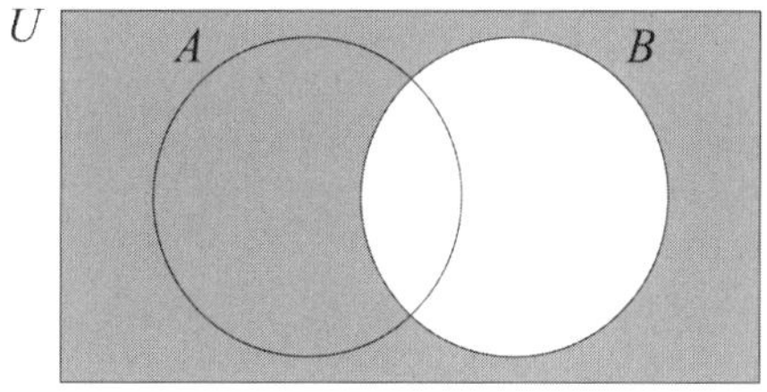

A or B or both

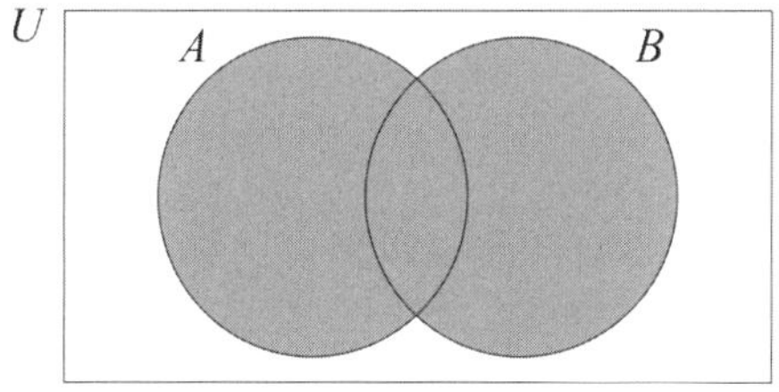

A or B but not both

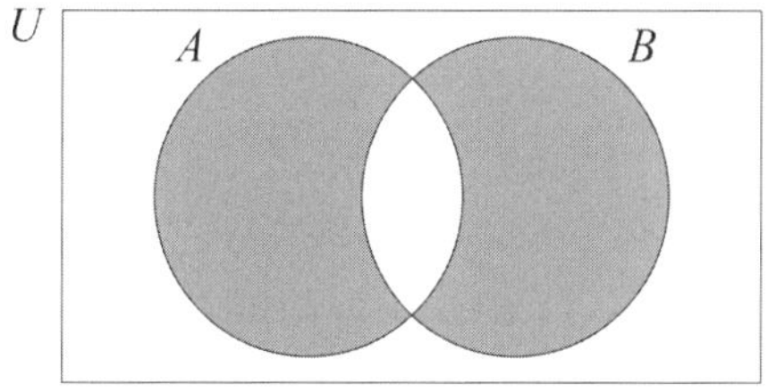

A and B

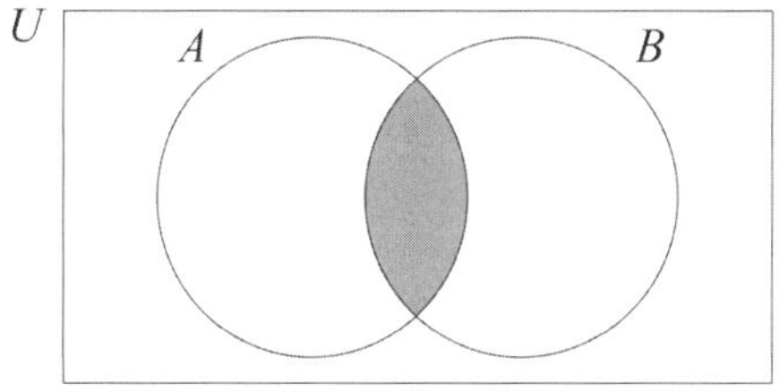

Neither A nor B

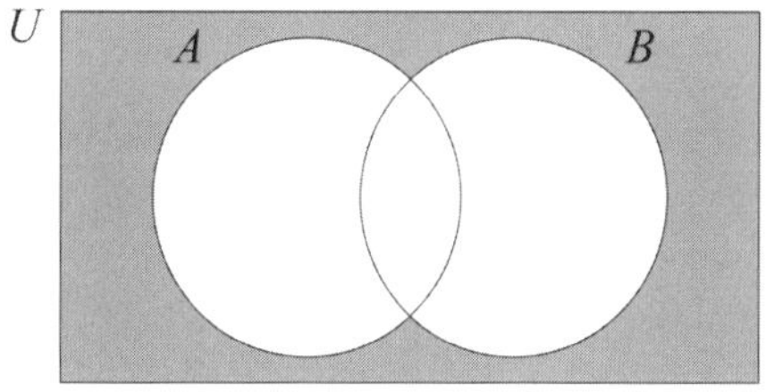

Example

The Venn diagram below shows the results of a survey of teachers who were asked whether they like drinking tea or coffee.

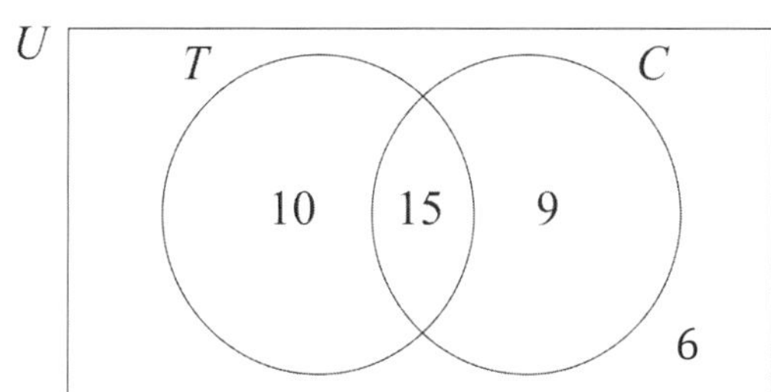

Find the probability that a randomly selected teacher from this group likes drinking:

a. tea

b. coffee but not tea

c. tea or coffee or both

d. tea or coffee but not both

e. neither tea nor coffee.

✓ Solution

Working	Explanation
a. $\Pr(\text{tea}) = \frac{25}{40}$ $= \frac{5}{8}$	$10 + 15 = 25$ teachers like drinking tea. 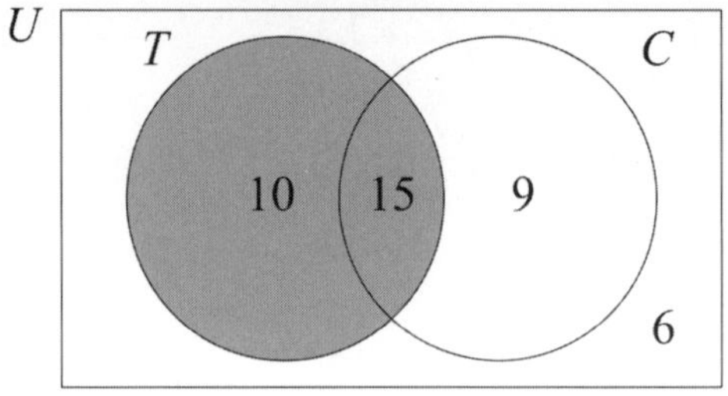 U T C 10 15 9 6 The total number of teachers is $10 + 15 + 9 + 6 = 40$. Hence 25 out of 40 teachers like drinking tea. Simplify the fraction.
b. $\Pr(\text{coffee but not tea}) = \frac{9}{40}$	9 teachers like drinking coffee but not tea. 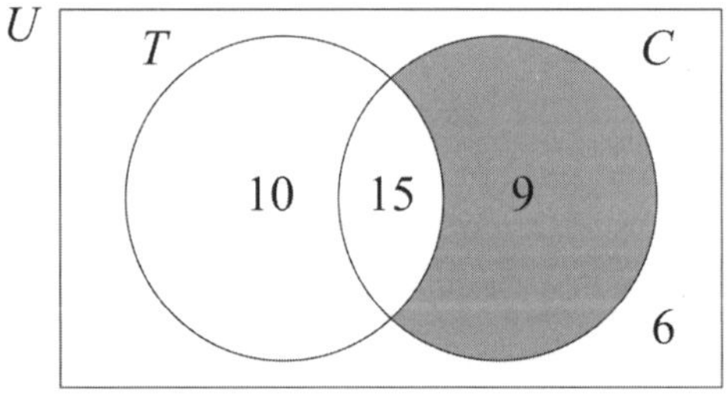 U T C 10 15 9 6 Hence 9 out of 40 teachers like drinking coffee but not tea.
c. $\Pr(\text{tea or coffee or both}) = \frac{34}{40}$ $= \frac{17}{20}$	$10 + 15 + 9 = 34$ teachers like drinking tea or coffee or both. 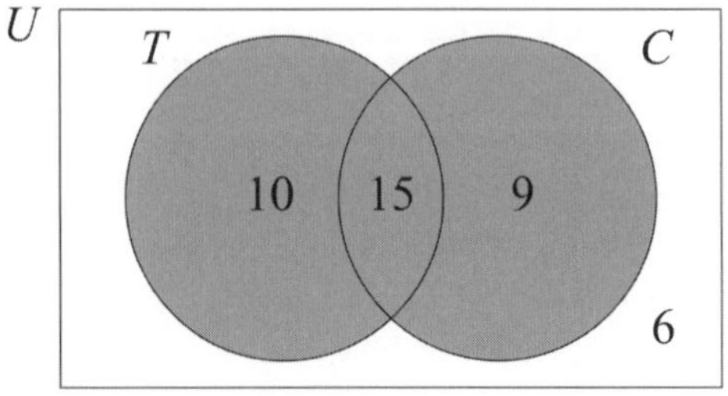 U T C 10 15 9 6 Hence 34 out of 40 teachers like drinking coffee, tea or both. Simplify the fraction.

d. Pr(tea or coffee but not both) $= \frac{19}{40}$	$10 + 9 = 19$ teachers like drinking tea or coffee but not both. 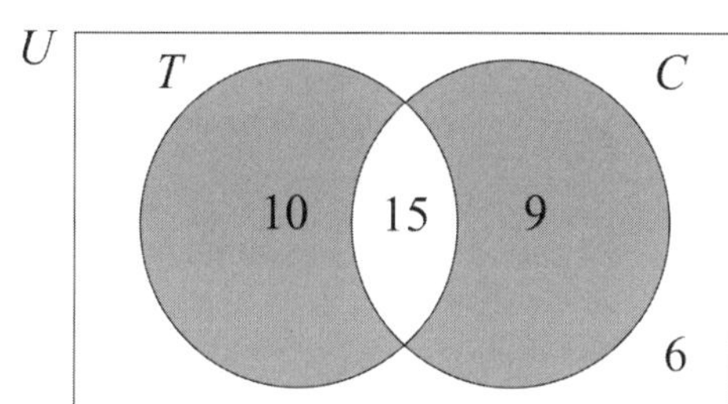 Hence 19 out of 40 teachers like drinking tea or coffee but not both.
e. Pr(neither tea nor coffee) $= \frac{6}{40}$ $= \frac{3}{20}$	6 teachers like neither tea nor coffee. 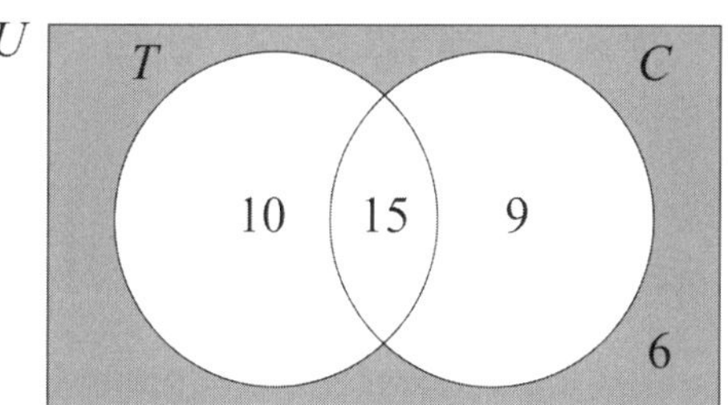 Hence 6 out of 40 teachers like drinking neither tea nor coffee. Simplify the fraction.

Mutually exclusive events are events that cannot occur together. If events A and B are mutually exclusive then Pr(A and B) $= 0$. In a Venn diagram, the sets would have no overlap (as shown below).

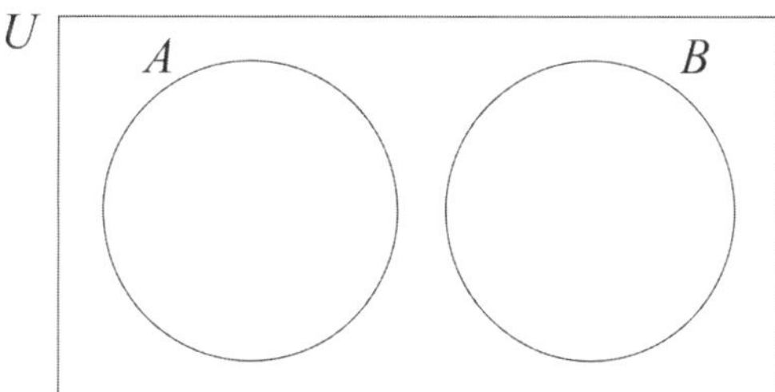

For example, suppose a letter is selected at random from the word BALLOON and it is noted whether it is a vowel or a consonant. Since a letter is either a vowel or a consonant, the set containing the vowels and the set containing the consonants do not overlap. Hence the events 'selecting a vowel' and 'selecting a consonant' are mutually exclusive.

Exercise 11.5.1

Consider the following Venn diagram showing the number of students in a class who study art (A) and/or history (H).

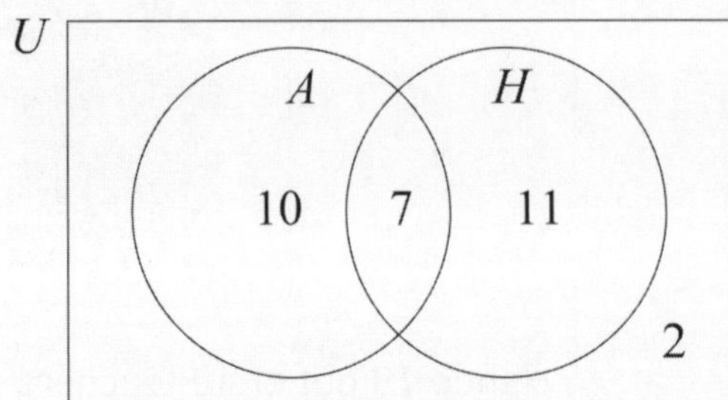

Calculate the probability that a student chosen at random from the class:

a. studies art

b. studies history but not art

c. studies both subjects

d. studies neither subject.

Exercise 11.5.2

In a group of 30 students, 5 students belong to both the Maths Club and the Public Speaking Club, 10 belong to the Maths Club only and 9 belong to the Public Speaking Club only.

a. Represent this information in a Venn diagram.

b. Determine the probability that a randomly selected student belongs to:

  i. the Maths Club

  ii. the Public Speaking Club only

  iii. neither club

  iv. both clubs.

11.6 Two-way tables

A two-way table is a way of organising categorical data into rows that represent one type of data and columns that represent another type of data.

The table below is an example of a two-way table. It gives a summary of the membership of a bowling club.

	Casual	Competition
Adult	**56** The number of adults who are casual members	**44** The number of adults who are competition members
Child	**24** The number of children who are casual members	**16** The number of children who are competition members

We can calculate probabilities from a two-way table by dividing the number in the category of interest by the total of the entries in the table.

Example

A shop receives a delivery of sports tops in three colours and three sizes. The table below shows the number of each colour and each size received in the delivery.

	Green	**Yellow**	**Blue**
Small	25	31	40
Medium	40	26	32
Large	12	24	20

A sports top is selected at random from the delivery. What is the probability that it is:

a. green **b.** medium **c.** large and blue?

✓ Solution

Working	Explanation
a. Number of green shirts $= 25 + 40 + 12$ $= 77$	Find the total number of green shirts by adding the numbers in the green column.
Total number of shirts $= 250$	Add all numbers in the table to find the total number of shirts.
$\text{Pr(green)} = \frac{77}{250}$	The probability of selecting a green shirt is the number of green shirts divided by the total number of shirts.
b. Number of medium shirts $= 40 + 26 + 32$ $= 98$	Find the total number of medium shirts by adding the numbers in the medium row.
$\text{Pr(medium)} = \frac{98}{250}$ $= \frac{49}{125}$	The probability of selecting a medium shirt is the number of medium shirts divided by the total number of shirts. Simplify the fraction.
c. Number of large and blue shirts $= 20$	The number of shirts that are large and blue is found in the cell where the large row and blue column intersect.
$\text{Pr(large and blue)} = \frac{20}{250}$ $= \frac{2}{25}$	The probability of selecting a shirt that is large and blue is the number of large blue shirts divided by the total number of shirts. Simplify the fraction.

Information that can be displayed in a Venn diagram can also be displayed in a two-way table. The table below gives a summary of how to interpret the information displayed in a two-way table.

	A	A'	Total
B	The number of elements in both sets A and B.	The number of elements in set B that are not also in set A.	The total number of elements in set B.
B'	The number of elements in set A that are not also in set B.	The number of elements in neither set A nor set B.	The total number of elements not in set B.
Total	The total number of elements in set A.	The total number of elements not in set A.	The total number of elements

Example

The two-way table below shows the number of people at a workplace who like sweet biscuits and/or savoury biscuits.

	Sweet biscuits	Not sweet biscuits	Total
Savoury biscuits	20	10	30
Not savoury biscuits	6	4	10
Total	26	14	40

One person is selected at random. What is the probability that they like:

a. sweet biscuits

b. both sweet and savoury biscuits

c. savoury biscuits but not sweet biscuits?

✓ Solution

Working	Explanation
a. $\text{Pr(sweet)} = \frac{26}{40}$ $= \frac{13}{20}$	The total number of people who like sweet biscuits is 26 out of a total of 40 people. Simplify the fraction.
b. $\text{Pr(both types)} = \frac{20}{40}$ $= \frac{1}{2}$	20 out of the total of 40 people like both sweet and savoury biscuits. Simplify the fraction.
c. $\text{Pr(savoury but not sweet)} = \frac{10}{40}$ $= \frac{1}{4}$	10 people out of a total of 40 people like savoury biscuits but do not like sweet biscuits. Simplify the fraction.

Exercise 11.6.1

Marika has a box of cards in various shapes and colours.

	Red	White	Blue
Triangle	5	1	4
Circle	4	6	3
Square	2	4	3

She selects a card at random and notes its colour and shape. What is the probability that it is:

a. red

b. a square

c. a blue triangle

d. a circle?

Exercise 11.6.2

The two-way table below shows the number of students in a class who like milk chocolate and/or dark chocolate.

	Milk chocolate	Not milk chocolate	Total
Dark chocolate	8	2	10
Not dark chocolate	10	4	14
Total	18	6	24

One student is selected at random from the class. Determine the probability that the student likes:

a. milk chocolate

b. both milk chocolate and dark chocolate

c. neither milk chocolate nor dark chocolate.

11.7 Tree diagrams

A tree diagram is a way of listing all possible outcomes for a probability experiment that involves more than one action, such as spinning a spinner and then tossing a coin, or tossing one coin after another. Branches in the diagram show the outcome of each possibility in the experiment.

Example

The spinner shown below is spun twice.

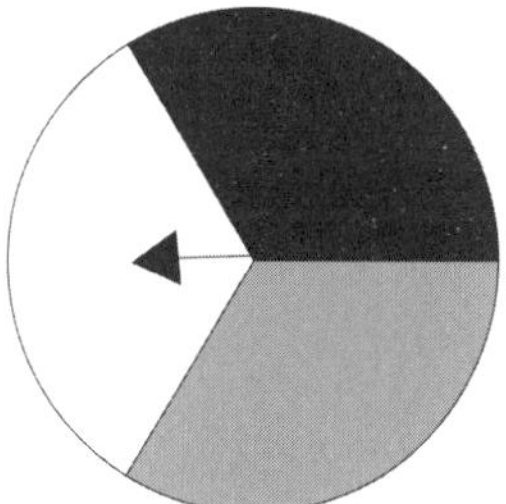

a. Use a tree diagram to list all possible outcomes of the experiment.

b. What is the probability of spinning the same colour on both spins?

✓ *Solution*

Working	Explanation
a. 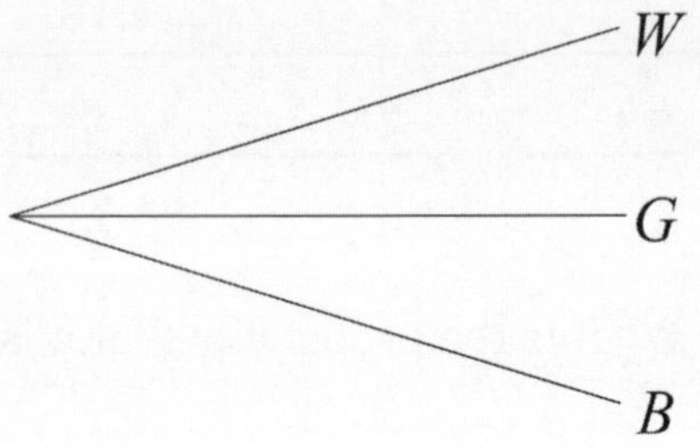 W G B	The first three branches represent the possible outcomes of the first spin: white (W), grey (G) or black (B).
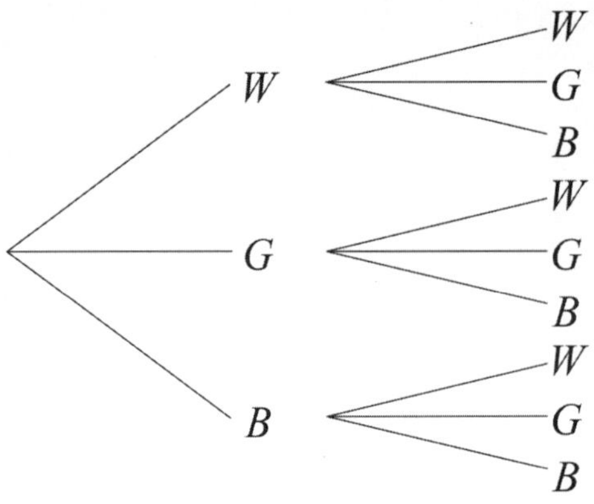 W — W, G, B G — W, G, B B — W, G, B	On the second spin we can also spin white (W), grey (G) or black (B), so we add three more branches after each of the branches for the first spin.
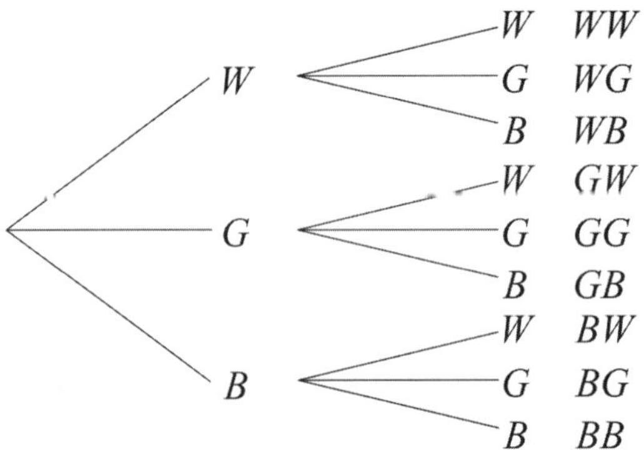 W — W WW, G WG, B WB G — W GW, G GG, B GB B — W BW, G BG, B BB	We now list all possible outcomes in the experiment at the end of each path through the tree.
b. $\Pr(\text{same on each spin}) = \frac{3}{9}$ $= \frac{1}{3}$	There are three outcomes with the same colour on each spin: WW, GG and BB. There are nine outcomes in total. Therefore the probability is 3 divided by 9. Simplify the fraction.

Exercise 11.7.1

Dean spins the following spinner once and then tosses a fair coin.

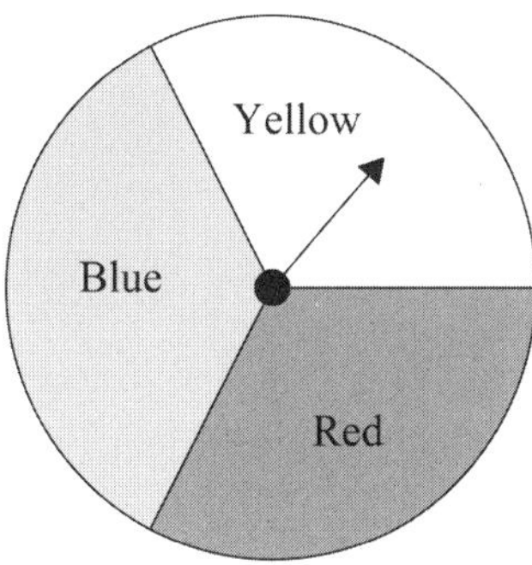

a. Use a tree diagram to list all possible outcomes of this experiment.

b. Find the probability that he:

- **i.** spins red and tosses a head
- **ii.** spins blue and tosses a tail.

Exercise 11.7.2

A fair coin is tossed three times. Find the probability of tossing:

a. three heads

b. two tails then a head

c. exactly two heads

d. at least two tails.

Answers

Exercise 11.1.1

a. impossible b. even chance c. certain d. very unlikely

Exercise 11.1.2

a. {white, black, grey}

b. $\{2, 4, 6, 8, 10, 12, 14, 16, 18\}$

c. {Jan, Feb, Mar, Apr, May, Jun, Jul, Aug, Sep, Oct, Nov, Dec}

Exercise 11.2.1

a. $\frac{2}{5}$ b. $\frac{1}{4}$

Exercise 11.2.2

a. $\frac{1}{30}$ b. $\frac{1}{5}$ c. $\frac{7}{30}$ d. $\frac{4}{15}$

Exercise 11.3

a. 0.2 b. $\frac{7}{12}$

Exercise 11.4.1

a. $U = \{1, 3, 5, 7, 9, 11, 13, 15, 17, 19\}$

b. $A = \{3, 9, 15\}$

c. $B = \{13, 15, 17, 19\}$

d. U

A: 3, 9
A and B: 15
B: 13, 17, 19
Outside: 1 5 7 11

Exercise 11.4.2

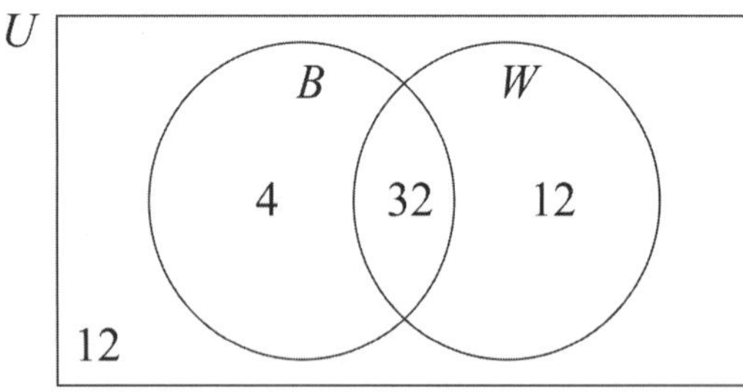

Exercise 11.5.1

a. $\Pr(A) = \frac{17}{30}$

b. $\Pr(H \text{ but not } A) = \frac{11}{30}$

c. $\Pr(\text{both}) = \frac{7}{30}$

d. $\Pr(\text{neither}) = \frac{1}{15}$

Exercise 11.5.2

a.

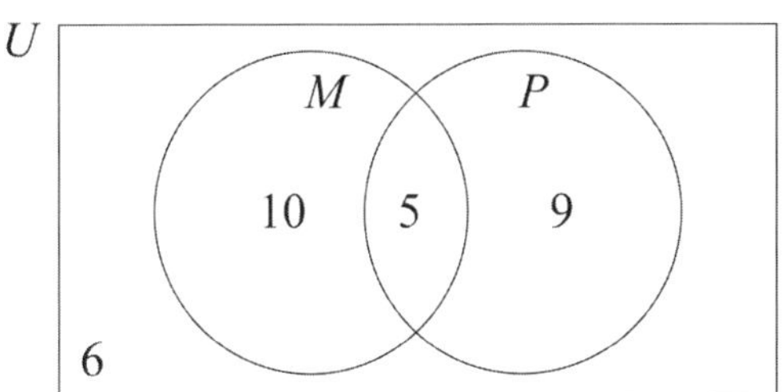

b. i. $\Pr(M) = \frac{1}{2}$

ii. $\Pr(P \text{ only}) = \frac{3}{10}$

iii. $\Pr(\text{neither}) = \frac{1}{5}$

iv. $\Pr(\text{both}) = \frac{1}{6}$

Exercise 11.6.1

a. $\Pr(\text{red}) = \frac{11}{32}$

b. $\Pr(\text{square}) = \frac{9}{32}$

c. $\Pr(\text{blue triangle}) = \frac{1}{8}$

d. $\Pr(\text{circle}) = \frac{13}{32}$

Exercise 11.6.2

a. $\Pr(\text{milk}) = \frac{3}{4}$

b. $\Pr(\text{both}) = \frac{1}{3}$

c. $\Pr(\text{neither}) = \frac{1}{6}$

Exercise 11.7.1

a.

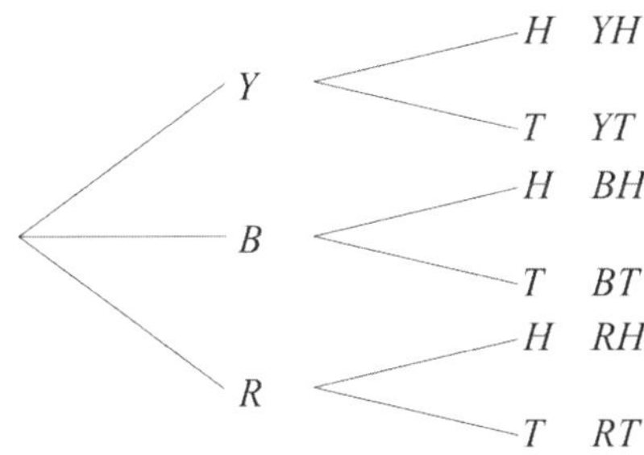

b. i. $\Pr(RH) = \frac{1}{6}$

ii. $\Pr(BT) = \frac{1}{6}$

Exercise 11.7.2

a. $\Pr(HHH) = \frac{1}{8}$

b. $\Pr(TTH) = \frac{1}{8}$

c. $\Pr(\text{exactly 2 heads}) = \frac{3}{8}$

d. $\Pr(\text{at least 2 tails}) = \frac{1}{2}$

Chapter 12 – Linear graphs

12.1 The Cartesian plane

The Cartesian plane is a way of representing points in two-dimensional space by their distance from two number lines:

- a horizontal number line called the ***x*-axis**
- a vertical number line called the ***y*-axis**.

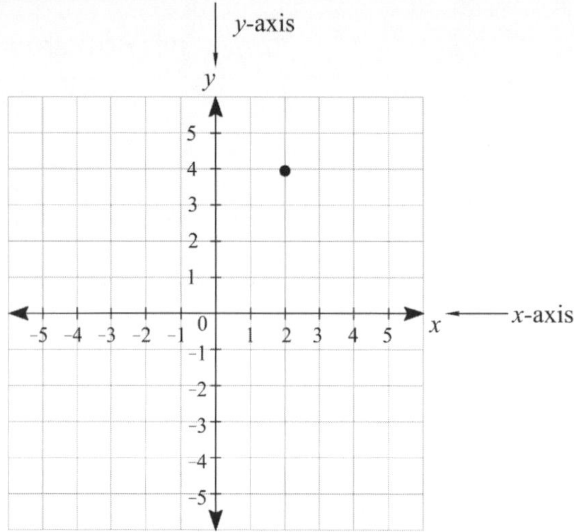

The position of a point on the Cartesian plane is given by a combination of two coordinates:

- the ***x*-coordinate** of a point is its position on the horizontal number line
- the ***y*-coordinate** is its position on the vertical number line.

The coordinates of a point are given as two numbers separated by a comma and enclosed in brackets. The x-coordinate is the first number and the y-coordinate is the second number.

The coordinates of the point plotted on the Cartesian plane at the right are

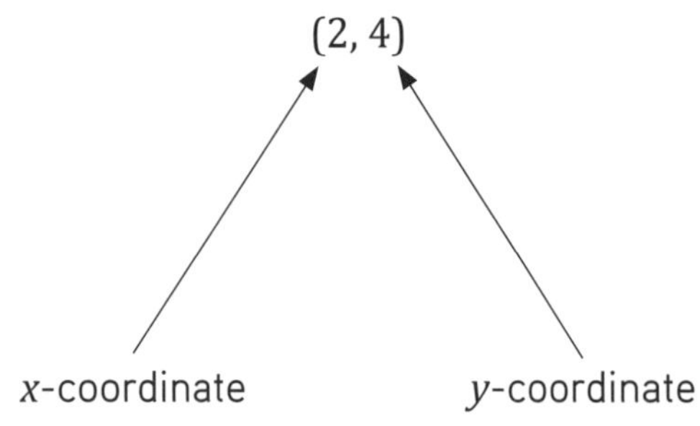

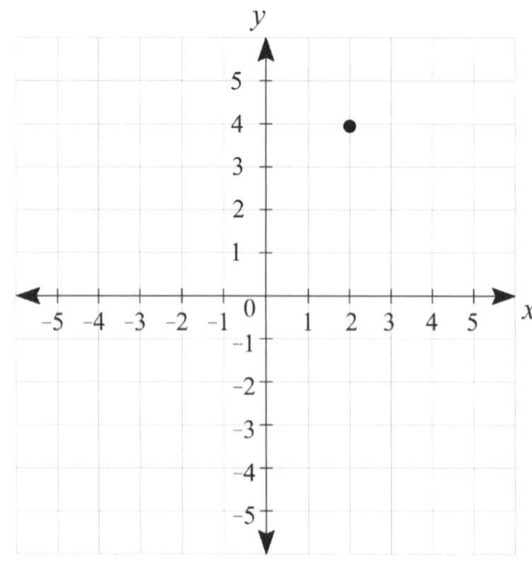

The point $(0, 0)$ is called the **origin**. This is the point where the x-axis and the y-axis intersect.

Example

What are the coordinates of points A, B, C, D and E on the following Cartesian plane?

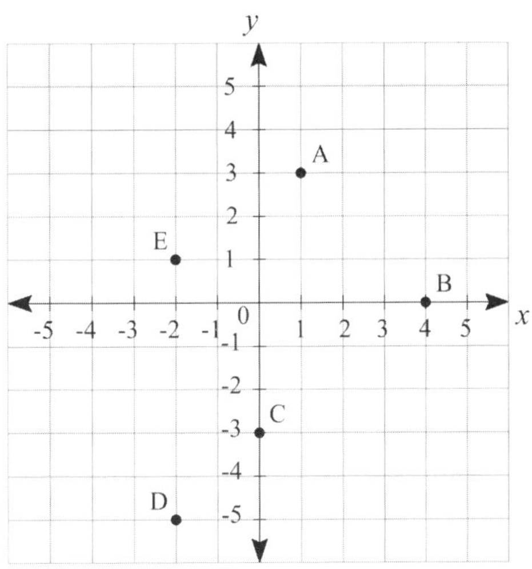

✓ Solution

Working	Explanation
$A = (1, 3)$	A lies at 1 on the x-axis and 3 on the y-axis.
$B = (4, 0)$	B lies at 4 on the x-axis and 0 on the y-axis.
$C = (0, -3)$	C lies at 0 on the x-axis and -3 on the y-axis.
$D = (-2, -5)$	D lies at -2 on the x-axis and -5 on the y-axis.
$E = (-2, 1)$	E lies at -2 on the x-axis and 1 on the y-axis.

Exercise 12.1

What are the coordinates of points A, B, C, D and E on the Cartesian plane below?

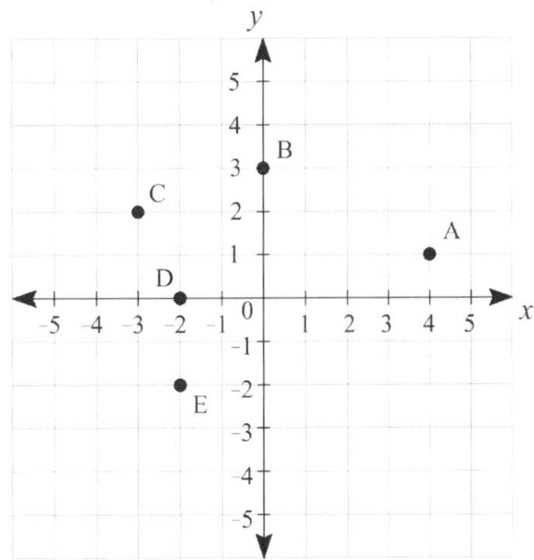

12.2 Graphs from tables of values

A table of values can be used to find points that lie on the graph of a rule. For each value of x in the table, the rule can be used to find the corresponding value of y.

Each corresponding pair of x and y values are coordinates. These coordinates can be plotted on the Cartesian plane and a line drawn through them to form a graph.

Linear graphs from tables of values

When a rule connecting x and y is linear, the points on the graph lie on a straight line.

Example

a. Complete the following table of values for the rule $y = 2x - 1$.

x	-3	-2	-1	0	1	2	3
y							

b. List the values in the table as coordinates.

c. Plot the graph of $y = 2x - 1$.

✓ Solution

Working	Explanation
a. $x = -3: y = 2 \times -3 - 1 = -6 - 1 = -7$ $x = -2: y = 2 \times -2 - 1 = -4 - 1 = -5$ $x = -1: y = 2 \times -1 - 1 = -2 - 1 = -3$ $x = 0: y = 2 \times 0 - 1 = 0 - 1 = -1$ $x = 1: y = 2 \times 1 - 1 = 2 - 1 = 1$ $x = 2: y = 2 \times 2 - 1 = 4 - 1 = 3$ $x = 3: y = 2 \times 3 - 1 = 6 - 1 = 5$	Substitute each value of x into the rule $y = 2x - 1$ to find the corresponding y value and complete the table of values.
b. $(-3, -7)$, $(-2, -5)$, $(-1, -3)$, $(0, -1)$, $(1, 1)$, $(2, 3)$, $(3, 5)$	Each value of x and the corresponding value of y make up a coordinate: (x, y). List all the coordinates.

x	-3	-2	-1	0	1	2	3
y	-7	-5	-3	-1	1	3	5

c. 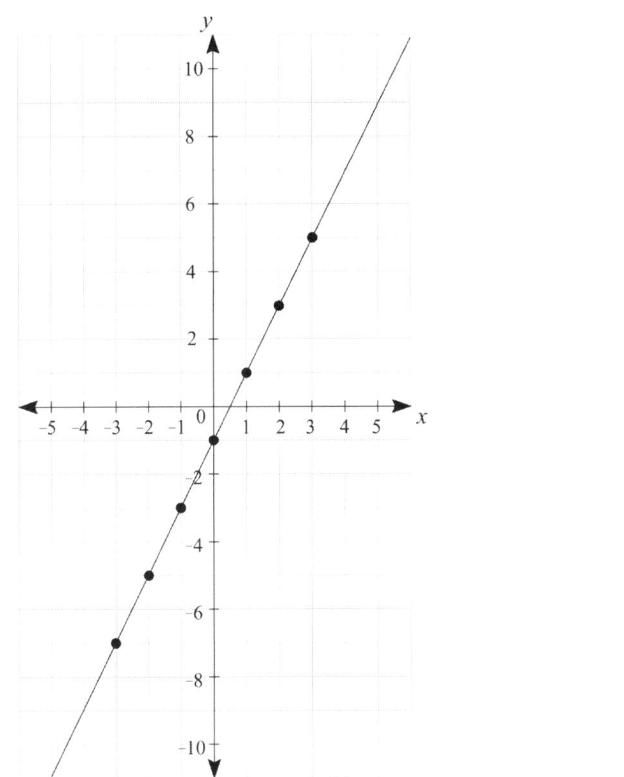	Plot each point and then rule a straight line through the points. The line is the graph of $y = 2x - 1$.

Exercise 12.2.1

Consider each of the following rules.

a. $y = x + 3$ **b.** $y = 2x - 3$ **c.** $y = -3x + 1$

For each rule:

i. Complete a table of values using the following x-values.

x	-3	-2	-1	0	1	2	3
y							

ii. List the values in the table as coordinates.

iii. Plot the graph.

Determining if a point lies on a graph

A point will lie on a graph if its x-coordinate and y-coordinate satisfy the rule for the graph.

We can determine if a point lies on a graph by plotting the graph or using the rule.

Example

Determine if the point $(4, -1)$ lies on the graph of $y = 3 - x$.

✓ Solution

Working	Explanation
$y = 3 - x$ $= 3 - 4$ $= -1$ Therefore $(4, -1)$ lies on the graph of $y = 3 - x$.	The x-coordinate of the point $(4, -1)$ is 4. Substitute $x = 4$ into the rule $y = 3 - x$. The result is $y = -1$, the same as the y-coordinate of the point. Hence the point lies on the graph.

Example

Determine if the point $(-1, 2)$ lies on the graph of $y = 3 - x$.

✓ Solution

Working	Explanation
$y = 3 - (-1)$ $= 3 + 1$ $= 4$ Therefore $(-1, 2)$ does not lie on the graph of $y - 3 - x$.	The x-coordinate of the point $(-1, 2)$ is -1. Substitute $x = -1$ into the rule $y = 3 - x$. The result is $y = 4$. This is not the same as the y-coordinate of the point. Hence the point does not lie on the graph.

Exercise 12.2.2

Determine if each of the following points lies on the graph of $y = x - 4$.

a. $(0, 4)$ **b.** $(2, -2)$ **c.** $(-5, -9)$

Exercise 12.2.3

The graph of $y = 4 - 2x$ is shown below.

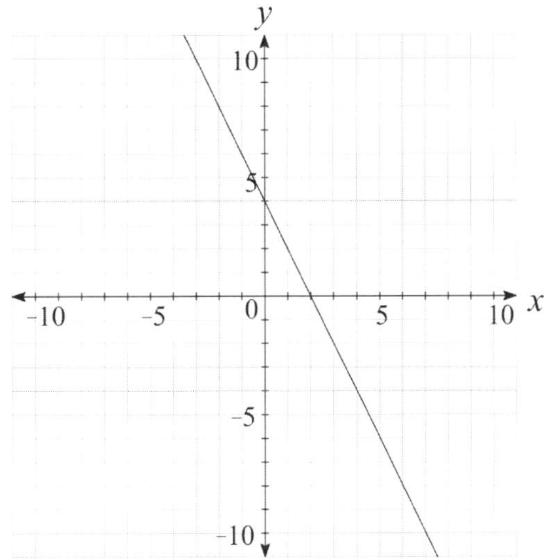

For each of the following points, determine whether it lies on, above or below the graph.

a. $(0, 2)$ **b.** $(5, -6)$ **c.** $(-3, 3)$ **d.** $(6, 2)$

Non-linear graphs

A non-linear graph is one where points on the graph do not lie in a straight line.

Example

From the table of values below, plot the graph and determine if it is linear or non-linear.

x	-3	-2	-1	0	1	2	3
y	9	4	1	0	1	4	9

✓ *Solution*

Working	Explanation
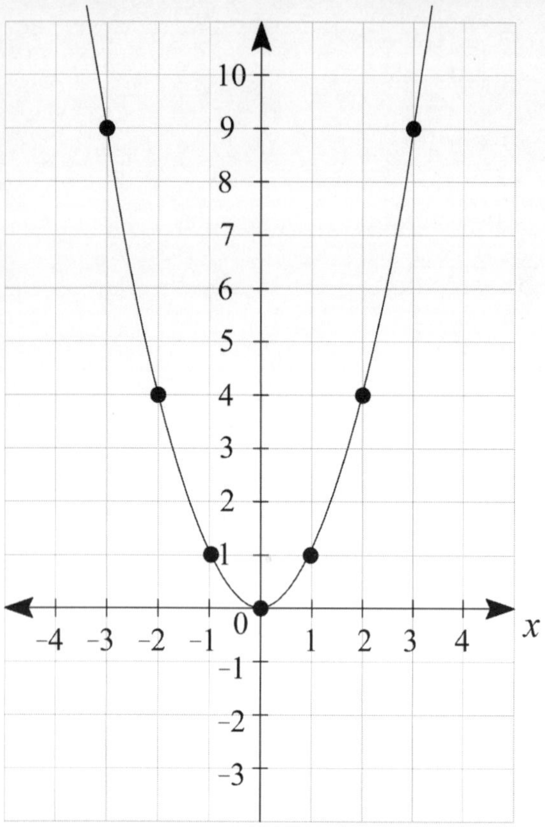	Plot the points $(-3, 9)$, $(-2, 4)$, $(-1, 1)$, $(0, 0)$, $(1, 1)$, $(2, 2)$, $(3, 9)$. Connect the points.
The graph is non-linear.	The points lie on a curve, not on a straight line.

Example

From the table of values below, plot the graph and determine if it is linear or non-linear.

x	-3	-2	-1	0	1	2	3
y	$\frac{1}{2}$	1	$\frac{3}{2}$	2	$\frac{5}{2}$	3	$\frac{7}{2}$

✓ ***Solution***

Working	Explanation
	Plot the points $\left(-3, \frac{1}{2}\right)$, $(-2, 1)$, $\left(-1, \frac{3}{2}\right)$, $(0, 2)$, $\left(1, \frac{5}{2}\right)$, $(2, 3)$, $\left(3, \frac{7}{2}\right)$ To plot the fractional values, convert them to mixed numbers: $\frac{3}{2} = 1\frac{1}{2}$, $\frac{5}{2} = 2\frac{1}{2}$, $\frac{7}{2} = 3\frac{1}{2}$ Connect the points.
The graph is linear.	The points lie on a straight line.

Exercise 12.2.4

State whether each of the following graphs is linear or non-linear.

a.

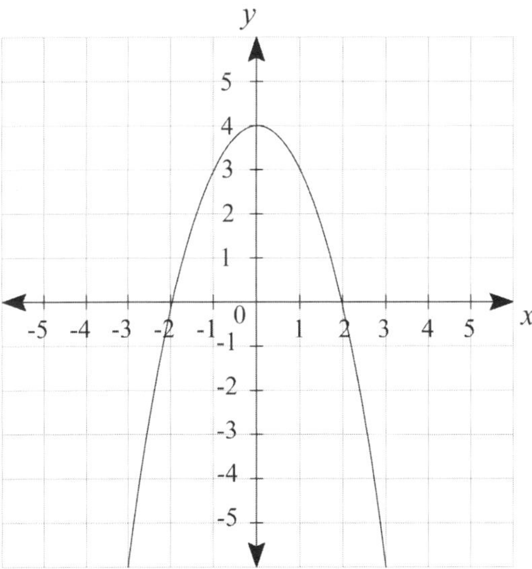

b.

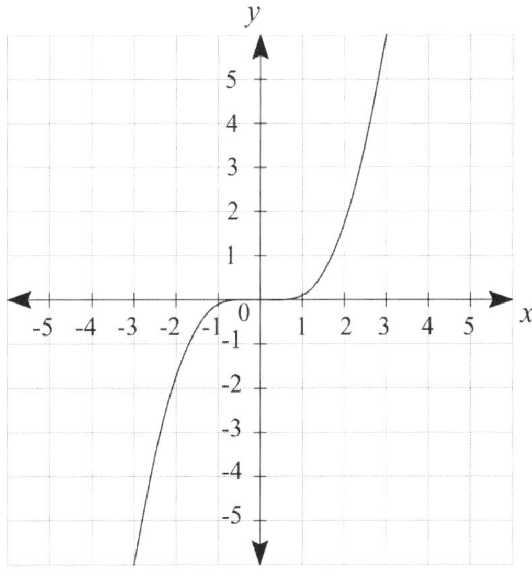

c.

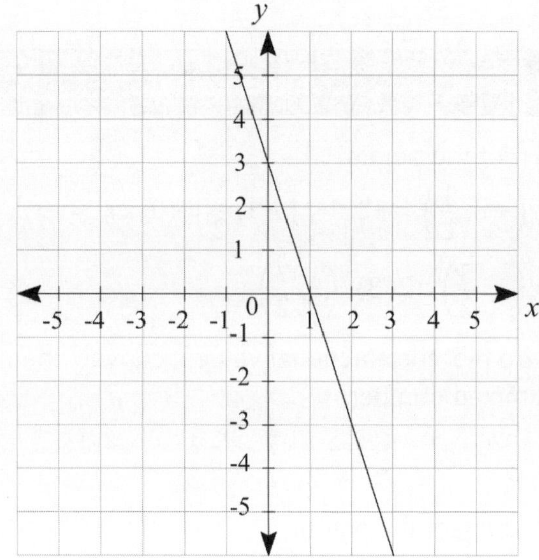

d.

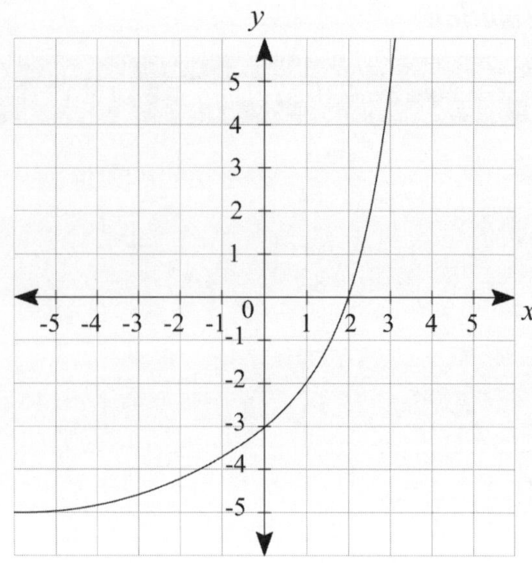

12.3 Linear rules from tables of values

The rule for a linear graph has the form $y = mx + c$, where m and c are numbers.

We refer to m as the coefficient of x and c as the constant.

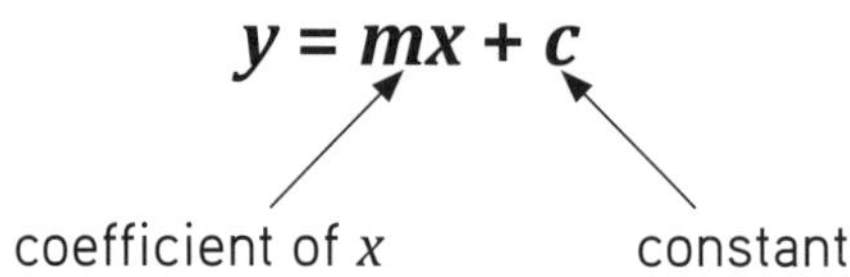

c is the value of y when $x = 0$.

y changes by m, each time x increases by 1.

Example

Find the linear rule for the following table of values.

x	−2	−1	0	1	2
y	−1	2	5	8	11

✓ Solution

Working	Explanation
When $x = 0, y = 5$. Therefore $c = 5$.	A linear rule has the form $y = mx + c$. c is the value of y when $x = 0$.
+1 +1 +1 +1 <table><tr><td>x</td><td>−2</td><td>−1</td><td>0</td><td>1</td><td>2</td></tr><tr><td>y</td><td>−1</td><td>2</td><td>5</td><td>8</td><td>11</td></tr></table>+3 +3 +3 +3 $m = 3$	y changes by m each time x increases by 1.
$y = mx + c$ $y = 3x + 5$	Write the rule with the values of m and c.

Example

Find the linear rule for the following table of values.

x	0	1	2	3	4
y	−10	−12	−14	−16	−18

✓ Solution

Working	Explanation
$c = -10$	The rule has the form $y = mx + c$. c is the value of y when $x = 0$.
+1 +1 +1 +1 <table><tr><td>x</td><td>0</td><td>1</td><td>2</td><td>3</td><td>4</td></tr><tr><td>y</td><td>−10</td><td>−12</td><td>−14</td><td>−16</td><td>−18</td></tr></table>−2 −2 −2 −2 $m = -2$	y changes by m each time x increases by 1.
$y = mx + c$ $y = -2x - 10$	Write the rule with the values of m and c.

If m is negative and c is positive, we can change the order of the terms in a linear rule. For example:

$$\boldsymbol{y} = -5\boldsymbol{x} + 2 \text{ is the same as } \boldsymbol{y} = 2 - 5\boldsymbol{x}$$

Exercise 12.3

Determine the linear rule for each of the following table of values.

a.

x	−2	−1	0	1	2
y	−2	1	4	7	10

b.

x	−2	−1	0	1	2
y	−9	−7	−5	−3	−1

c.

x	0	1	2	3	4
y	30	31	32	33	34

d.

x	0	1	2	3	4
y	100	80	60	40	20

12.4 Features of linear graphs

A linear graph is a straight line. The line could have positive slope, have negative slope, be horizontal or be vertical.

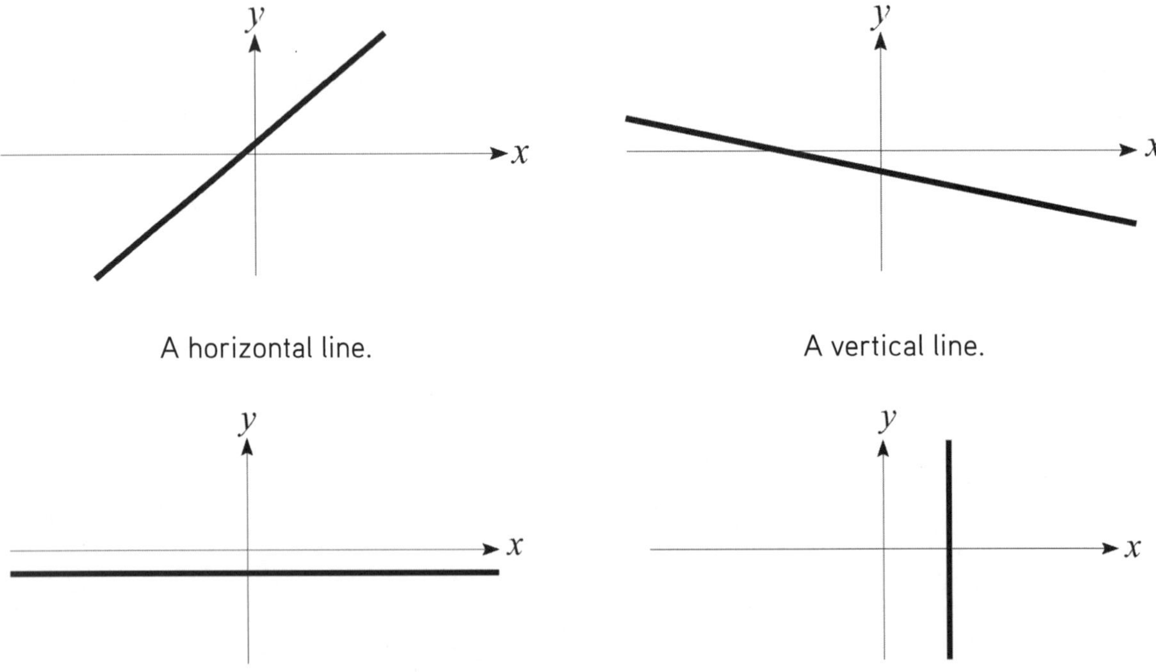

Where a straight line has a positive slope or a negative slope, the rule for the line has the form $y = mx + c$ where m is not equal to zero.

If m is positive then the graph has positive slope and the graph slopes up from left to right. If m is negative, the graph has negative slope and the graph slopes down from left to right.

The value of c tells us where the graph crosses the y-axis.

Example

For the linear rule $y = 2x + 3$, determine:

a. if the graph has positive or negative slope

b. the coordinates of the point where the graph crosses the y-axis.

✓ *Solution*

Working	Explanation
a. $y = 2x + 3$ $m = 2$ The graph has positive slope.	$y = mx + c$ Determine the value of m. m is positive, so the graph has positive slope.
b. $c = 3$ The graph crosses the y-axis at $(0,3)$.	Determine the value of c. c tells us the value of y where the graph crosses the y-axis.

 **Exercise 12.4**

For each of the following linear rules determine if the corresponding graph has positive or negative slope, and find the coordinates of the point where the graph crosses the y-axis.

a. $y = 5x - 2$ **b.** $y = -4x - 1$ **c.** $y = 6 - 3x$

12.5 Vertical and horizontal lines

All points on a **vertical line** have the same x-coordinate.

The equation of the vertical line shown below is $x = 2$.

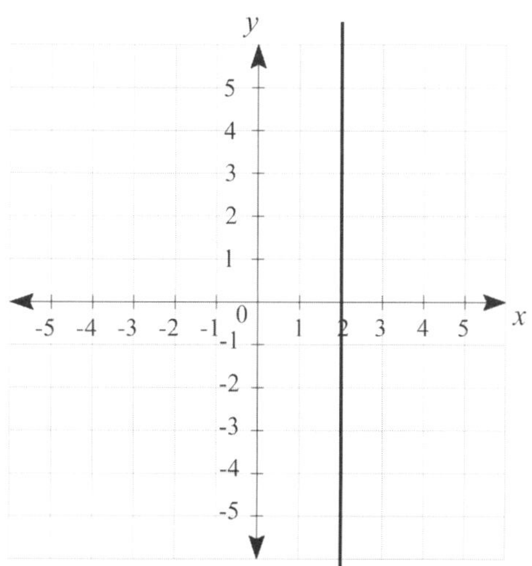

All points on a horizontal line have the same y-coordinate.

The equation of the horizontal line below is $y = -3$.

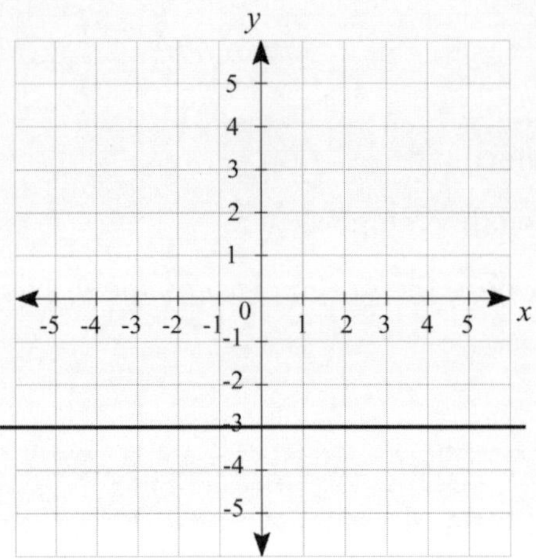

Example

Determine the equation of each of the following straight lines.

a.

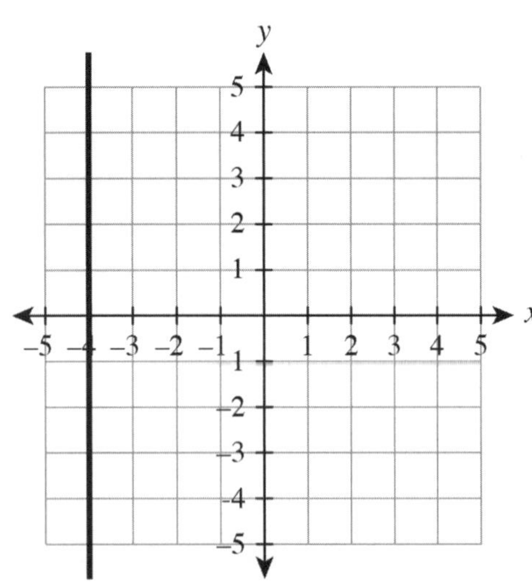

b.

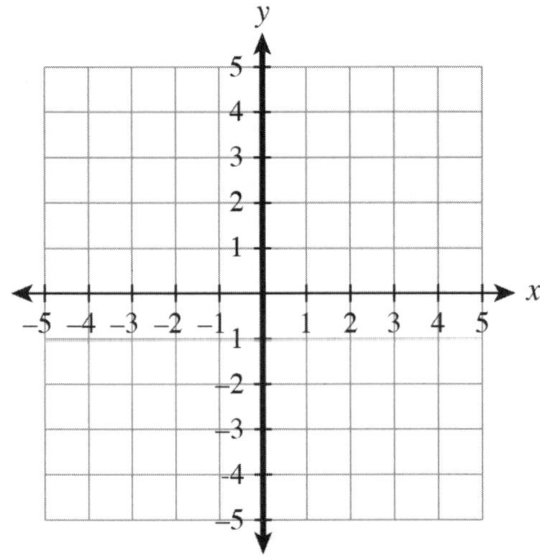

c.

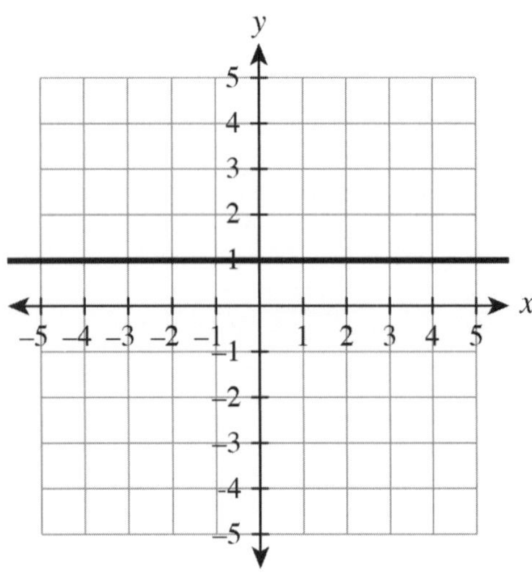

d.

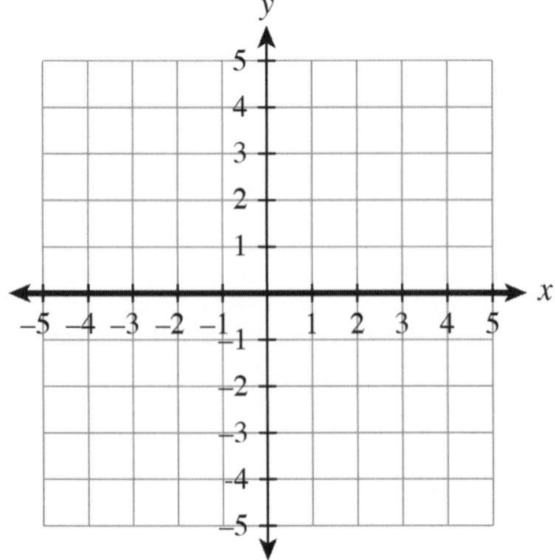

✓ ***Solution***

Working	Explanation
a. $x = -4$	The graph is a vertical line and all points on the line have an x-coordinate of -4.
b. $x = 0$	The graph is a vertical line on the y-axis. Every point on the line has an x-coordinate of 0.
c. $y = 1$	The graph is a horizontal line and all points on the line have a y-coordinate of 1.
d. $y = 0$	The graph is a horizontal line on the x-axis. Every point on the line has a y-coordinate of 0.

Exercise 12.5

Write down the equation of each of the following straight lines.

a.

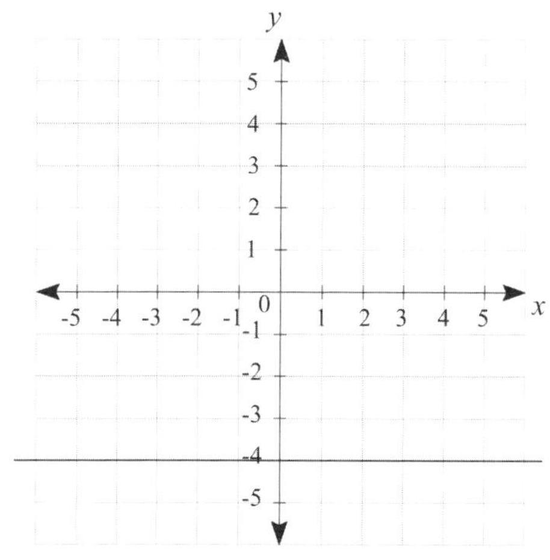

b.

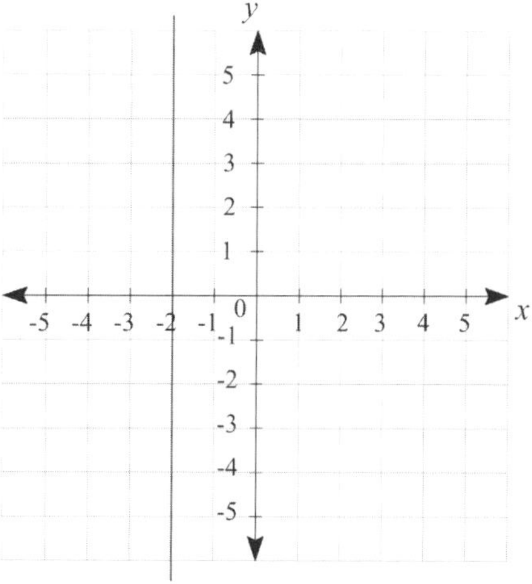

12.6 Graphing straight lines using intercepts

A point where a graph crosses the y-axis is referred to as a y-intercept. At a y-intercept $x = 0$.

A point where a graph crosses the x-axis is referred to as an x-intercept. At an x-intercept $y = 0$.

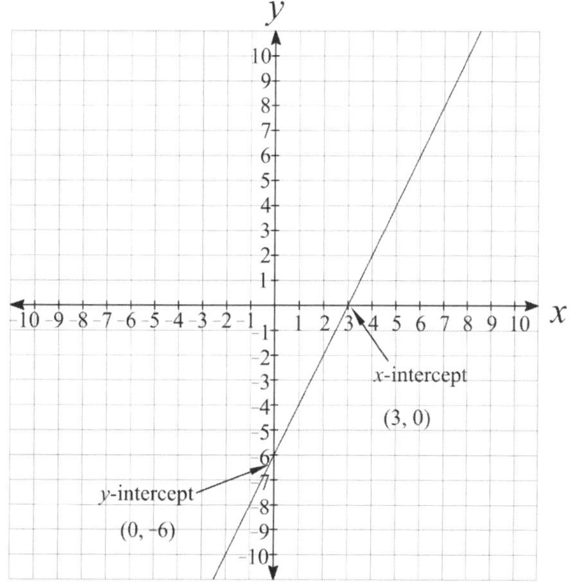

Example

Sketch the graph of $y = -2x + 4$ by finding the coordinates of the x-intercept and the coordinates of the y-intercept.

✓ *Solution*

Working	Explanation
$y = -2x + 4$ $c = 4$ y-intercept $= (0, 4)$	The rule is written in the form $y = mx + c$, so c is the y-intercept. Write the intercept as coordinates.
$0 = -2x + 4$ $-4 = -2x$ $\frac{-4}{-2} = x$ $x = 2$ x-intercept $= (2, 0)$	Let $y = 0$ to find the x-intercept. Solve for x by first subtracting 4 from both sides. Divide both sides by -2. Write the intercept as coordinates.
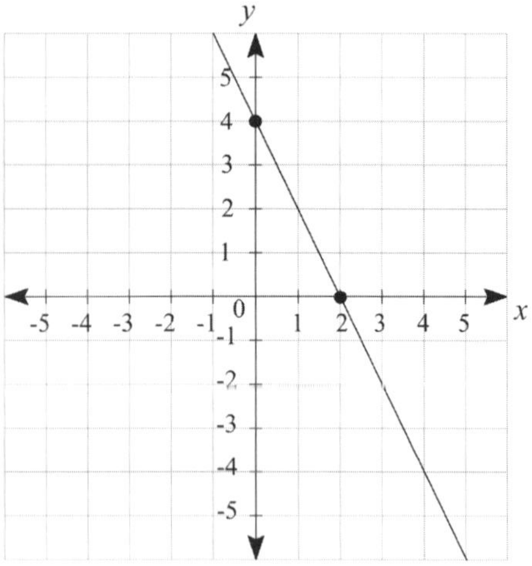	Plot the points $(0, 4)$ and $(2, 0)$ and draw a straight line through the points.

The rule for a linear graph can also be expressed in the form $ax + by = c$.

Example

Sketch the graph of $5x - 2y = 10$ by first finding the coordinates of the x- and y-intercepts.

✓ ***Solution***

Working	Explanation
$5x - 2y = 10$ $5x = 10$ $x = 2$ x-intercept $= (2, 0)$	Let $y = 0$ to find the x-intercept. Divide both sides of the equation by 5. Write the intercept as coordinates.
$-2y = 10$ $y = -5$ y-intercept $= (0, -5)$	Let $x = 0$ to find the y-intercept. Divide both sides of the equation by -2. Write the intercept as coordinates.
y 10 9 8 7 6 5 4 3 2 1 -1 -2 -3 -4 -5 -6 -7 -8 -9 -10 -10 -9 -8 -7 -6 -5 -4 -3 -2 -1 1 2 3 4 5 6 7 8 9 10 *x*	Plot the points $(0, -5)$ and $(2, 0)$ and draw a straight line through the points.

Exercise 12.6

Sketch a graph of each of the following linear rules by finding the coordinates of the x-intercept and y-intercept.

a. $y = 3x - 9$ **b.** $y = 4 - 4x$ **c.** $2x + 3y = 6$ **d.** $y - 4x = 12$

12.7 Applications of linear graphs

Linear functions and their graphs can be used as models in many practical situations. To make it clear what variables are being modelled, it is important that each axis of a graph is labelled with the correct variable.

Example

An electrician charges an \$80 call-out fee and then \$120 per hour.

a. Complete the following table.

Number of hours worked (n)	0	1	2	3	4
Cost in dollars (C)					

b. Plot a graph of cost (C) against the number of hours worked (n). Use a scale of 1 from 0 to 4 for the horizontal axis and a scale of 20 from 0 to 600 on the vertical axis.

✓ Solution

Working	Explanation
a. 0 | 1 | 2 | 3 | 4 80 | 200 | 320 | 440 | 560	The cost for 0 hours is \$80 (i.e. the call-out fee). For 1 hour the cost is $80 + 120 = \$200$. For 2 hours the cost is $80 + 2 \times 120 = \$320$. For 3 hours the cost is $80 + 3 \times 120 = \$440$. For 4 hours the cost is $80 + 4 \times 120 = \$560$.
b. C 600 500 400 300 200 100 1 2 3 4 n	Construct a graph with C on the vertical axis and n on the horizontal axis. Plot the points: (0, 80), (1, 200), (2, 320), (3, 440), (4, 560). Draw a straight line through the points.

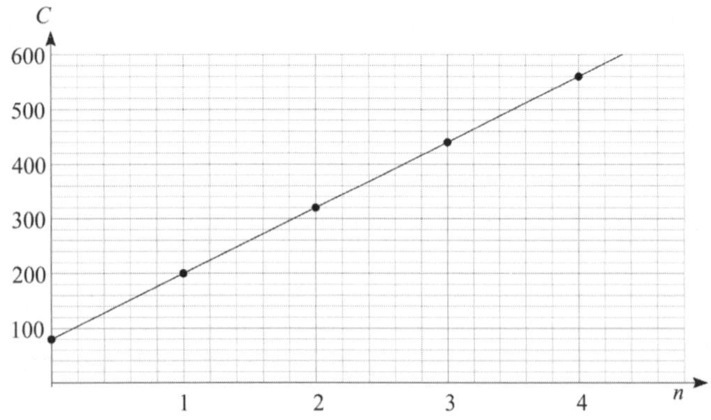

Exercise 12.7

Sabrina's rainwater tank has sprung a small leak. The tank originally contained 800 litres of water and water leaks from the tank at a constant rate of 2 litres per minute.

a. Copy and complete the following table.

Time (minutes)	0	40	80	120	160
Volume (litres)					

b. Plot a graph of volume in litres against time in minutes. Use a scale of 0 to 800 on the volume axis and 0 to 400 on the time axis.

c. How long does it take for the tank to empty?

d. How much water remains in the tank after 180 minutes?

Answers

Exercise 12.1

a. (4, 1) b. (0, 3) c. (−3, 2) d. (−2, 0) e. (−2, −2)

Exercise 12.2.1

a.

i.

x	−3	−2	−1	0	1	2	3
y	0	1	2	3	4	5	6

ii. (−3, 0), (−2, 1), (−1, 2), (0, 3), (1, 4), (2, 5), (3, 6)

iii.

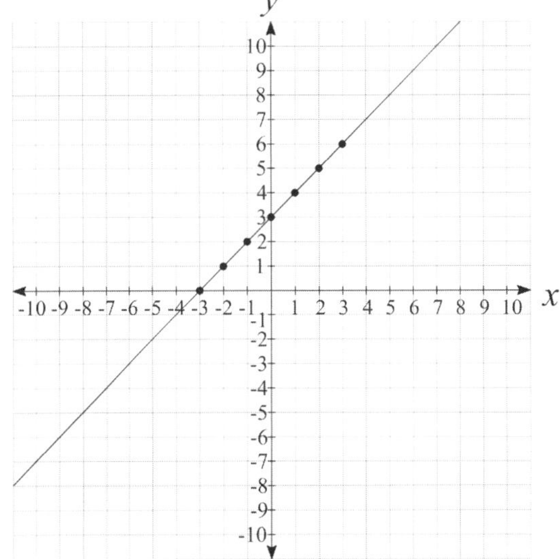

b.

i.

x	-3	-2	-1	0	1	2	3
y	-9	-7	-5	-3	-1	1	3

ii. $(-3, -9)$, $(-2, -7)$, $(-1, -5)$, $(0, -3)$, $(1, -1)$, $(2, 1)$, $(3, 3)$

iii.

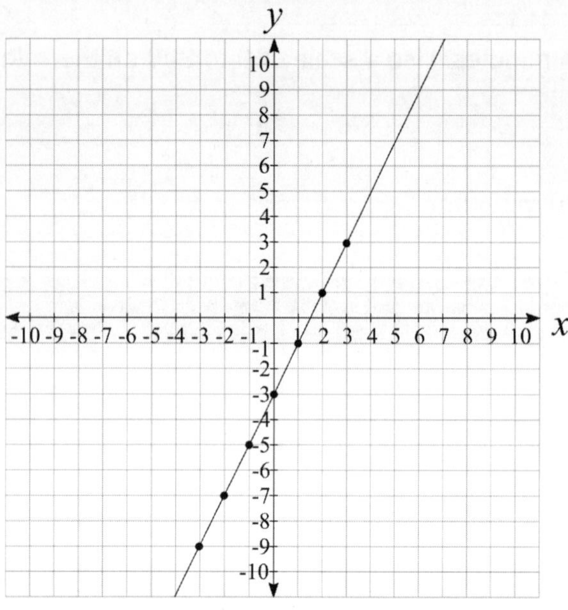

c.

i.

x	-3	-2	-1	0	1	2	3
y	10	7	4	1	-2	-5	-8

ii. $(-3, 10)$, $(-2, 7)$, $(-1, 4)$, $(0, 1)$, $(1, -2)$, $(2, -5)$, $(3, -8)$

iii.

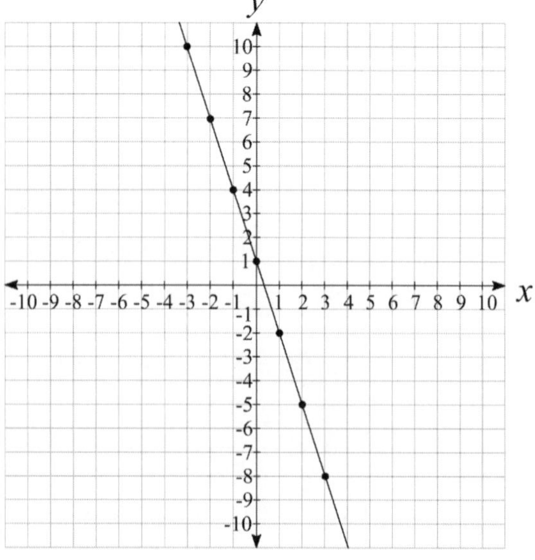

Exercise 12.2.2

a. no b. yes c. yes

Exercise 12.2.3

a. below b. on c. below d. above

Exercise 12.2.4

a. non-linear b. non-linear c. linear d. non-linear

Exercise 12.3

a. $y = 3x + 4$ b. $y = 2x - 5$ c. $y = x + 30$ d. $y = -20x + 100$

Exercise 12.4

a. positive slope, $(0, -2)$ b. negative slope, $(0, -1)$ c. negative slope, $(0, 6)$

Exercise 12.5

a. $y = -4$ b. $x = -2$

Exercise 12.6

a.

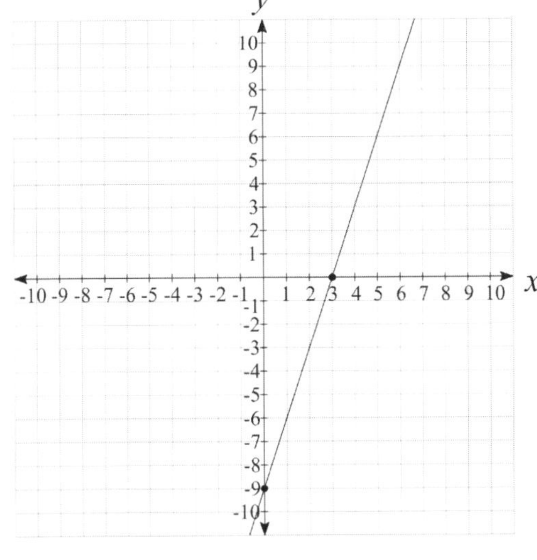

b.

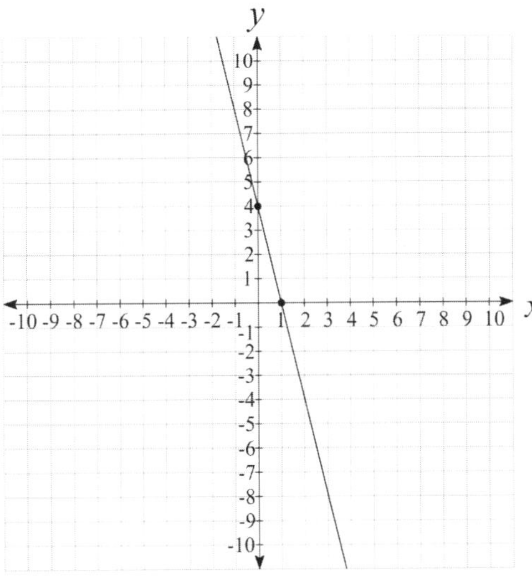

c.

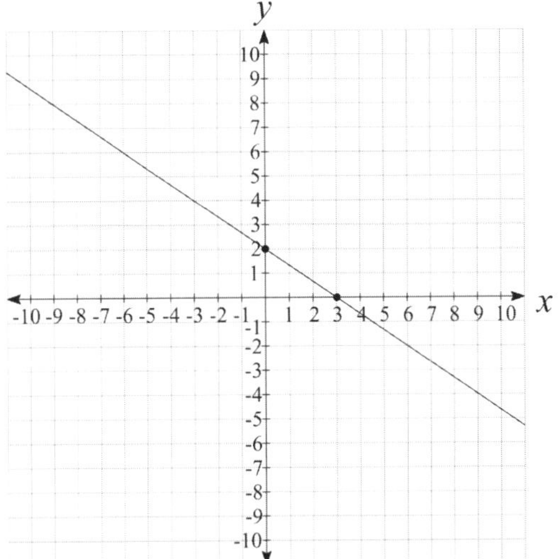

d.

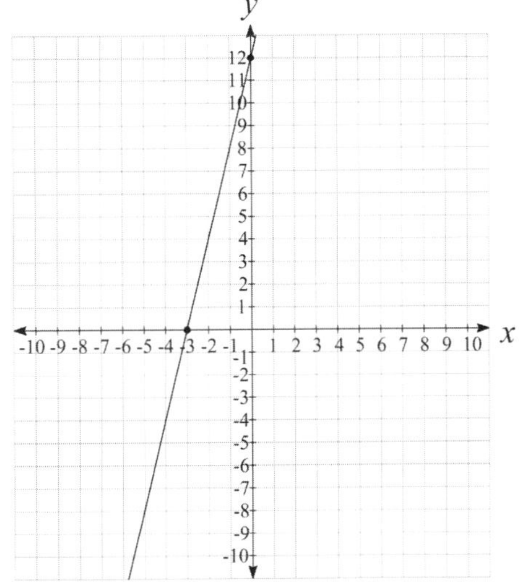

Exercise 12.7

a.

Time	0	40	80	120	160
Volume	800	720	640	560	480

b.

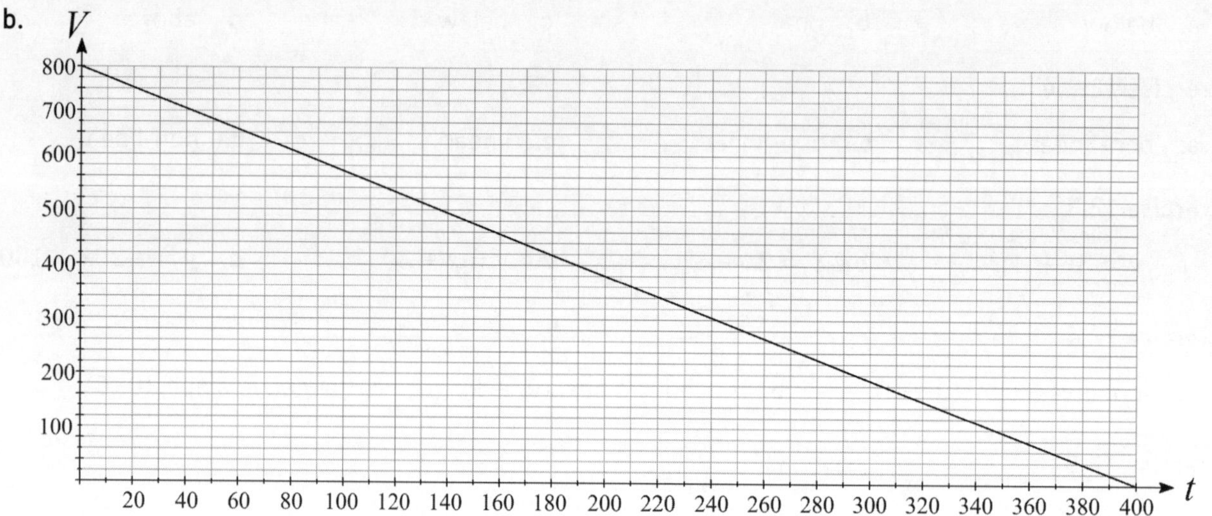

c. 400 minutes

d. 440 litres

Chapter 13 – Transformations and congruency

A shape can be transformed by reflection, translation or rotation.

13.1 Reflection

When we reflect a shape over a line, we create a mirror image of the shape. Each point in the shape is reflected at right angles over the line of reflection (also known as the mirror line). The size of the original shape remains unchanged.

By convention, the image of a point labelled A in the original shape is labelled A' in the reflection, the image of a point B is labelled B' and so on.

In the following diagram, triangle $A'B'C'$ is a reflection of triangle ABC over the mirror line.

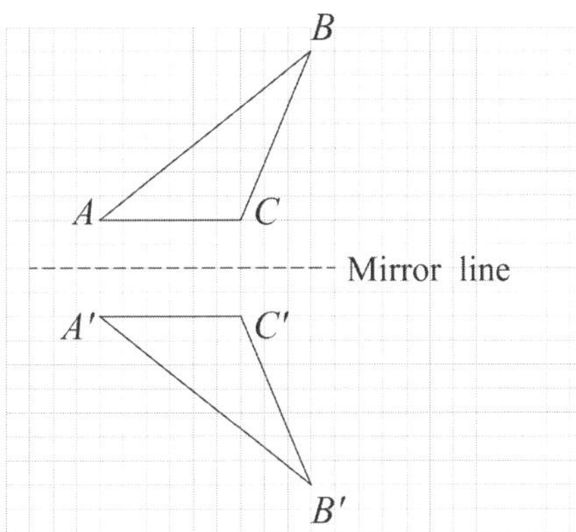

Example

Draw the image of each of the following shapes after it is reflected over the mirror line. (The mirror line is the dashed line.)

a.

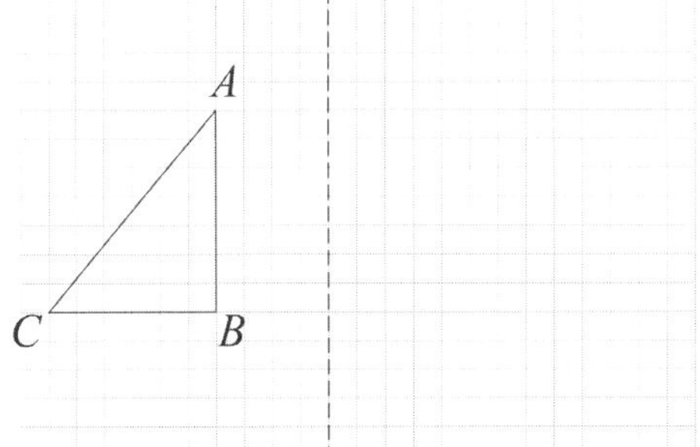

b.

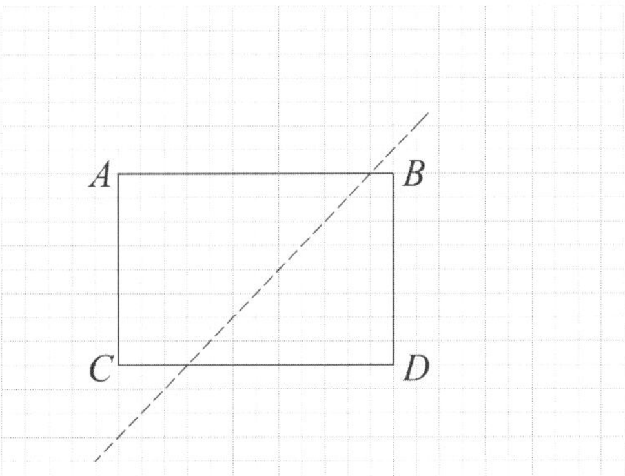

✓ Solution

Working	Explanation
a. 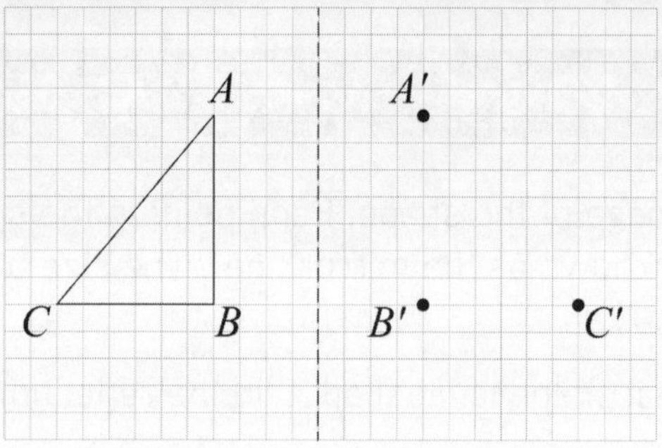	Reflect each vertex over the mirror line at right angles to the mirror line. Label the image of each vertex with the same letter as the original shape followed by the prime symbol (′).
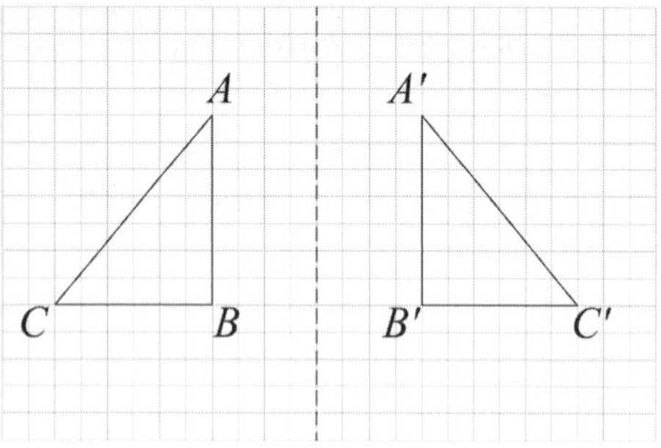	Join the three vertices using straight lines.
b. 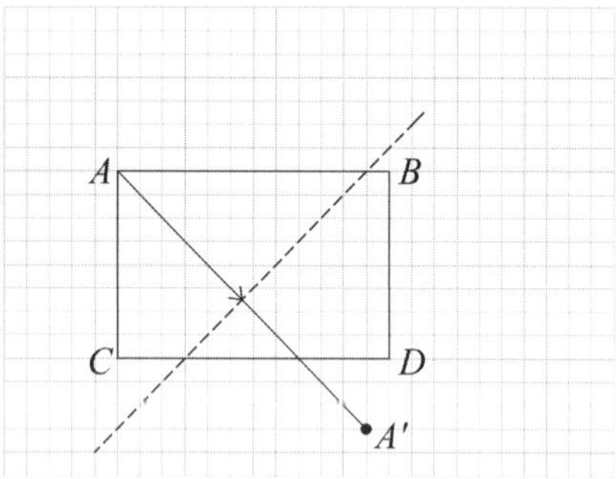	Reflect vertex A over the mirror line at right angles to the mirror line. Label the image of this vertex A'.
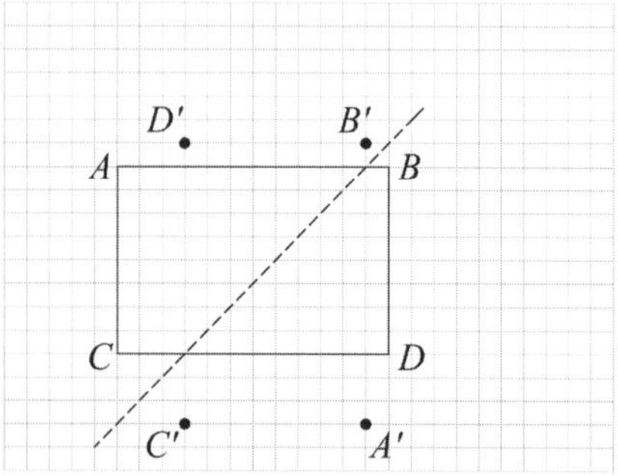	Repeat this procedure for the other three vertices.
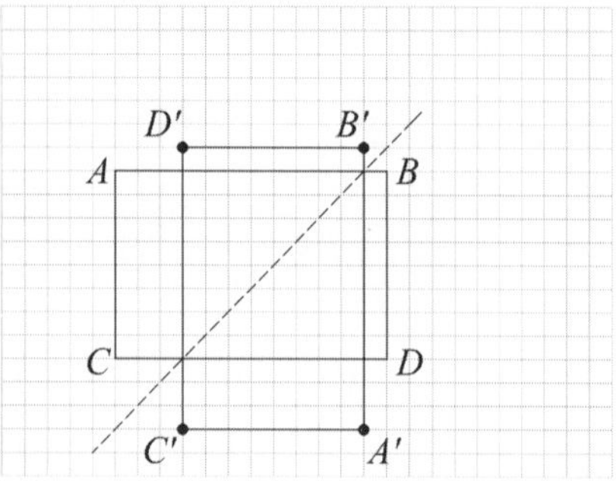	Join the four vertices using straight lines.

Points on the Cartesian plane can be reflected using the same technique.

Example

a. Find the coordinates of the image of point $A(3, 2)$ when it is reflected over the x-axis.

b. Find the coordinates of the image of point $B(-4, -3)$ when it is reflected over the y-axis.

✓ Solution

Working	Explanation
a. The image of $A(3, 2)$ is $A'(3, -2)$.	Plot the point $A(3, 2)$. The x-axis is the mirror line, so reflect the point over the x-axis at right angles to the axis.
b. The image of $B(-4, -3)$ is $B'(4, -3)$.	Plot the point $B(-4, -3)$. The y-axis is the mirror line, so reflect the point over the y-axis at right angles to the axis.

Exercise 13.1.1

Draw the image of each of the following shapes after it is reflected over the dashed mirror line.

a.

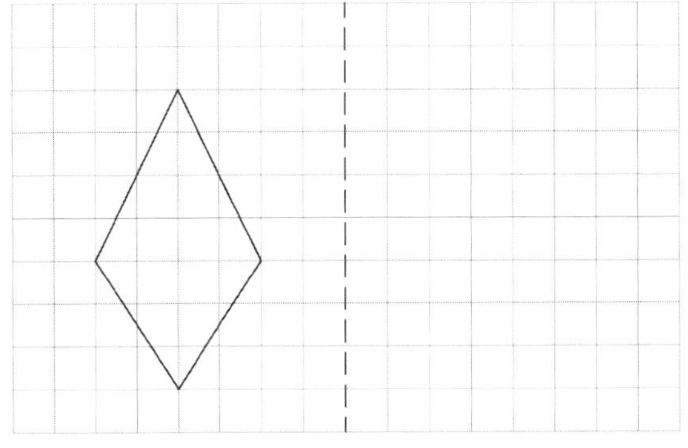

b.

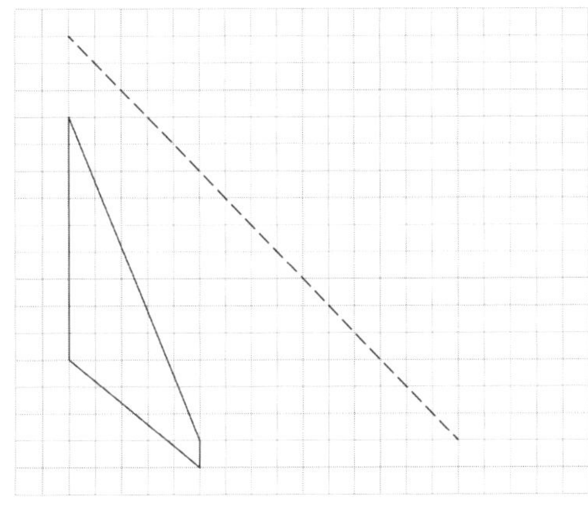

Exercise 13.1.2

Consider the following points.

a. $(4, 1)$ b. $(-1, 2)$ c. $(-1, -4)$ d. $(0, 5)$ e. $(-3, 0)$

Find the image of each point when it is reflected over the:

i. x-axis ii. y-axis.

13.2 Translation

When we translate a shape, each point is moved the same distance and in the same direction.

A translation vector (h, k) tells us how far to move a shape horizontally and vertically.

If h is positive the translation is to the right. If h is negative the translation is to the left.

If k is positive the translation is vertically up. If k is negative the translation is vertically down.

For example:

- The translation vector $(3, -2)$ tells us to move the shape 3 units to the right and 2 units down.
- The translation vector $(-4, 1)$ tells us to move the shape 4 units to the left and 1 unit up.

Example

Describe the translations given by each of the following translation vectors.

a. $(-2, 5)$ b. $(0, -6)$

✓ *Solution*

Working	Explanation
a. $(-2, 5)$ describes a translation of 2 units left and 5 units up.	The first number in the vector gives the translation right or left. Since this is negative, the translation is to the left. The second number in the vector gives the translation up or down. Since this is positive, the translation is up.
b. $(0, -6)$ describes a translation of 6 units down.	The first number in the vector gives the translation right or left. Since this is zero, there is no translation right or left. The second number in the vector gives the translation up or down. Since this is negative, the translation is down.

Example

Draw the image of triangle ABC after translation by vector $(1, -3)$.

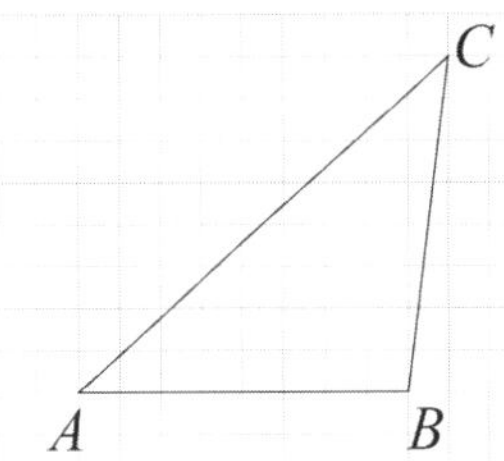

✓ ***Solution***

Working	Explanation
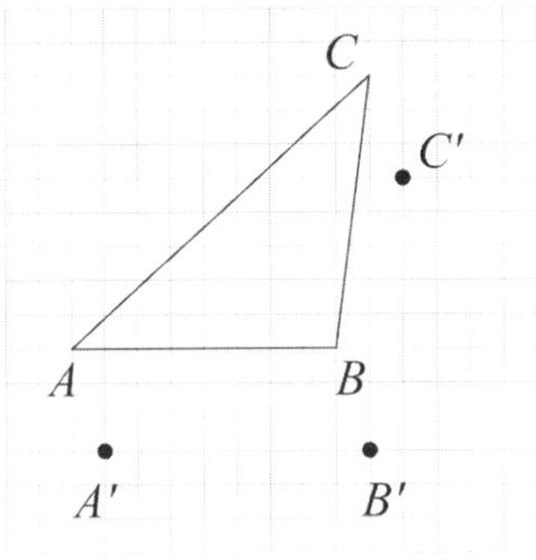	Translate each vertex 1 unit right and 3 units down. Label the image of A as A', the image of B as B' and the image of C as C'.
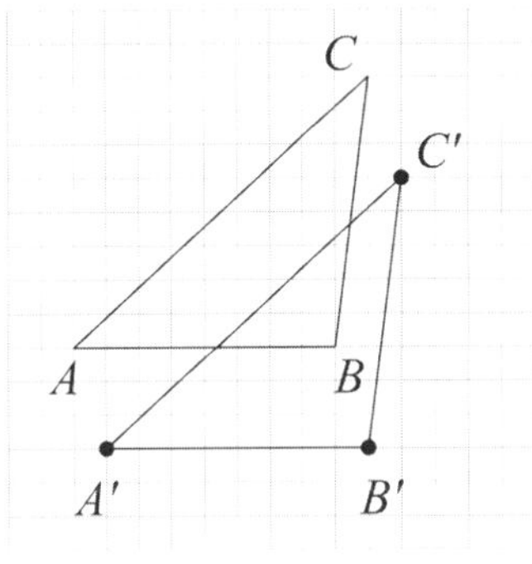	Connect the translated vertices with straight lines to create the image of the original triangle.

Points in the Cartesian plane can also be translated using translation vectors.

Example

Find the coordinates of point $A(3, -4)$ after translation by the following vectors.

a. $(-2, 3)$

b. $(5, -4)$

✓ ***Solution***

Working	Explanation
a. $(3, -4) \rightarrow (3 - 2, -4 + 3)$ The image of the point $(3, -4)$ is $(1, -1)$.	The translation vector $(-2, 3)$ translates the point 2 units left and 3 units up. Subtract 2 from the x-coordinate and add 3 to the y-coordinate to find the coordinates of the image of the point.
b. $(3, -4) \rightarrow (3 + 5, -4 - 4)$ The image of the point $(3, -4)$ is $(8, -8)$.	The translation vector $(5, -4)$ translates the point 5 units right and 4 units down. Add 5 to the x-coordinate and subtract 4 from the y-coordinate to find the coordinates of the image of the point.

Exercise 13.2.1

Describe the translations that result from each of the following translation vectors.

a. $(-2, 1)$

b. $(-3, 0)$

c. $(1, -5)$

Exercise 13.2.2

Find the coordinates of the image of point $A(-5, 2)$ after a translation by each of the vectors in the previous exercise (**Exercise 13.2.1**).

Exercise 13.2.3

Draw the image of quadrilateral $ABCD$ after translation by the vector $(-3, 2)$.

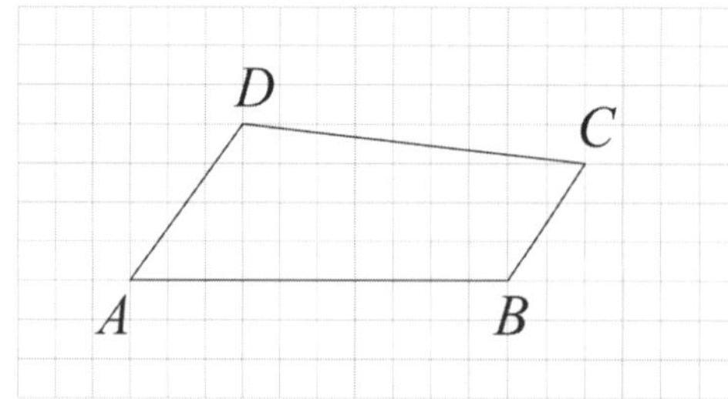

13.3 Rotation

When we rotate a shape about a point, every point on the object moves in a circular path about that point. A shape can be rotated in a clockwise direction or an anticlockwise direction.

A full rotation about a point is $360°$, so if a shape is rotated $360°$ about a point, it will end up back in its original position.

A $90°$ rotation is a quarter of a full rotation and a $180°$ rotation is half a full rotation.

When we rotate a vertical line $90°$ in either direction, it becomes a horizontal line. Similarly, when we rotate a horizontal line $90°$ it becomes a vertical line.

Example

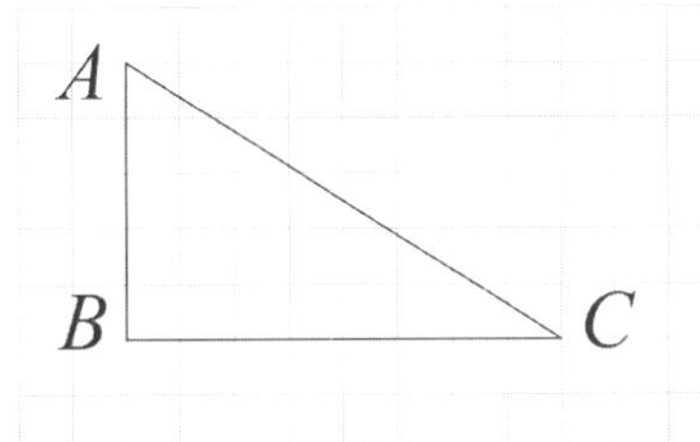

Rotate triangle ABC:

a. $90°$ clockwise about A

b. $180°$ anticlockwise about A.

✓ Solution

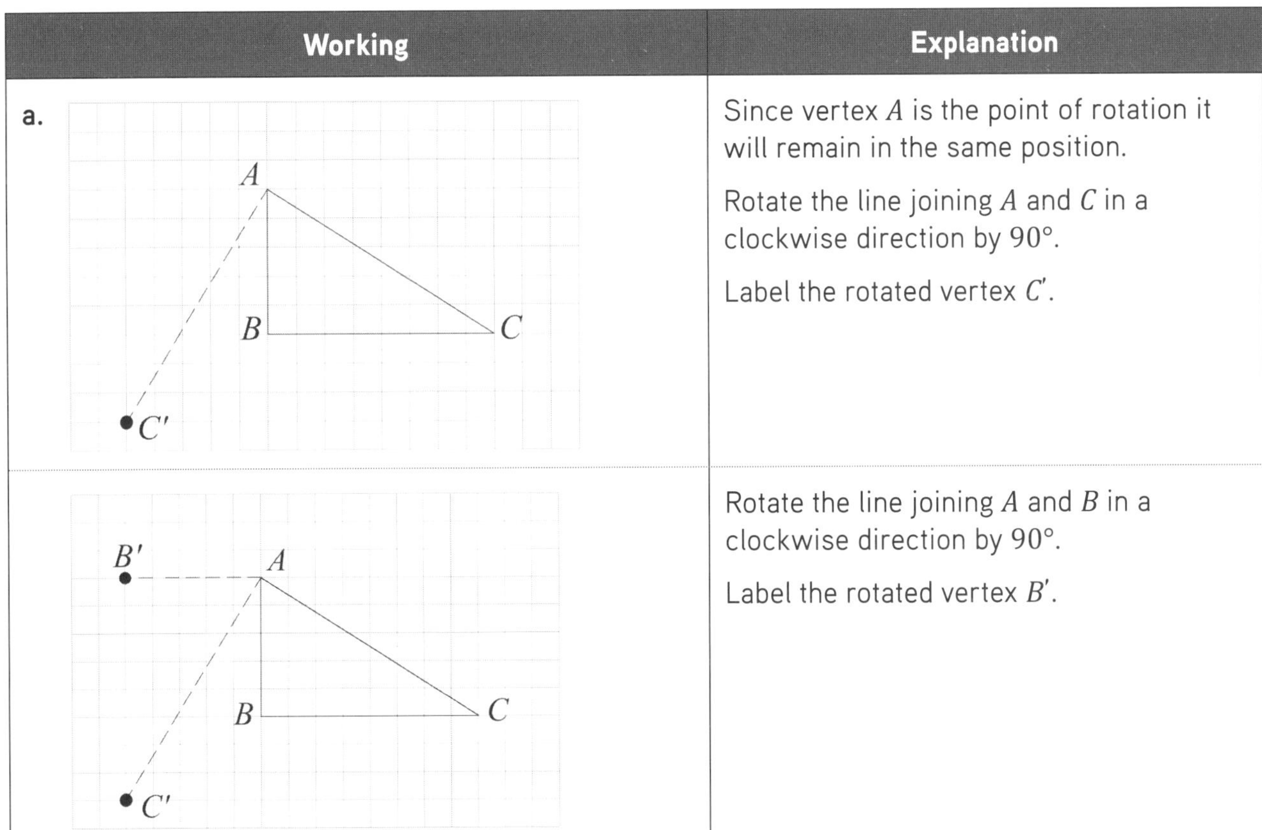

Working	Explanation
a.	Since vertex A is the point of rotation it will remain in the same position. Rotate the line joining A and C in a clockwise direction by $90°$. Label the rotated vertex C'.
	Rotate the line joining A and B in a clockwise direction by $90°$. Label the rotated vertex B'.

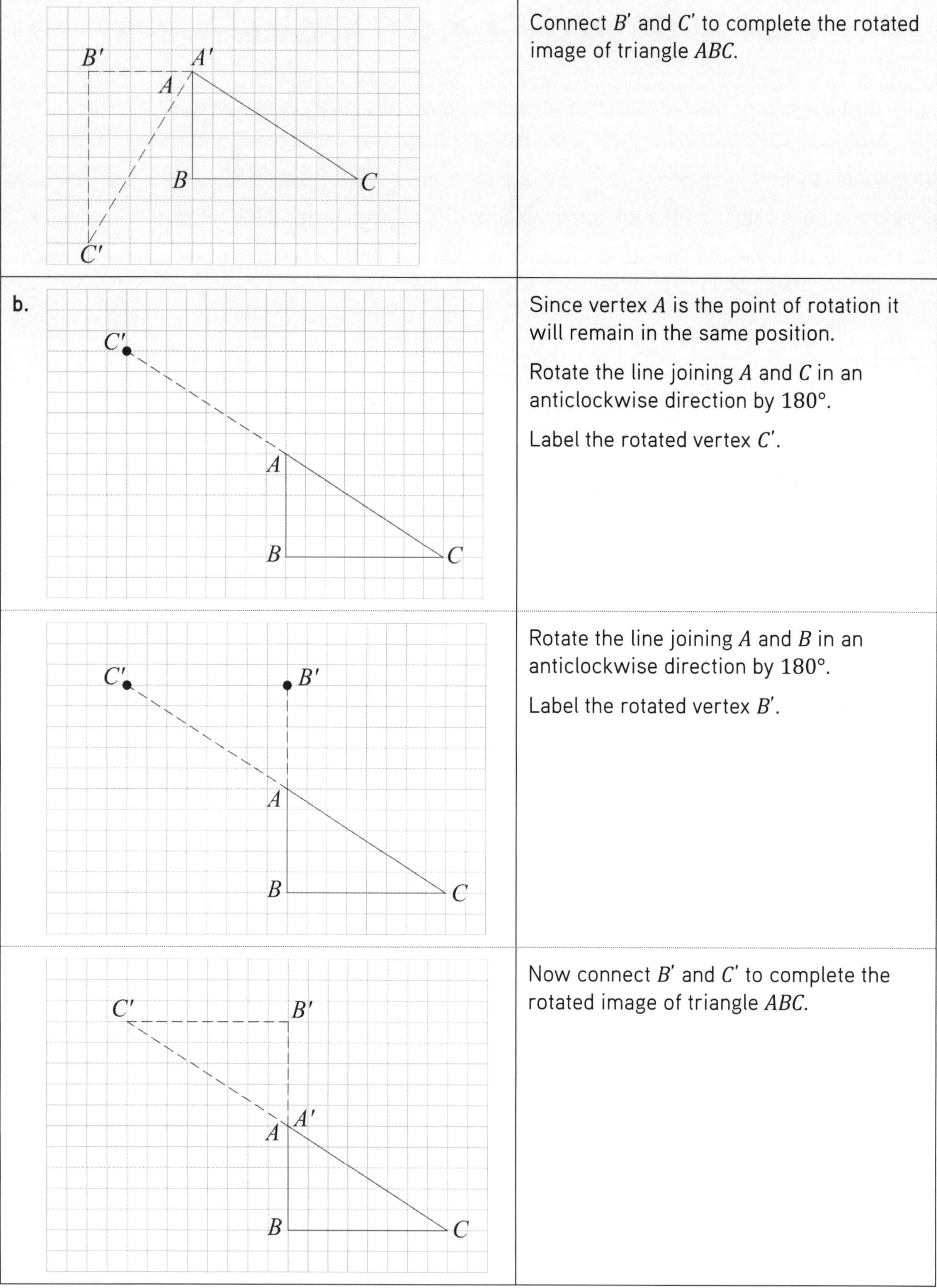

Connect B' and C' to complete the rotated image of triangle ABC.

b.

Since vertex A is the point of rotation it will remain in the same position.

Rotate the line joining A and C in an anticlockwise direction by 180°.

Label the rotated vertex C'.

Rotate the line joining A and B in an anticlockwise direction by 180°.

Label the rotated vertex B'.

Now connect B' and C' to complete the rotated image of triangle ABC.

Points in the Cartesian plane can be rotated using the same technique.

Example

Rotate rectangle $PQRS$ 90° clockwise about the origin.

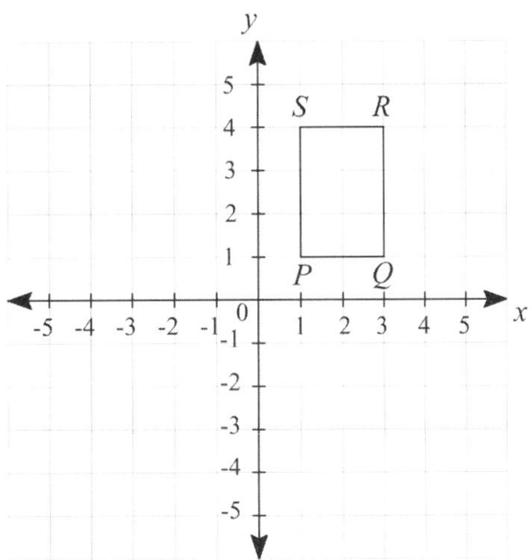

✓ *Solution*

Working	Explanation
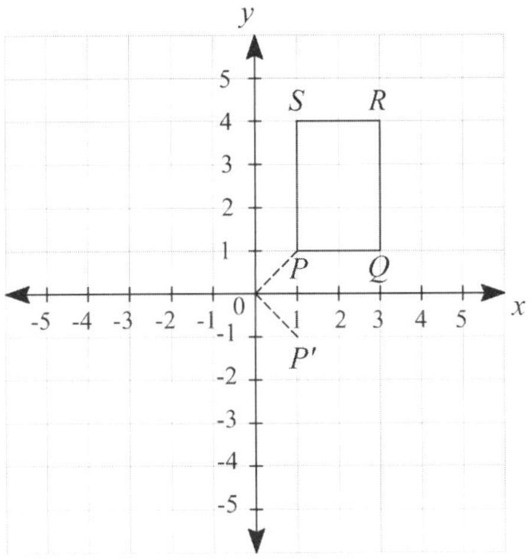	Rotate the line joining 0 and P in a clockwise direction by 90°. Label the rotated point P'.
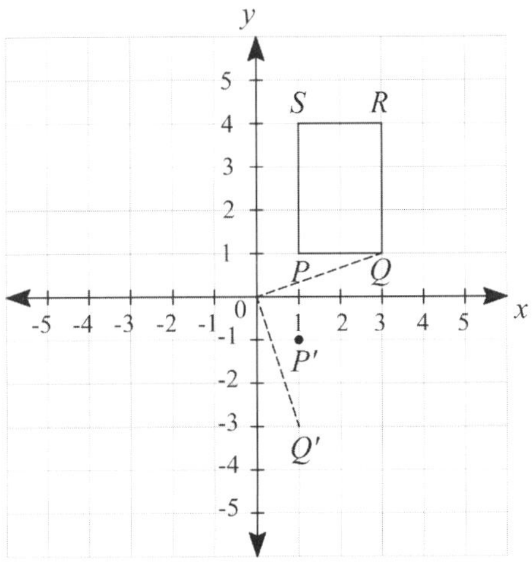	Rotate the line joining 0 and Q in a clockwise direction by 90°. Label the rotated vertex Q'.

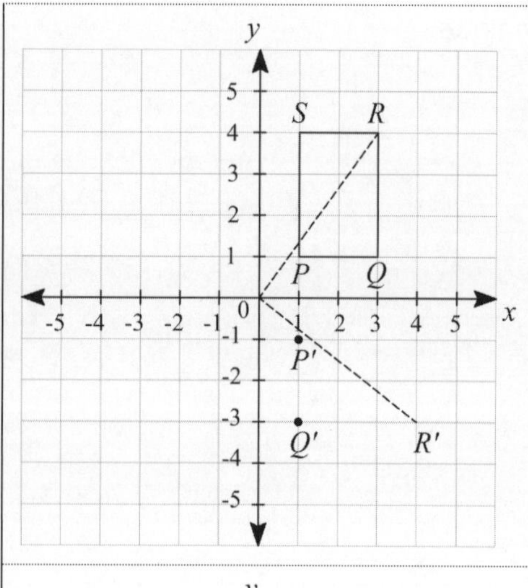	Rotate the line joining 0 and R in a clockwise direction by 90° Label the rotated vertex R'.
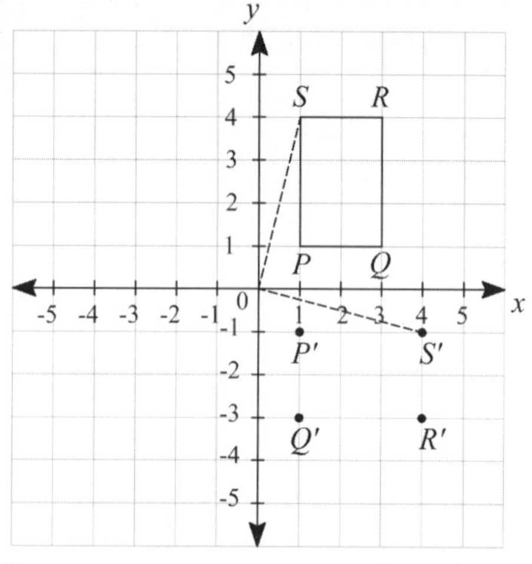	Rotate the line joining 0 and S in a clockwise direction by 90°. Label the rotated vertex S'.
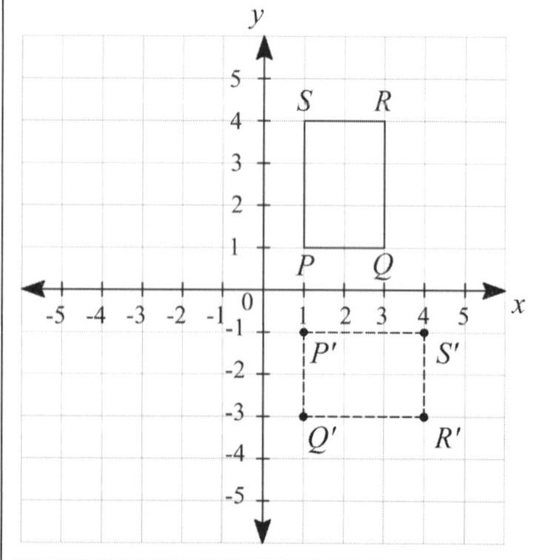	Connect the four rotated vertices to create the rotated rectangle.

Exercise 13.3.1

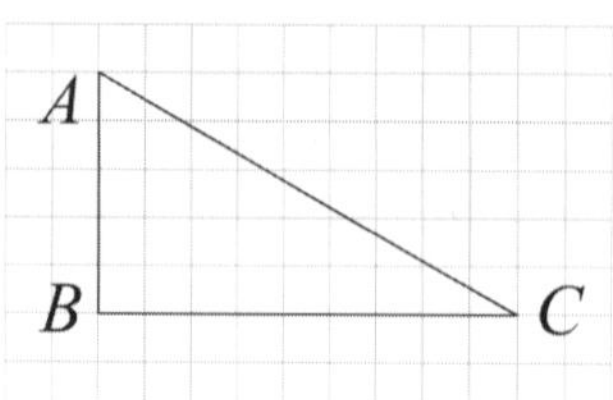

Rotate the triangle ABC:

a. 90° anticlockwise about point C

b. 180° clockwise about point C.

Exercise 13.3.2

Rotate rectangle $PQRS$ 90° anticlockwise about the origin.

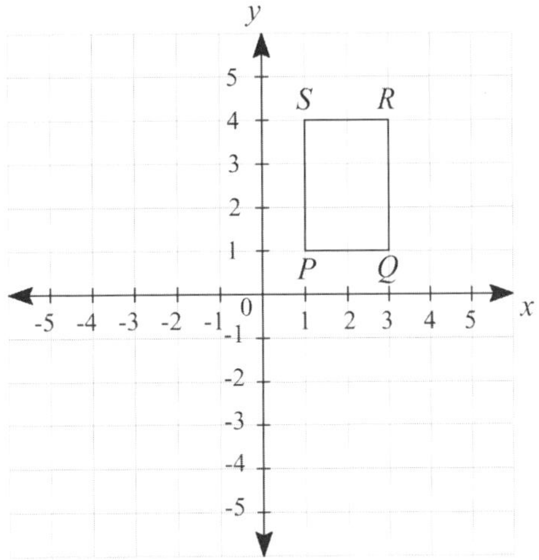

13.4 Congruency and similarity

Congruent figures are identical. Two figures are congruent if they are the same shape and the same size. The symbols ≡ and ≅ both mean 'is congruent to'.

Two figures are congruent if one can be transformed into the other using reflection, translation and rotation.

In congruent figures, corresponding sides have the same length and corresponding angles have the same size. For example, the three kites in the diagram below are congruent because they are the same shape and the same size.

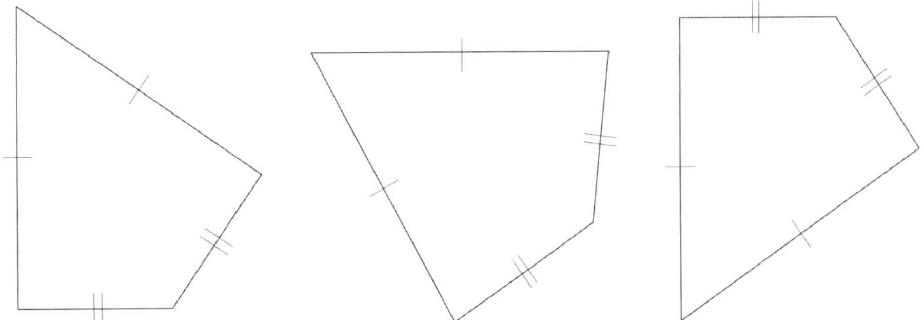

If two figures have the same shape but different sizes, they are said to be **similar**.

The equilateral triangles below have the same shape but are different in size, so they are similar but not congruent.

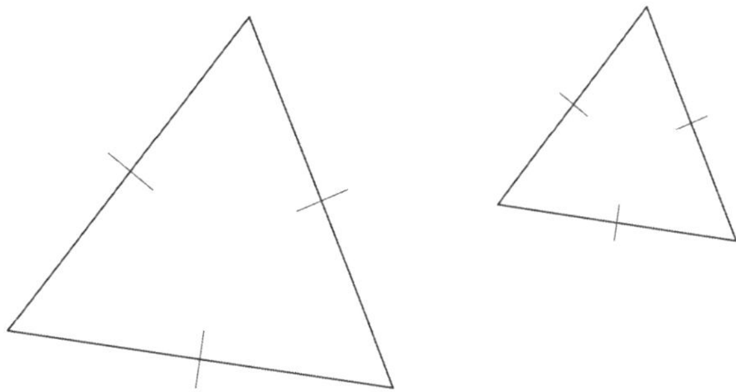

Example

In the following diagram the quadrilateral $ABCD$ has been reflected to give the quadrilateral $PQRS$.

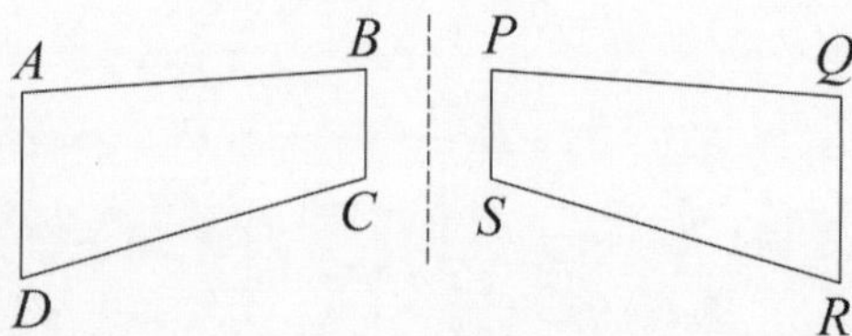

a. Are the two quadrilaterals congruent? Give a reason for your answer.

b. Name the vertex in quadrilateral $PQRS$ that corresponds to vertex B in quadrilateral $ABCD$.

c. Name the side in quadrilateral $PQRS$ that corresponds to the side CD in quadrilateral $ABCD$.

✓ Solution

Working	Explanation
a. The two quadrilaterals are congruent because they are the same shape and same size.	Reflecting a shape does not change its shape or size.
b. Vertex P corresponds to vertex B.	Vertex P is the reflection of vertex B.
c. Side SR corresponds to CD.	Vertex S is the reflection of vertex C and vertex R is the reflection of vertex D.

Exercise 13.4.1

In the following diagram the quadrilateral $ABCD$ has been translated to give the quadrilateral $EFGH$.

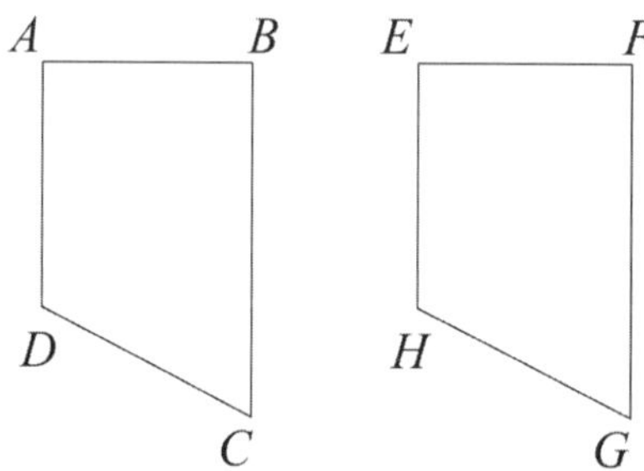

a. Are the two quadrilaterals congruent? Give a reason for your answer.

b. Name the vertex in quadrilateral $EFGH$ that corresponds to vertex D in quadrilateral $ABCD$.

c. Name the side in quadrilateral $EFGH$ that corresponds to the side AD in quadrilateral $ABCD$.

Exercise 13.4.2

In the following diagram the triangle ABC has been rotated to give the triangle PQR.

a. Name the side in ABC that corresponds to the side QR in PQR.

b. Name the angle in PQR that corresponds to BAC in ABC.

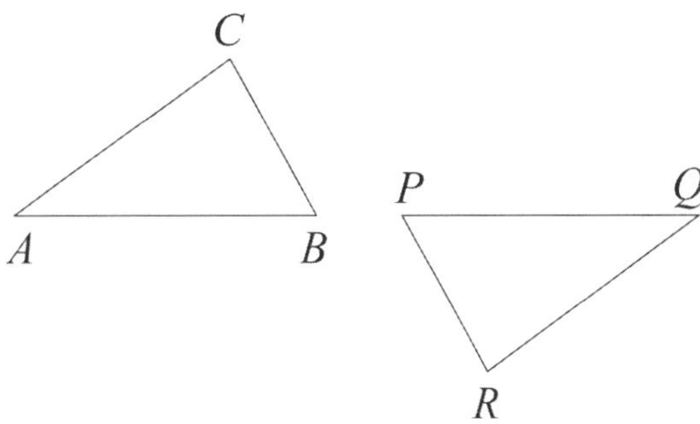

13.5 Congruent triangles

Congruent triangles have exactly the same size and shape.

There are five tests to determine if two triangles are congruent. They are explained in the following table.

Side–Side–Side (SSS) The lengths of all corresponding sides are equal.	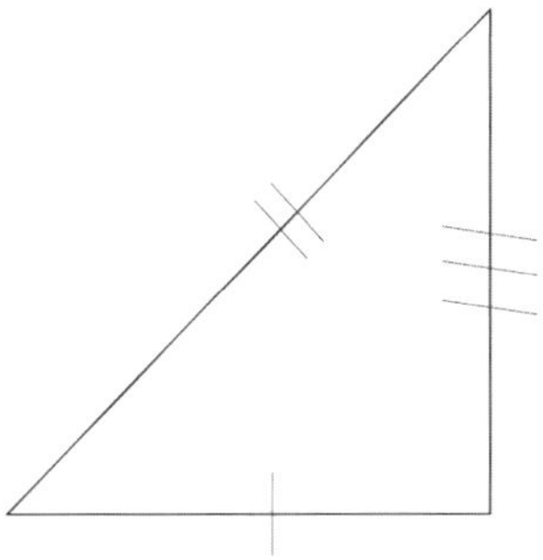	(SSS) ≡	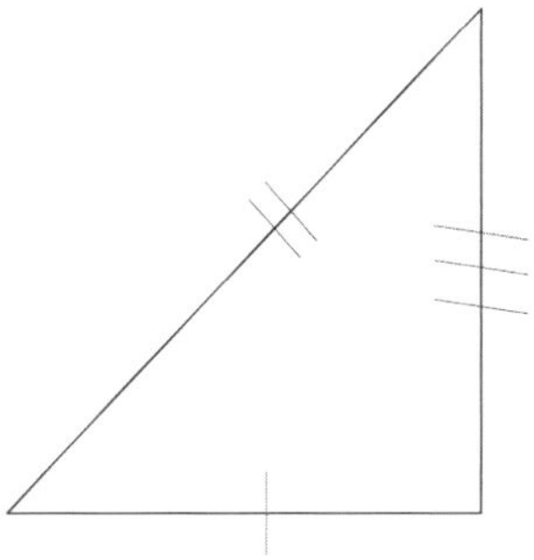
Angle–Side–Angle (ASA) Two pairs of corresponding angles and the corresponding sides between them are equal.	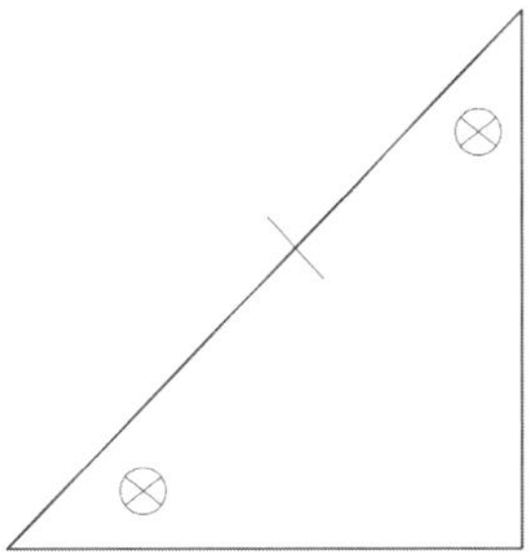	(ASA) ≡	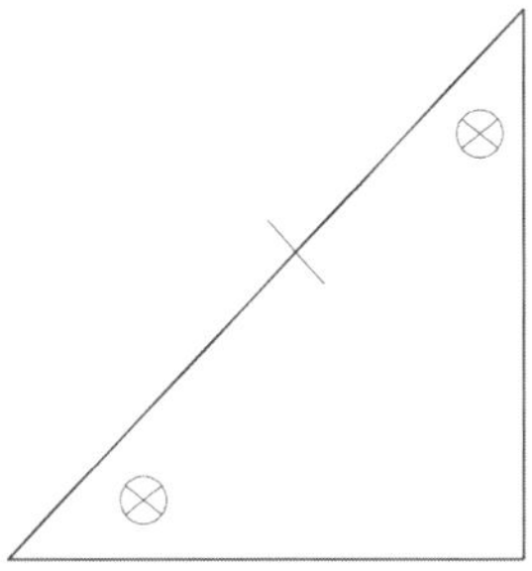
Side–Angle–Side (SAS) Two pairs of corresponding sides and the corresponding angles between them are equal.	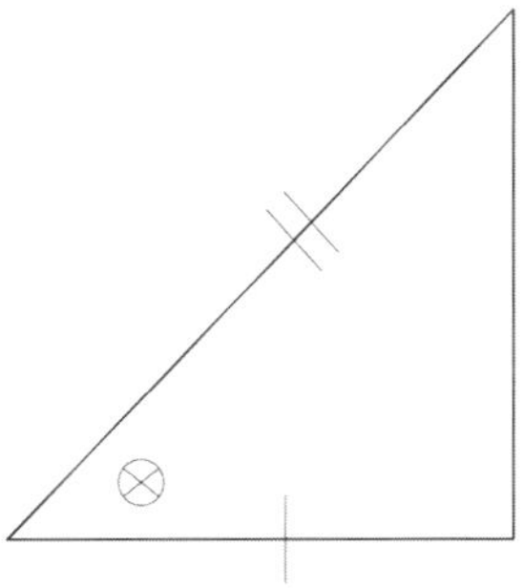	(SAS) ≡	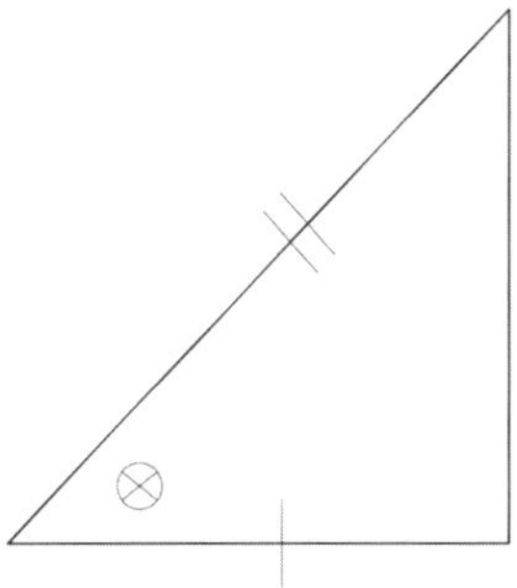

Angle–Angle–Side (AAS) Two pairs of corresponding angles and one pair of corresponding sides (but not the sides between the angles) are equal.		(AAS) $\equiv$	
Right-Angle–Hypotenuse–Side (RHS) In two right-angled triangles, the length of each hypotenuse is the same and one pair of corresponding sides are equal.		(RHS) $\equiv$	

Example

Prove that the pair of triangles shown below are congruent.

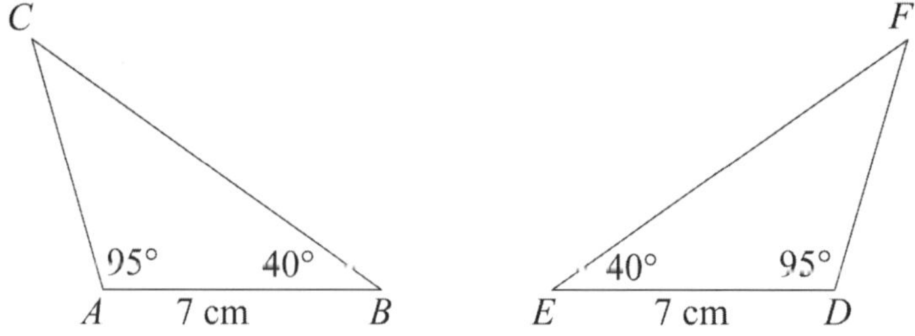

✓ *Solution*

Working	Explanation
$AB = DE$	AB and DE both have the same length: 7 cm.
$\angle CBA = \angle FED$	An angle in each triangle is 40°.
$\angle CAB = \angle FDE$	An angle in each triangle is 95°.
$\Delta ABC \equiv \Delta DEF$ by ASA	Write a congruency statement for the triangles. List the vertices in corresponding order when naming the triangles. $\equiv$ means 'is congruent to'. Give a reason. In this case the sizes of two angles and the length of the side joining them are the same in both triangles, so the ASA test of congruency has been met.

Exercise 13.5.1

Write the name of the congruency test that proves that each pair of triangles below are congruent.

a.

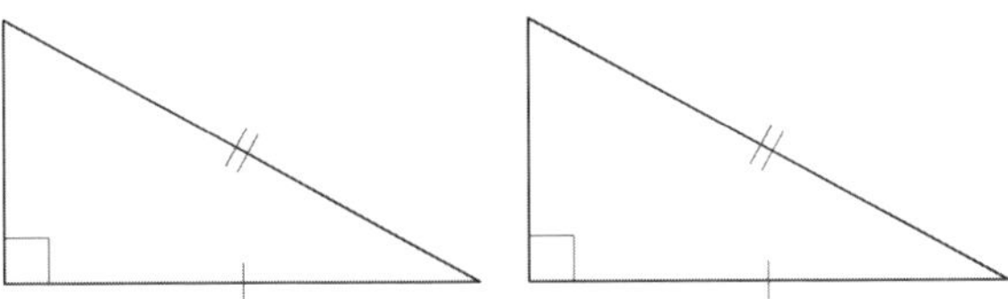

b.

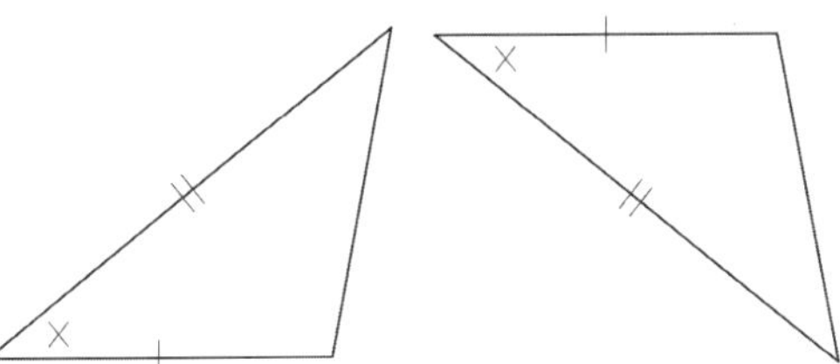

Exercise 13.5.2

Prove that the pair of triangles below are congruent.

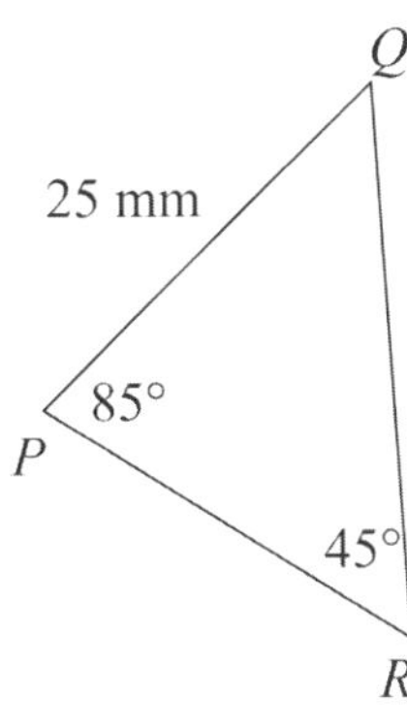

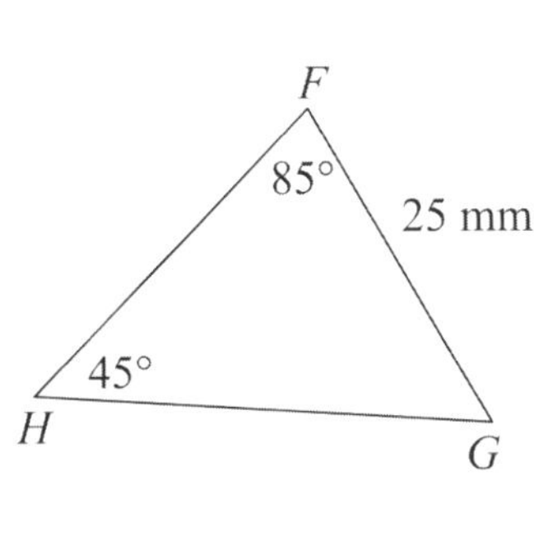

Answers

Exercise 13.1.1

a.

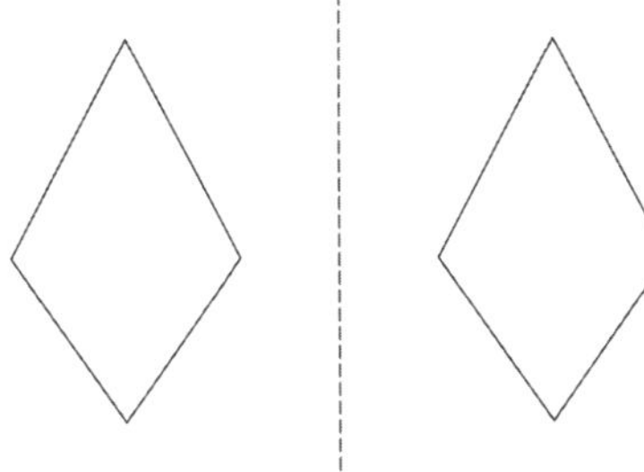

b.

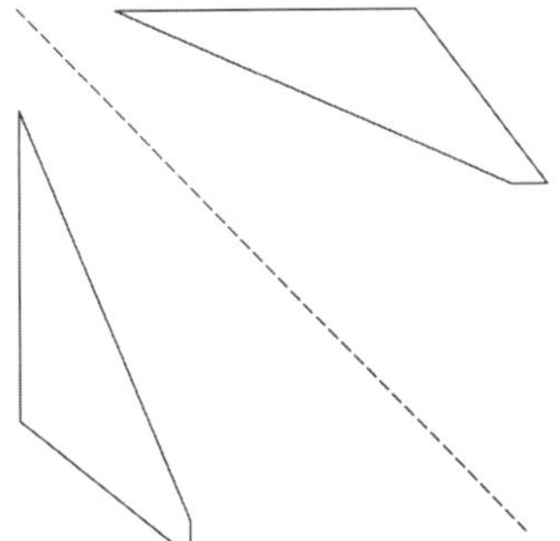

Exercise 13.1.2

a. i. $(4, -1)$ ii. $(-4, 1)$

b. i. $(-1, -2)$ ii. $(1, 2)$

c. i. $(-1, 4)$ ii. $(1, -4)$

d. i. $(0, -5)$ ii. $(0, 5)$

e. i. $(-3, 0)$ ii. $(3, 0)$

Exercise 13.2.1

a. a translation of 2 units left and 1 unit up

b. a translation of 3 units left

c. a translation of 1 unit right and 5 units down

Exercise 13.2.2

a. $(-7, 3)$ b. $(-8, 2)$ c. $(-4, -3)$

Exercise 13.2.3

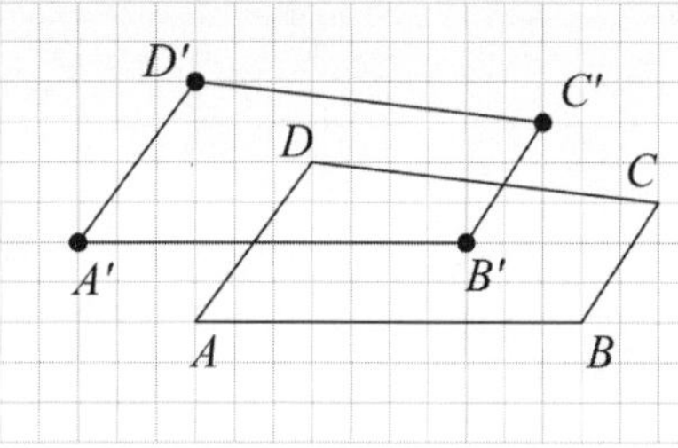

Exercise 13.3.1

a.

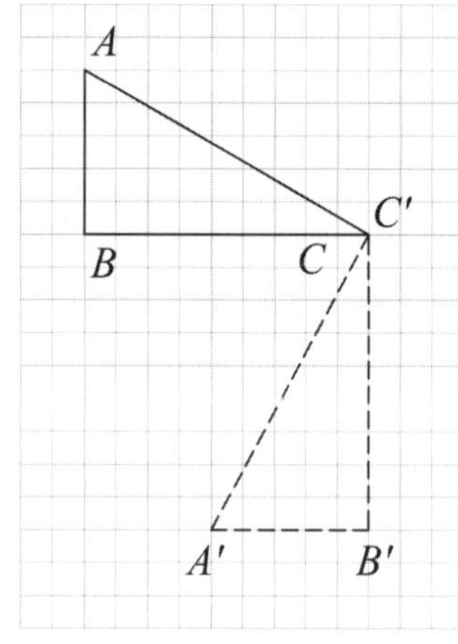

b.

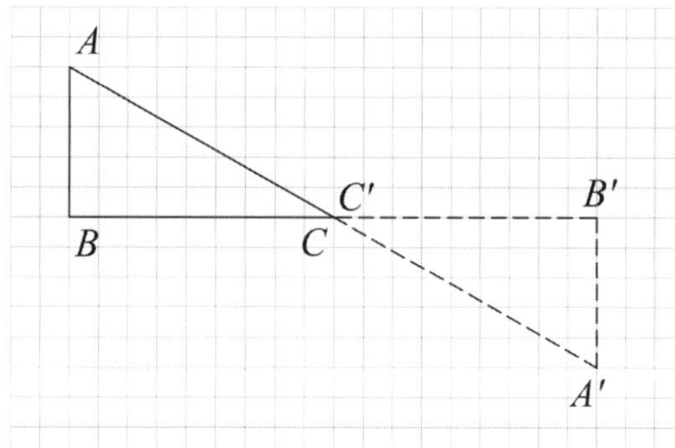

Exercise 13.3.2

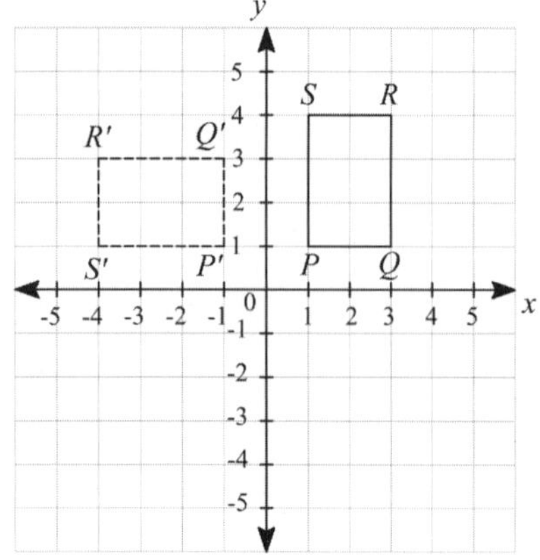

Exercise 13.4.1

a. Yes. They have the same size and the same shape.

b. vertex H

c. EH

Exercise 13.4.2

a. AC

b. $\angle PQR$

Exercise 13.5.1

a. RHS

b. SAS

Exercise 13.5.2

$PQ = FG$, $\angle QPR = \angle GFH$, $\angle QRP = \angle GHF \therefore \Delta PQR \equiv \Delta FGH$ by AAS

Chapter 14 – Algorithms

An algorithm is a step-by-step process or set of rules that can be followed to solve a problem or make a decision.

The example below is an algorithm to determine the congruence of triangles using the RHS test.

Step 1 Do both triangles contain a right angle?

If YES, go to Step 2.

If NO, write 'The RHS congruence test cannot be used to determine the congruence of these triangles' and ignore Steps 2 and 3.

Step 2 Is the length of the hypotenuse the same in both triangles?

If YES, go to Step 3.

If NO, write 'The triangles are not congruent'.

Step 3 Are the lengths of one pair of corresponding sides the same?

If YES, write 'The triangles are congruent by RHS.'

If NO, write 'The triangles are not congruent.'

Example

Use the algorithm above to determine if the triangles below are congruent by the RHS test.

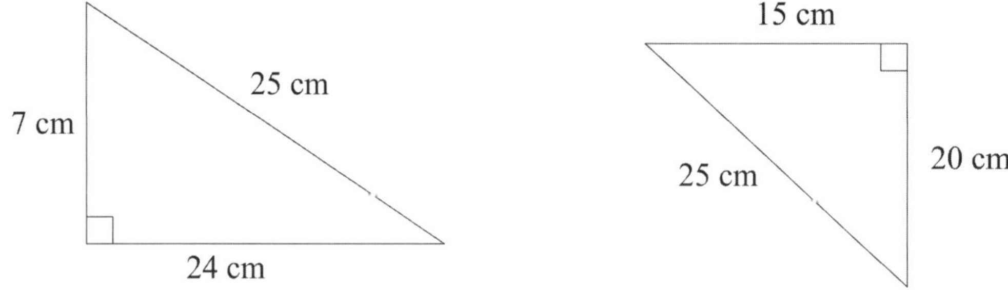

✓ ***Solution***

Working	Explanation
Both triangles contain a right angle.	Step 1: Do both triangles contain a right angle? Follow the 'YES' instruction.
The length of the hypotenuse is 25 cm in both triangles.	Step 2: Is the length of the hypotenuse the same in both triangles? Follow the 'YES' instruction.
The lengths of corresponding sides are not the same, so the triangles are not congruent.	Step 3: Are the lengths of one pair of corresponding sides the same? Follow the 'NO' instruction.

The algorithm below can be used to find the area of a triangle given the lengths of its three sides.

Step 1 Let the lengths of the sides be a, b and c.

Step 2 Calculate $\frac{a+b+c}{2}$ and let the answer be s.

Step 3 Calculate $s - a$.

Step 4 Calculate $s - b$.

Step 5 Calculate $s - c$.

Step 6 Calculate $s \times (s-a) \times (s-b) \times (s-c)$ and let the answer be x.

Step 7 Calculate $\sqrt{x}$.

Step 8 Area $= \sqrt{x}$ and include units with your answer,

Example

Use the algorithm above to calculate the area of the following triangle correct to 2 decimal places.

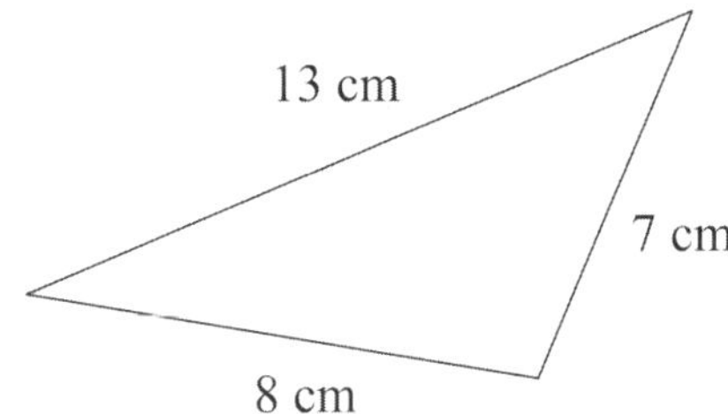

✓ Solution

Working	Explanation
$a = 7, b = 8, c = 13$	**Step 1:** Let the lengths of the sides be a, b and c.
$s = \frac{7+8+13}{2} = 14$	**Step 2:** Calculate $\frac{a+b+c}{2}$ and let the answer be s.
$s - a = 14 - 7 = 7$	**Step 3:** Calculate $s - a$.
$s - b = 14 - 8 = 6$	**Step 4:** Calculate $s - b$.
$s - c = 14 - 13 = 1$	**Step 5:** Calculate $s - c$.
$x = s \times (s-a) \times (s-b) \times (s-c)$ $= 14 \times 7 \times 6 \times 1$ $= 588$	**Step 6:** Calculate $s \times (s-a) \times (s-b) \times (s-c)$ and let the answer be x.
$\sqrt{x} = \sqrt{588} = 24.2487...$	**Step 7:** Calculate $\sqrt{x}$.
Area $= 24.25$ cm^2	**Step 8:** Area $= \sqrt{x}$ and include units with your answer,

Exercise 14.1

Use the algorithm for calculating the area of a triangle to find the area of a triangle with side lengths 15 cm, 20 cm and 29 cm correct to two decimal places.

Answer

Exercise 14.1

139.94 cm^2